PRAISE FOR

PERSISTENCE:
THE POWER TO MAKE CHANGE

Light the fire. Pour the tea. Pull up the quilt and settle in. Pat Bakalian's memoir reads like a long talk with an old friend - warm and
intimate, engaging and instructive. Valuable lessons in political activism mix with reflections on family, personal responsibility and the
joy of staying open to the wonders of daily life. Every woman who has
ever doubted her ability to lead in the public arena will take heart as
Pat rises above financial hardship, family estrangement and professional ups and downs to become the wise and full-throated warrior
for women that she was meant to be.

~ MARY V. HUGHES, Political strategist, Hughes & Company,
Founder, Close the Gap California

———

Pat Bakalian's memoir is one that all women will identify with, telling the story of how a shy young girl transformed into an outspoken
activist for women's rights. She shows how each one of us can contribute to the greater good, regardless of our experiences, and how to
overcome any self-imposed limits. For all women who want to help
others but don't know where or how to start, Pat will show you how.

~ LORI SOKOL, Ph.D. Executive Director and
Editor-in-Chief *Women's eNews*

In telling her story from a challenging childhood through to her current life as a strong, independent woman and political activist Pat Bakalian's *Persistence: The Power to Make Change* is exemplary of the struggles of girls and women to come into the power of their own lives. As a now seasoned feminist political activist and electoral strategist this book could not be more timely or instructive as we face off against the current administration for the 2020 Presidential elections. Read it! Be inspired! Take action!

~ BETTINA APTHEKER, Professor Emerita, Feminist Studies Department University of California, Santa Cruz and author of *Intimate Politics: How I Grew Up Red, Fought for Free Speech and Became a Feminist Rebel*

———

Pat Bakalian reminds us of the value of every voice, encouraging the seeds of bravery within us that make change possible because we choose to stand up.

~ ANITA FINLAY, Actor, Activist and Author of *Dirty Words on Clean Skin*

———

Woven throughout Pat's touching and inspiring memoir is her mother's voice telling her to trust the Universe and that is exactly what she has done. *Persistence: The Power to Make Change* is one women's story of how she grew in her ability to make a difference in the lives of people in her own way – all the while "Trusting the Universe." I was privileged to see this first hand when she worked for the U.S. Center for Disease Control and Prevention. Her courage was/is inspiring and her spirit is indomitable.

~ CATHERINE DODD, Former District Director, Congresswoman Nancy Pelosi, Regional Director, U.S. Health and Human Services Region IX and Board Chair, National Committee to Preserve Social Security and Medicare

Pat Bakalian's memoir is more than one woman's story. It's an invitation to recover the history, both personal and political, of a generation of women that often seems eclipsed or dismissed nowadays. That generation struggled through post-war expectations and gave birth, in themselves and for the generations that have followed, to the possibilities that exist for women today. Whether you lived through those times or not, you will be delighted to find a real and recognizable voice offer an alternative—warmly, candidly and non-polemically—to the labels and generalizations of the "second wave" of feminism.

~ SUSAN BORDO, Professor Emerita, Gender and Women's Studies, University of Kentucky and the author of many books, most recently *The Destruction of Hillary Clinton: Untangling the Political Forces, Media Culture, and Assault on Fact that Decided the 2016 Election*

———

Reading Pat's life story is inspiring and motivating. It's a lifetime of activism from fundraiser to mother and community activist to feminist activist. She bravely shares her and her mother's personal experiences of having an abortion before the passage of Roe v. Wade which clearly shows why we need to fight for women's reproductive rights now more than ever.

~ SOPHIA YEN, MD MPH CEO, Co-Founder Pandia Health, Founder Silver Ribbon Campaign to Trust Women and lifelong #reprorights activist/feminist

———

Persistence: The Power to Make Change is written in such a way that it draws you in. Although my life and that of the author are markedly different, the underlying issues and struggles felt so familiar that is was as if we were travelling this path together. The honesty was profound, so raw yet without coming off as bitchy, which is difficult to do.

~ PATRICIA KEITH-SPIEGEL, PhD author of *Ethics in Psychology and the Mental Health Professions* and Professor Emerita, California State University, Northridge

And thoughts from two of my daughters

I never really knew what kind of work you did. I loved learning about your life from such a different perspective. A lot of the stories rang a bell, but at the time my teenage self never really understood what your work meant to you, or to the community, or to women's empowerment. You succeeded in writing a very touching, inspiring and thoughtful book. You have come so far in your ability to look back, forgive and learn from your experiences. I'm so glad you wrote this book!
~ SARA BAKALIAN WILDMAN

———

The way my mom tells the story about overcoming her insecurities is something I think a lot of people can relate to. I certainly can as I struggle with my own. As an adult now, I loved reading about her growth as an activist. This book is not just a great gift to our family but I think it is also a gift to anyone who reads it.
~ LESHA ELIZABETH BAKALIAN

PERSISTENCE

PERSISTENCE

THE
POWER
TO
MAKE CHANGE

A Memoir by

PAT BAKALIAN

Persistence:
The Power to Make Change

ISBN: 978-1-7333522-1-5

Published by

Big Hat Press
  Lafayette, California
  www.bighatpress.com

There is no doubt that I am a product of white privilege. I have become more acutely aware of that fact through the process of writing this book. We can't change the color of our skin, where we were born, or the family we were born into. But with self-awareness we can overcome, in our personal lives, some of the cards we were dealt and do what we can to help others who are less fortunate.

Included in my book is a resource for you – a compilation of organizations doing important work to make our world a better, healthier, safer and more tolerant place for all of us to live.

DEDICATION

In loving memory to my mother, Barbara Dawes Vogl (1924-2009), who saw the person I was to become and always supported me throughout my journey.

To my strong, resilient, and caring daughters Kelly, Sara and Lesha. You have made me the person I am today.

To John, the love of my life. I am incredibly grateful for our crazy and unusual life.

And to dedicated, committed volunteers everywhere helping to make our small planet a more equitable and safe place for everyone.

TABLE OF CONTENTS

PREFACE

MY KALEIDOSCOPE

When your heart is beating fast, oh that is inner applause.
~ Frances Moore Lappe, American Researcher and Author

I contemplated the enormous ballroom, overwhelmed by the prospect of filling it with people, arranging for food, banners, and balloons. Staging a large-scale fundraiser was like planning a wedding — on steroids! My thoughts turned toward the program, and that's when it hit me that *I would have to speak* —stand up all-alone in front of hundreds of people and say something worthwhile. The idea petrified me. "Oh my god!" I thought. "Just let me stay behind the scenes, where I'm comfortable and know how to have fun."

For the last six months, my friend Shana and I had worked our butts off on an enormous fundraising dinner for two organizations, the California Abortion Rights Action League and our local Reproductive Rights Network. We reached out to elected officials, key leaders in the community, activists, churches, community groups and service organizations, got them to sponsor tables and fill them with their friends. We arranged for the venue and a zillion logistical details. We were two passionate, committed women, and threatening phone calls had only fanned the flames of our resolve. Now, in October 1989, we were about to welcome more than 500 people to "A Choice Dinner" at the Cocoanut Grove Ballroom on the famous Boardwalk in Santa Cruz, California.

When the day came, I was in my element, laughing, chatting, and schmoozing with the people — a strategy that allowed me to ignore the panic rising in my stomach. But nerves have a way of asserting themselves. A clumsy move in the restroom just before my big moment sent the end of one of the long sleeves of my elegant black jumpsuit swooping into the toilet, thankfully just after I had flushed it. It was sopping wet. Frantic, I blotted the darn thing with paper towels and had at it with the hand blower. With the clock ticking, I pulled myself together and made my way through the crowd to the stage, hoping no one could see the evidence of my mishap. I was scared to death.

Then, with total control, I strode into the spotlight and graciously welcomed a ballroom full of guests to our gala evening.

I didn't know that at that moment I was also stepping into a new life. On that long-ago evening I began to shed the shyness and uncertainty that kept my outgoing personality under wraps and inhibited my efforts to make a difference in the world.

The life that brought me to that moment had not been a traditional one; neither were the adventurous decades that followed. Looking back, I now see how my journey led me to overcome my insecurities and develop the confidence to act on my passions and find my personal power as a feminist social activist.

In the late 1980s, I was a middle-aged woman without a career or any real personal direction, hiding behind my role of wife and mother. Gradually emerging from my husband's shadow, I began to look outward for an identity of my own. But it was only when events catapulted me toward a larger destiny that I took significant steps out of the safe world I had built.

This book and the story it relates all started with my mother - a remarkable woman with a fascinating life. She was complex, energetic, talented, worldly and altruistic. A child of the Great Depression, Mom learned to be a submissive wife, a mother, a smiling and unobtrusive homemaker. She bore the burdens of a destructive marriage and the social stigma of having a child — my sister — with severe mental disabilities. And then, somehow, she walked out of the stereotypical woman's role of the 1950s and '60's to assert herself as a person with her own thoughts, dreams and passions.

Mom's transformative life was not typical of her generation. She was a new-age thinker and ahead of her time. Even at age 84 — not long before she died — she was working on a new sort of *Whole Earth Catalog*. She called it *newPATTERN*, and envisioned it as an interactive website, a "hub" for people working on innovative social and economic ways of living in this world as the old ways were breaking down. She wanted to introduce her readers to a positive view of the future, encouraging more people to think differently. It would connect people with each other in real time to share what was already happening, reinforcing and encouraging hope and action on a global scale.

My mother's experience of emergence and empowerment ultimately became a catalyst for me to tell my own story. In her 80s, Mom began compiling audio memoirs. Meeting once a week with her friend Savanah, she told stories from her life while Savanah asked questions and recorded the conversations. When Mom died in 2009, twenty-four tapes of her talking about her life were mine — a remarkable gift. As I listened with increasing eagerness to those recordings, I began to see her accomplishments through new eyes. "The world deserves to hear about this woman", I thought. Using the recordings as my main source, I was determined to produce her written memoirs.

Savanah, who had loved my mom, immediately jumped on board the project. But, like life itself, this book did not evolve in a straight line. It began to morph into a mother-daughter story. But that didn't work, either, because there were too many moving parts, and too many holes that Mom was not here to fill. It finally became clear that the tale I needed to tell was my own, interwoven with my mother's but eventually establishing a separate tapestry. That choice was confirmed when writing this book turned out to be a path to my own healing.

Amazingly, besides those prized twenty-four tapes, I also possessed seventy letters my dad had written to me over a seventeen-year period. They reveal the painful, dysfunctional relationship I had with him all of my life. I needed to understand how his controlling, manipulative behavior and inability to express love for me played a role in my life. I needed to understand how my mom, playing out her second adolescence as I was going through my first, affected my development. Her life intertwined with mine, and influenced me so profoundly that even now she continues to live through me.

I also needed to look at the economic roller-coaster ride I took with my husband and how it prodded me into emerging from my shell. The decisions I made led from one adventure to the next and have made me the person I am today.

I have tried to be as honest and open as I could, sometimes revealing hard truths that part of me would rather keep secret. I have tried to rediscover the little girl, the teenager, the young woman I was, what made me do what I did and reach the decisions I made in my life, and how I see things differently now. It has taken me many years to shed the image I had of myself as an introverted, self-conscious, scared, incapable woman, to see myself differently and to find out what I was capable of. I have realized I have always been an extrovert but made decisions throughout my life as if I was an introvert.

In the process of reflecting on the influences of my parents as well as the male-dominated society of the 1950s and '60s in which I grew up, I have released the pressure of hidden feelings and subconscious beliefs that no longer serve me. But I hope the story I've told here is not just for my own benefit. I hope it will resonate, not only with readers from my generation, but also with women of all ages. None of us, after all, is a stranger to personal experiences and social messages that can undermine our power. Each of us is on a journey that can lead either to disappointments and isolation or to self-realization and the joys and challenges of being involved in the community in which we live. Having traveled both of those forks, I share my journey in hopes that it will provide others with insight and inspiration.

Creating a memoir requires reliving the memories. It also means seeing them from a different perspective. A memoir is about an author's memories. Some might see things differently. That is their right and their choice. Mom wanted to name her memoirs *Kaleidoscope,* because she often experienced profound clarity with the slightest shift in perspective. Since beginning this journey, my perspective has changed more than a little. I see the past with different eyes. My heart is fuller and my body is calmer. I could not have reached this place without the challenges I faced, and on some level I know I chose my route. "This is your journey now, and later it will be someone else's," my mom told me. She always advised me to "trust the process and focus on the journey." To my surprise, the journey of writing this book has helped me more than I could have ever imagined.

I am supremely grateful I was able to spend the time it took and happy that I had the persistence to finish what for a long time was known in my household as "this darn thing." It has been an adventure. I hope it is one for you too.

Pat Bakalian

CHAPTER 1

EARLIEST INFLUENCES

Life shrinks and expands in proportion to one's courage.

~ Anais Nin, French-American diarist,
essayist, novelist, and writer

My parents' marriage was not a good one. Mom's tapes revealed much I never knew. She said:

> *I lived on the brink of going crazy for quite a few years of my marriage. If I hadn't been masochistic, I wouldn't have been able to survive.*

This was the woman who mothered me, my role model. I felt sad for her and frustrated because I wanted to know more, but she wasn't here to answer my questions. What made her say this? What was going on during this time of her life? Who made her feel this way? I also began to wonder how her feelings and behavior affected me as a child.

It was 1960. Mom was thirty-six, I was eleven, my intellectually disabled sister Susie was nine, and my two brothers Peter and Steve were seven and five. Back then few women sought divorces, so Mom was definitely outside her comfort zone when she said she was "doing what she knew she had to do."

When I got my divorce I knew it was the first adult decision I'd ever made. I knew my family wouldn't accept it — no one in my family had gotten divorced except an aunt who was talked about in whispers. But I knew I had to for my mental health and for the kids' sake too. I couldn't put my finger on it, but I remember knowing by getting divorced I was breaking the chain.

It feels like I've had two lives — before and after the divorce. After the divorce it was an adult life because I was now willing to take the consequences for what I did. Before I was always the little girl who could get out of things. I hadn't developed a character. I was good at doing what was expected of me.

It is hard to imagine young women now days ever feeling and saying anything like this. It was a very different era.

My dad, Charles Weiner Vogl was born in 1919. He grew up in Chicago in the 1920s and 30s, the oldest child and only son (he had a younger sister named Ruth) of Jewish parents who had immigrated to America from Czechoslovakia before World War I. His father, Otto Vogl, followed his love, Margaret Weiner, to the United States, where they married not long afterward.

Margaret's brother, my great uncle Charles Weiner, was the owner of the Victor Tape Company, which he founded in Prague in 1898. In 1915 he moved to America, settled in Chicago and re-branded his business the Chicago Printed String Company. My Grandpa Otto Vogl and Charles became business partners and developed a patent for a process that printed names on tape and ribbons — "advertising tape" or binding ribbon that marketed a product or company.

They developed their own machines, began experimenting with decorative ribbons and eventually got into the gift-wrapping business, inventing the pleated curling ribbon that curls when drawn over a sharp edge. I learned much later in my life and am proud to say that Chicago Printed String was one of the first profit-sharing companies in the country long before that concept was popularized.

In 1939 the company began sending its "Tie-Tie" girls to department stores to conduct gift-wrapping classes, which led to a whole new service offered to shoppers. In the 1960s the company began leasing machines that mass-produced fancy bows. With a multi-colored array of hundreds of different kinds of paper and thousands of varieties and sizes of ribbons and bows, Chicago Printed String became the largest company of its kind in the United States. It eventually became CPS Industries and was sold in the 1970s to Papercraft Company out of Pittsburgh.

As a child I was thrilled each Christmas when we would get a huge box in the mail filled to the brim with beautiful colorful wrapping paper and shiny bows in all different sizes. (This was before such extravagance was commonplace!)

As Hitler rose to power, Grandpa Vogl did his best to get as many family members as he could out of Czechoslovakia. His economic success afforded him the wherewithal to bring to the United States relatives who almost surely would have died in the Nazi death camps.

Our family did not talk about this family history so my knowledge is sparse. I am still not sure why. After my dad passed away I did learn that Grandpa helped Dad's cousins Joe and Nora Vogl. My cousin Judy, who lived close to our grandparents and saw them every weekend while she was growing up, shared with me what she remembered: "Grandma's family was here as far as I know. Grandpa's family was still in Czechoslovakia. He had eight siblings. I know Grandpa brought his sister Kamila and her husband, Leopold, to the United States. I think that four or five were murdered, along with most of their families. Our grandparents never spoke about that. Leopold died in the early 1950's, so I don't have many memories of him. Kamila was tiny, lived in a small walk-up flat and made women's fashionable hats for a living. My mother (my aunt Ruth) once told me that all the linen tablecloths and napkins that she inherited from her mother (our grandma) were purchased by our grandparents in order to get money into the country to bring more relatives out."

Grandpa and Grandma Vogl were formal and reserved. To me as a child, they felt cold and distant, but Grandpa always seemed a bit friendlier. "Grandpa" I would say "Can I touch your wooden leg?" He would smile down at me and say "Sure." As I knocked on his hollow sounding wooden leg he told me how he got it in a car accident. Grandma was a small, thin woman with pale white skin who, until the day she died, had jet-black hair and always wore dark red lipstick. She was not the friendly, warm grandma type. As I approached my teen years I thought of her as the Wicked Witch of the West from the *Wizard of Oz*.

Judy went on to say: "I think that our grandparents did not have a good and open relationship. In part it was because of the era and their European background. But it was also because their interests were so different. Grandpa deeply loved Grandma, but I don't think this was reciprocal. And so they didn't talk and I know they had separate bedrooms."

This kind of upbringing - my dad growing up in a house that was quiet and repressed, with lots of unspoken anger and resentment - explains a lot to me. In those days children were raised to be seen, and not heard. As a child growing up in that environment, my dad learned to be silent and keep his feelings, hopes, dreams, disappointments, ambitions and hurts to himself.

When Grandpa Vogl died in the late 50's I was ten years old. We were living in Palo Alto, California. Grandma would come to visit us from Chicago, each time taking us to Blum's restaurant and ice cream parlor in the newly opened Stanford Shopping Center, one of the first upscale open air shopping malls in the country. Grandma let us order any one of their absolutely enormous ice cream sundaes, about the size of my head - the biggest ice cream sundae I had ever seen. That was her way of showing love. Never did she give me a warm hug, ask about how I was or who my friends were or what I liked to do. She used her money as a show of love. This is what my dad learned.

Mom's family couldn't have been more different. Barbara Ann Dawes was born in the manufacturing town of Beloit, Wisconsin, in 1924. She was the middle child of three girls born to Hazel Tiffany and Raymond Dawes, whose families can be traced back to the founding of this country.

Grandpa Dawes was a railroad engineer, able to provide for his family, even through the great depression. They lived in a two-story house in a middle-class neighborhood. Mom said "When I was a small child I watched my mom feed unemployed men who came to our back door asking for food during the Depression." I think this had a huge impact on her. Growing up in the Methodist faith, Mom learned that "you are your brother's keeper" and that helping others who are less fortunate is a part of what you do in life. She took those teachings to heart. This was always at the core of how she lived her life.

In 1925, right after Mom was born and just before the Depression, Grandpa followed a job opportunity to Florida. While living in Florida Mom got diphtheria; the family myth was that their "colored washer woman" saved her life before the doctor came by putting her in a tub of cold water. Mom said "I always felt that since God had saved me, God must have wanted me to do something good with my life" when it was actually the "colored washer woman" who saved her life.

I grew up hearing how Grandpa and Grandma Dawes characterized each of their daughters in a sweet and complimentary stereotype: Merrilie, the oldest, was the smart one; Alice, the youngest, was the athletic one, and Mom in the middle was the cute, popular one. They loved their daughters but had no idea how limiting their praise was. My mother's exceptional intelligence was completely hidden from her until after her divorce and well into her adult life. While growing up she dutifully played her role as the pretty and popular one, which did nothing to bolster her self-confidence or self-esteem.

> *I was such a zombie when I was growing up. I just followed in lock step. I was a school leader but I was a personal follower. I followed what was expected of me completely. I never really knew myself.*

Growing up, we didn't live close to any of our grandparents. Grandpa Dawes had developed Alzheimer's disease in the late 50's, when I was still young, so I never really knew him. After he passed away, Grandma Dawes would come to visit us and was always warm and loving.

....

My parents met in Chicago. Chuck was an intern at the University of Chicago Medical Center and Barbara was a student nurse. After his internship he moved to Bowman, North Dakota, and became the only doctor in this tiny town of five hundred people with the nearest doctor or hospital a hundred miles away in Dickenson. She described her fork-in-the road this way.

I was trying to decide what I was going to do with my life. I was thinking I wanted to go to New York City and get a job with the airlines. At the time they only hired nurses [and only women as well]. I thought, oh boy this would be so much fun - but then Chuck talked me into moving to North Dakota to work as his nurse. So this was rather adventurous too. That was my fork in the road. Looking back I wouldn't have been able to handle New York City. I was much too immature.

Despite Mom choosing to follow Dad to Bowman, instead of taking a right turn to New York City, she always had an adventurous streak. This played itself out when she learned to fly a small plane, which took them both to farmhouses across the plains to deliver babies in the middle of the very cold North Dakota winters.

Eleven months after their wedding, in January 1949, I was born. It was a dark and snowy midwinter night. A snowplow came through their little town on its way to the big city of Dickenson. Taking advantage of this opportunity, Mom and Dad, packed two small suitcases, got into their car and followed the snowplow for the hundred-mile drive to the nearest hospital. I was born the next day.

Feeling the isolation of Bowman Mom would take me, when I was a baby, to visit Dad's parents in the big city of Chicago.

Their huge condo on Lake Shore Drive high above Lake Michigan was an exciting way to live …having a cook and a driver…the way the rich people lived. I enjoyed the conversation I had with Otto [my grandpa Vogl]. I liked him and felt he saw me as an intelligent woman. Getting up early with Pat, Otto and I would have breakfast together. One morning I fixed breakfast for him. When Margie [my grandma Vogl] saw I had fixed breakfast she was furious. This was what the maid was supposed to do. My family didn't have maids. I wasn't used to this kind of life. When Chuck and I got married, I always felt many of the Vogls were not happy. I was a Goya [not Jewish], and beneath his social status.

From the beginning, my parents' marriage was not an easy one. At one of their prenuptial parties one of dad's relatives, a psychiatrist, took my mom aside to tell her what an emotionally damaged child my dad had been. Subconsciously, Mom knew he was trying to warn her, but she was unable to fully hear him.

About 18 months after I was born we moved to Ann Arbor, Michigan, where Susie and Peter were born, then on to Missoula, Montana. While living there, Dad was drafted into the army. His job would be to give medical examinations to new recruits at Fort Hood in Columbia, South Carolina - but first he had to go to Texas for basic training. That left Mom, who was now five months pregnant on her own to take care of three small children. I was five at the time. Susie was three but not developed to the level of a normal three-year old, so still in diapers and not speaking. Peter, also in diapers, was only two. My youngest brother, Steve, would arrive a few months later.

Ever since I was a very young child Mom relied on me. She had to. Children come into the world with a personality of their own. Lucky for Mom I came into this world with the "caretaking gene". As I heard Mom relay her stories of enlisting me to help her care for my younger siblings, it struck me how young I was at the time, and how alone she must have felt.

With Dad gone and our belongings on their way to South Carolina, Mom reached out to her older sister. "Visiting Merrilie on the way would break up the long trip." She thought. Aunt Merrilie and Uncle John and the five children they had at the time (they eventually had seven children), lived in Rockford, Illinois. Mom booked a sleeping compartment on a train from Missoula to Rockford, a 1200-plus-mile trip. For her own survival she had the porter open the top berth and lock the door to our compartment so Susie, Peter and I couldn't get out. With me being in charge of my younger sister and brother, Mom collapsed into the upper berth to get much needed rest.

> *We had all our meals in there. I didn't dare let Susie out to run up and down the train; at five months pregnant I wasn't very good at running after her.*

With Susie still in diapers and not talking, my parents, by then, had come to grips with the fact that she was (as they called it in those days) mentally retarded. She has never had speech and has always worn diapers. Susie and I were less than two years apart and looked very much alike as babies and toddlers. One rarely remembers those early years, but family pictures tell the story of Susie and I having fun together which makes me often wonder what my life would have been like if my little sister had not been so severely mentally disabled. As a mom and grandma now I can only imagine how hard this must have been for both my parents. On Mom's tapes she shared this story of one of her experiences:

> *When Susie was a baby she looked completely normal; that's why it took us so long to realize she was retarded. We thought she was just developing slowly. She was born when*

*Chuck was in Pediatric residency. We used to go to depart-
ment picnics and Susie would be in the playpen – she was so
cute. I noticed the head of the department would spend an
awful lot of time playing with her and observing her, seeing
signs we weren't emotionally able to accept yet. It's so helpful that your conscious mind can protect you until you're
ready. Susie always had a very good personality. She wasn't
like some children who can't do things and get angry – with
her, she was always completely accepting. She has a love that
seems to come through her.*

After both of my parents died I became Susie's guardian and
spending time with her is very special to me. Mom was right *"She
has a love that seems to come through her."* She is a loving, sweet
woman. She is real. There is nothing fake or insincere about her,
what you see is what you get which is so refreshing and heartwarm-
ing to be around.

After a week or two at Aunt Merrilie's and Uncle John's, Mom
booked a flight from Chicago to Columbia to meet up with Dad. Unable to get four seats together on the plane, she gave me the job of
taking care of my rambunctious, squirmy two-year-old brother, Peter
sitting about six rows up from her and Susie.

For me this story highlights how submissive Mom was to the
rigid rules of her situation and the lack of her own voice in getting
what she needed. It illustrates so clearly the difference between wom-
en of her generation and mine. How insensitive and unthinking people were towards women with small children in those days and how
Mom didn't think she had choices or the right to speak up. Why didn't
she insist on seats together for her family?

South Carolina was a turning point in Mom's life and her marriage to my dad. It was 1955, and the U.S. Supreme Court had ruled

the year before in Brown v. Board of Education that separate schools for black and white children were unequal and unconstitutional. At the same time, Vocational Rehabilitation Amendments were passed authorizing federal grants to expand programs available to people with physical and mental disabilities.

In the 50's, disabled children and their parents were stigmatized. Most mentally challenged children and adults were put in large institutions with atrocious living conditions or hidden away in their homes. There were few if any special programs in the schools, and little money or attention was being paid to mentally challenged children. Then President Kennedy, whose sister was mentally challenged, signed the Community Mental Health Act to provide federal funding for community mental health centers and research facilities devoted to the research and treatment of mental retardation.

Wanting to help her daughter, Mom's natural but much-buried activist tendencies were slowly being awakened and itching to come out.

> *My friends and I decided our retarded children needed a nursery school. We contacted the Junior League and got acquainted, suggesting this would be a good project for them. Our children were nursery-school age, so, with their help, we opened a nursery school enrolling some black retarded kids as well, which made our school the first integrated school in the area at the time. That was a big thing for them* [the Junior League] *to swallow and probably affected them a lot.*
>
> *Chuck would get furious with me because I was on the phone too much and would leave the kids with Gracie* [the black housekeeper we had].
>
> *It wasn't so much that he did not like what I was doing; it was he did not like what I was becoming. I was be-*

coming somebody, and this was threatening to him. This was
something I wanted to do. I was doing it for my child and
learning ways to be able to accept having a retarded child.

With her energies expanding into a new and challenging arena
and her intelligence finally starting to be unlocked, she became involved in the newly formed National Association for Retarded Children. Then she got an important call from her father-in-law. Grandpa
Vogl, in his own altruistic and generous way, wanted to set up a research foundation for mentally challenged children. He recognized
Mom's fervor and the way she got things done. He asked her if she
would take on the job of finding the people and place to make this
happen. I can only imagine the excitement my mom must have felt,
not just for the wonderful development in her quest to improve the
lives of children like Susie, but for the confidence her father-in-law
showed in her. She was actually being valued for something besides
her role as a wife and a mother.

Stanford Medical School had a children's health facility with a
nursery school for mentally challenged children. Mom went to Palo
Alto to see what they were doing for the kids and recommended it to
Grandpa for the research foundation he was planning.

"The Universe Works" was Mom's lifelong mantra, and this was
one of those times when it applied. Not the type to calculate all con-
tingencies and prepare plans A, B and C., she was acting on pure con-
viction to help her daughter and other people's children. She didn't
have to sum up her courage and talk herself into jumping into the
fray. She saw a need and what should be done to fill it, and she moved
forward. There was a sort of force within her that propelled her where
she needed to go. This was a repeated pattern in her life. The work
she did for mentally challenged kids was only the first of her many

accomplishments. Her altruistic drive had a great influence on me and my life.

This was a role outside Mom's station of wife and mother. She was changing, and Dad was not supportive. Mom said this was the beginning of Dad treating her even worse than he had before.

He would treat me real nice and then pull the rug out from under me…that kind of nasty, sadistic way of behaving. This was something I wanted to do and I was doing it for my child. I was changing, but was not as conscious of it as I wish I'd been.

What she was doing and discovering about herself turned out to be the beginning of the end of my parents' marriage.

. . . .

I was in second grade when we moved to Palo Alto. Both my parents agreed that resources for Susie would be better there. Having a mentally disabled child must have been extremely hard for them. What I saw, as Susie's older sister were my parents being accepting and loving with Susie and not at all publically ashamed which happened quite a lot back then. Because of their attitude I grew up being very comfortable having a sister who was not "normal." She was always a part of my life, but it wasn't always easy.

Susie lived at home until she was about seven and I was about nine. At times she did things that embarrassed me profoundly. Once, Susie was taking a bath while I had a friend over. The bathroom door was open and we could both see and smell that she had pooped in the bathtub. I was embarrassed and tried to pretend nothing was wrong.

Another time she could have been hurt — or worse. Peter, Steve and some neighborhood kids were playing in our back yard, opening and closing the side yard gate, through which Susie manage to get out. A neighbor spotted her riding her tricycle down the middle of a nearby street, and called the police, who came promptly, scooped her up and delivered her back to our house unharmed.

This must have terrified my parents and made them realize that Susie was becoming too much to handle and needed a safer, more supervised place to live. Moreover, as she got older they could tell she wasn't happy. So, after much consideration, they found a warm and caring home for mentally disabled children an hour's drive north of us in Marin County. It was much safer for her.

My life growing up in a middle-class neighborhood populated by two-parent families with lots of kids mirrored that of the idyllic Cleaver family in the popular television show *Leave it to Beaver*. All the neighborhood kids — including me and my friends Cathy and Elaine from across the street, and Donna and her little sister a couple of houses down — spent our days running freely from house to house.

My bedroom was painted light baby blue, from the walls to the wooden bed board, desk and vanity. Mom and I picked out curtains and a bedspread that I loved, in a fabric with figures of ballerinas in shades of blue, light tan and pink. As my brothers got older I had the brilliant idea of persuading my dad to put a lock on my door — and high up on the door, too, so my brothers couldn't reach it and sneak in while I was gone. Not so brilliantly, I didn't realize that they could simply stand on a chair to reach the lock. Worse, they could — and did! — easily lock me into my bedroom, making me furious.

Our family had a nice back yard. Dad built a brick patio, a barbecue and a long wooden picnic table. Mom designed a play area with a swing set over a large sandbox, in which I spent hours constructing rivers, islands, bridges and little towns.

My self-made clubhouse in the side yard next to the neighbor's fence was furnished with a rickety wood table, a chair mom didn't want, old blankets and pillows and drawing supplies. This was my special place. Across the street was a huge, empty lot with a large oak tree perfect for climbing, and tall grass perfect for hiding. We drew chalk roads, gas stations, and grocery stores on the sidewalks and up the driveways, where we rode our bikes and pretended to be in our own little town.

On the Fourth of July, the neighbors would get together in the cul-de-sac across the street, set up folding tables and chairs and roll out their portable barbecues. Adults drank wine and beer while we kids ran around until dark, playing with sparklers and other rather tame fireworks.

I'm not sure how my parents found Camp Trinity deep in the Trinity Mountains of Northern California, but I was happy they did. Dad volunteered to be the "camp doctor" for a couple of summers when I was about nine or ten. I loved our trips to the camp, stopping on the way at the legendary Nut Tree. It had started out as a modest fruit stand along I-80 in Vacaville between San Francisco and Sacramento in the early 1920s, literally right off the highway. The Nut Tree was the state's first major road stop, and it featured an amazing selection of candy and dried fruits, toys and trinkets and a miniature railroad that we loved to ride on. It was a kid's paradise.

I was proud that my dad was camp doctor but don't remember spending much time with either him or Mom while we were there. Daytime, I was having too good a time with my girlfriends, riding horses and swimming in the nearby swimming hole. And I was old enough to spend my nights on one of the "sleeping platforms" — a cabin, front side open to the redwoods, with a row of cots and an older teenage counselor to oversee our activities.

Divorce was uncommon in those years, and none of my friends had divorced parents. When mine divorced in 1960, my *Leave It to Beaver* world collapsed. I felt embarrassed, different — and profoundly sad. I didn't like it when someone called the house for Dad and I would have to say he didn't live there anymore. I didn't like it when he came to pick Peter, Steve and me up for our Sunday outings. Since he couldn't stand to be anywhere near Mom, he didn't bother coming to the front door and just stayed in the car, honking the horn loudly, announcing to the whole neighborhood that we were different. All I felt was shame and embarrassment.

Dad took us on picnics, occasionally swinging by the hospital first to check on patients while my brothers and I rode up and down the hospital elevators. He took us on weeklong trips that many kids don't get to experience. There were Sierra Club trips: canoeing in Idaho, riding the whitewater rapids in Oregon, and my favorite — rubber-rafting off the coast of Mexico. Unfortunately, being together on these weeklong trips did nothing to bring us closer. I know Dad wanted to spend time with us. He had the money and the inclination to give us these amazing experiences, for which I'm grateful. But he didn't know how to relate to me as a father. He was always comfortable with younger children, but now I was going through puberty, becoming a young woman. What's more, although I can't say for sure, it seems to me now that Dad's hatred of Mom colored our relationship.

It was she who initiated the divorce, as I discovered years later from the tapes. Perhaps the alarm first sounded for her when she learned that three area doctors' wives had committed suicide.

I knew if I'd stayed married, I would have not committed suicide, but I would have been in a mental hospital or an alcoholic or a drug addict.

I started being so depressed. I saw myself next to myself. I had the feeling of committing suicide but wouldn't do it because of the kids. That was when I started talking to Chuck [my dad]. *He was so terrified because talking about our marriage would have opened up a whole can of worms – the wounds of his childhood. He would have never survived.*

I married Chuck because he was safe, because he was not sexually demanding. Sexually he had problems. He didn't like women.

I did feel so grateful he was willing to pay for my psychoanalysis. My psychiatrist said he felt that I chose Chuck because he was less threatening to me sexually.

I tried to lean on him, he was never there – that's an image that stuck in my mind. It wasn't all his fault – it was me. I learned in analysis that I didn't lean because it was too frightening. That I would find out I didn't have anything to lean on. I never gave him the chance. We had a sado/masochistic marriage. It was not a good marriage.

We had four children and stayed together for 12 years. It took me nine months to get divorced because Chuck fought it. I was subpoenaed to go in front of the Judge to prove I had reasons to divorce him. Chuck was used to me being an auxiliary to him. I felt incredibly trapped like women who live in countries where women don't have a right to leave a bad marriage. I thought, what if the judge won't give me a divorce? What will happen then?

I was scared. I was still in analysis and told my therapist how frightened I was. Chuck still lived at the house but we slept in separate bedrooms. I remember going to bed with scissors under my pillow. I told Cam [Mom's therapist]

I was frightened because Chuck was never angry, it was all just under the surface and it is his possible explosion that was so scary.

As an adult, I had open conversations with Mom about all sorts of things, and much on her tapes was not new to me, but I knew nothing about what she went through with her husband.

My heart broke as I heard her describe her mental state, thoughts of suicide and fear of her husband. It made me angry to find out what she had to go through to get a divorce. I felt scared and wronged for her to learn she was trapped in a marriage with a psychologically and physiologically damaged man and had to "prove she had reasons to divorce him," most likely to a male judge. I was overwhelmed to learn what her life with my dad was really like.

At the same time I was grateful that she had the courage to leave her dysfunctional marriage. As a young child, I had no clue about the life Mom described on her tapes. I don't remember my parents sleeping in separate beds. I don't remember their angry exchanges. I did feel the uneasiness that filled our home but the way my subconscious chose to escape it was to pay it no attention, to focus on my own world of friends and school. I remember my little brother Steve spending most of his time watching TV in his bedroom. He even saved up money to buy his own small TV. Was that his escape route?

The tension between my parents lay beneath the surface. One night as I was falling asleep I heard them through my bedroom wall having what I considered a heated exchange. Afterwards, when Mom came to kiss me goodnight, I blurted out, "Are you and dad going to get a divorce?" Surprised and shocked she said, "Oh dear. No, of course not. Where did you get an idea like that?" The question of divorce may not yet have been forefront in her mind, but as a child I could pick up on the intensity of their voices and the tone of their exchange. That was the only time I can remember hearing anything close to an argument.

By the time Mom filed for divorce, Betty Friedan's 1963 *Feminine Mystique*, had not yet been published. Said to have sparked feminism's "second wave," the book named what so many women were experiencing at the time. On the surface, their lives were stable, giving the illusion of happiness. But the reality was that women were beginning to question their lot in life — for example, the prevailing concept that they existed on this planet only to fulfill a God-given role of wife and mother. It was a confusing time for Mom. Outwardly it looked like she had everything: household help, membership in the country club, she did not have to work outside the home. Why should she be dissatisfied? But she was starting to wake up. Not only that, she was starting to realize that it would cost her mightily. Cam, her therapist, warned her that the changes she was making in her life would cause her friends to drop her. He was right — they did.

Before starting therapy she didn't think there was anything wrong with her. She simply hoped that if she went, Dad would go too, and that he would change.

> *I was not such a great mother, but the man I married was such a bad father. I spent the whole hour talking about how bad my marriage was. At end of the hour Cam said "when can I see you again"? I said "who, me?" I had no idea I needed anything.*

Dad refused to go to therapy, but paid for mom to see Cam three times a week for three years. Almost 500 visits allowed mom to cover a lot of territory.

It is important to a child's mental and emotional development for parents to have a sense of who they are and express and share their feelings. In my parents' case, there was much anger, but neither one of them knew what they felt or how to express it. Their anger hid beneath the surface, but I could sense it in the tense, unnatural silence. They were both afraid that if they spoke, they would lose control and let spew an avalanche of feelings.

I grew up thinking this is the way all married people behave. I learned to stuff my feelings. I had no model for speaking up or communicating in a healthy way. Instead, I learned to hide from my true feelings, take everything in stride and be "the strong one." This would play out in my marriage and is still something I am working on.

My parents and grandparents on their wedding day

*Me with my little sister Susie before my parents found
out she was mentally disabled*

My sister, Susie and I a few years ago on one of our visits to Fresno to see her

CHAPTER 2

LIFE CHANGING

Wherever you go becomes a part of you somehow.

~ Anita Desai, Indian novelist

"Pat, go get your brothers and come to the living room. I have exciting news to tell you!"

It was 1962, just a few years after my parents' divorce, when Mom, without warning, launched a plan that pulled my world out from under me.

"Oh boy! We're getting a convertible!" I thought as I rushed to get Peter and Steve. The three of us bunched up on the living room couch like baby birds eager to be fed. I sat on the edge of my seat, anticipation killing me. Mom looked nervous but happy.

"I have decided that we are going to move to Switzerland."

Anticipation turned to shock.

"It will be for a year and will be a wonderful experience for you kids going to school in a different country. We'll take trips to places you would only learn about in your geography class here. I know it will be a big change — but it will be so exciting!"

I opened my mouth to protest, but no words came out. Was I hearing her correctly? Finally, I found my voice. "Mom" I said "Really? A whole year?"

"Yes, Pat. That's how to really get to know a place and its culture and people. It will be so good for all of us — a great change of pace."

"But, Mom, why can't we just go for a vacation? Why do we have to move there? I don't want to leave my friends."

"They will be here when you get back, Pat."

She was excited and firm — determined to uproot our whole family and in no mood to let me try to persuade her otherwise.

And I wasn't one to put up a big fight. I was a shy, insecure, self-conscious thirteen-year-old, terrified of being whisked away to a far distant land. I hated the idea but tried my best to put a good face on a bad situation. I tried to catch Mom's enthusiasm by bragging about the move to my friends — and it was a good thing I did, because it helped me prepare for an adventure that would change my life.

Her motivations for this grand adventure remained mysterious to me until I listened to her tapes many decades later.

I didn't have such a good reason — I was just jealous of my husband — that's the reason. He was taking off, traveling all over Europe, and here I was sitting home with the kids. I got so mad. He came to pick up the kids for their regular Sunday visit and told me he was going to go to Europe. After they left I went back to my bed and screamed and cried and beat the pillow because I wanted to go. In fact, I was thinking, one of the fantasies I had when I married him was the two of us would become medical missionaries in Africa. Why I ever thought he would do something like that I don't know. I always wanted adventure.

On the one hand she seemed to me like a child pitching a tem-per tantrum. On the other I admired her love of adventure and refusal to let anything hold her back.

....

Before we moved to Europe, throughout my elementary school years, I had been called "fatty Patty" even though I wasn't actually fat; I just wasn't skinny like some of the other girls in my class. And of course my name rhymed with "fatty." Like many young girls, I had always been self-conscious about my weight and appearance. So even though they didn't apply, these two cruel words stuck with me and skewed my self-image, even years later, after my baby fat was long gone.

I wasn't a good student. My body didn't like to sit still and read-ing didn't come easily to me. I wasn't good at spelling, either — al-ways earning the fewest stars on the teacher's wall chart, for the whole world to see. All of this undermined my self-confidence.

Dad worked most of the time, essentially absent even when he was physically around, and finding it hard to relate to his budding teenage daughter. Mom had her hands full with four kids close in age — one of which was severely disabled. In spite of her unstable marriage, she labored to keep up the appearance of a perfect, happy family. As a result, my parents didn't notice or pay much attention to me.

It was not until fifth grade that I had a teacher I liked — and even more importantly, one who liked me. Mr. Brown was warm and caring. Starved for this kind of attention from an adult male, I just soaked it up. Mr. Brown felt like the father I wished I had. He was the bright light in my life. His creative way of teaching — using all types of art — suited my way of learning. He recognized this, encouraged me, and took pride in my artistic ability. Studying California missions, our class built a huge wood-framed twelve-by-five-foot papier-mâché relief map of California, on which we plotted the locations of all twenty-one missions. Mr. Brown's teaching methods made this history real and much more interesting for a visual learner like me. I hated moving on from his class.

Now, at thirteen, I was just starting to establish my place among my peers. After seventh grade I was fully in the groove of junior high school and looking forward to not being on the lowest rung on the ladder. My baby fat was finally gone, and looking like a California surfer chick was a serious priority. Since I didn't get it from either my parents or myself, I searched for approval from outside sources — particularly from boys. They became the center of my universe. I constantly thought, "Do they like me? Are they going to talk to me? Do they think I am cute?"

This was the era of the Beach Boys — surf, cars, bronze bodies and rock 'n' roll. I bleached my light brown hair blond and ironed it even though it was already straight. I slathered on baby oil, roasting myself in the back yard to get that perfect California tan. Adolescent hormones raging, all I wanted to do was hang out with boys.

This was my state of mind when Mom decided to snatch me away to Switzerland, which might as well have been another planet.

Besides grieving all I would be leaving behind, I was scared by what I was getting into. Bewildered, I asked my friends "I only speak English. How am I going to talk to the other kids? How will I understand them? Do my school work? How will I know what the boys are saying to me?" Of course, they were no help — none of them had experiences of their own to draw from. I never talked to Mom about my worries, keeping them stuffed deep down in my gut as I had been trained to do. Besides, despite being busy making all the arrangements, she didn't seem to have any idea what to expect for any of us. She was just barreling ahead with her plans.

From the perspective of an adult I have to hand it to her. I'm amazed at Mom's bravery. At 38 she was young and beautiful, fresh out of a grueling divorce, without an identity in sight. This was before her intellectual awakening, before her hippie days, before any drug-induced illusions she might have developed at a later stage of her life. In so many ways her world had been pulled out from under her, too. And yet, although she was in the throes of tremendous insecurity, she was planning to cart three of her young children off to a foreign country. (By that time, Susie was living in a good home for mentally disabled children, getting the care and attention she needed. She was safe and happy, and Dad was there to visit her regularly while we were gone.)

Looking back now, I wonder how my dad felt about having his kids whooshed away to Europe for such a long time. Did it help fuel his lifelong anger toward Mom? Did it affect his behavior towards me when I grew to be a woman?

Meanwhile, as I was struggling to get my head straight about the upcoming adventure, the logistics of it were starting to fall into place. A friend of Mom's had opened a travel agency and asked her to work for him. Thus she learned how to make arrangements for travel abroad. A neighbor's niece, Norie, visiting her aunt from the Netherlands, became our au pair. Her boyfriend had attended school in Switzerland and suggested to Mom a specific destination and school for us to attend.

Stars were aligning on the economic scene, as well. Dad paid alimony and child support, so Mom had a comfortable income. Her expenses were low because she owned our house free and clear; Grandpa Vogl had bought it as a gift for my parents and Mom got it in the divorce agreement. She decided that while we were abroad she would rent out our house to visiting professors at Stanford University, which would add to her income. The dollar was strong, so living in Switzerland would be less expensive than in the States. Everything was falling into place. As far as Mom was concerned, the Universe was working!

But for me everything was happening too fast, and keeping my feelings to myself did not make it any easier. Today, as I look at a photo of Mom, my brothers and me on our living room couch just before we left, I am struck at how telling it is. Mom, Peter and Steve were sitting up straight with big smiles, radiating excitement. I was slouching and looking nervous, insecure, and totally uncomfortable — like I was anticipating my next dentist appointment. My mouth was trying to smile, but the rest of my face wasn't going along.

Let it be noted that even in this state of mind, traveling over the Atlantic on an ocean liner — the SS Rotterdam — did feel like an adventure. Thirteen-year-old romantic that I was, to ease my anxiety I turned my efforts to trying to ignite a shipboard romance like the ones I had seen in the movies. I became absorbed in my appearance — clothes, hair, body, face — it all had to add up to a cool teenager. This actually turned out to be an effective diversion from my anxiety. But there was one complication. Before we left on the trip, Mom thought it would be a special treat for the two of us to go to the beauty parlor together and have our hair done. I got a permanent — I'm not sure why. Now, while scoping out the cute boys on board, I was mortified by the unexpected frizziness exploding on my head. The permanent was causing the damp sea air to turn my golden curls to yellow fuzz. Not the best look!

Despite their pre-voyage confidence, onboard my two little brothers now seemed unsettled and scared. In those days ships didn't offer all the activities for young kids that they do now. Without suitable diversions my dear siblings became wild, running around, climbing on chairs and acting like little monkeys. This was terribly annoying to the sophisticated young lady I believed myself to be, and I wanted nothing to do with them. Once again stuffing my feelings, I tried my best to look totally together and happy while keeping a lookout for that shipboard romance, which never came to pass.

Disembarking at Rotterdam, we all felt bewildered and lost among the thousands of people milling around trying to gather their belongings in what looked like the biggest warehouse I had ever seen. I was overwhelmed, trying to act grown up, but inside I just wanted to cling to my "mommy" for security. Mom shares this story:

I had taken my mother's steamer trunk. I thought, "I'm going on a steamer, I'm going to take a steamer trunk." It was really great. It was like taking a closet with you. When we were at the dock I could see all the baggage. No one spoke English. I was trying to tell the guy that the steamer trunk was mine. I was getting frustrated. Then I turned around and there was Robert smiling with two huge bouquets of flowers. He had flown over to meet us and had flowers for Pat and me. He was such a romantic guy.

Ah, Robert! Back in the states, Mom had been dating him. He was suave, handsome, warm, charming and paid attention to me, which I really liked. I could see that Mom was completely surprised to see him and relieved to have his support. For me, seeing him standing there with his big warm smile made everything feel okay. My worries disappeared. And it didn't hurt that he was thoughtful enough to bring me, as well as Mom, a beautiful bouquet of brightly colored flowers. Peter and Steve were chasing around, discharging their energy — and, likely, anxiety — the way little boys do. But for once they didn't bother me. My shoulders dropped, I suddenly felt a sense of ease. With a huge smile on my face I gave Robert a big hug. Life seemed perfect just for that moment.

Robert helped gather up our luggage and the steamer trunk and stowed them in the warehouse while we joined him for our first meal in Europe. He took us to a quaint outdoor café and afterwards had the maître d' call for a cab that would accommodate us and all our worldly belongings. Robert had been to Europe many times for business so it was easy for him to negotiate this stage of our trip. I'm sure Mom had no clue what to do once we arrived, and can only guess what trouble we'd have gotten into without him. Robert waved us off before heading to a business meeting. He said he'd see us after we got settled in Lausanne.

....

The taxi weaved down the narrow streets to Norie's parent's home, Mom seated in the front, the three of us kids quietly in the back, peering out the windows wondering what was next for us. It was a warm August afternoon, the sky was bright blue, and there was not a cloud to be seen. I remember Mom exclaiming, "This city is so clean, and look at all the bicyclers!"

Mom had become acquainted with Norie's family through letters they exchanged while Norie worked as our au pair. They had happily and graciously invited us to stay with them for a couple of days, and now they greeted us with warm and welcoming hugs. It was a perfect initiation to life in a foreign country. Their home was where my education to a wider world than Palo Alto got started. Mom shared this about our visit on her tapes:

> This wasn't too long after WWII, in which the Dutch were ravaged by the Nazis. One night we were all watching TV and a German man came on. I remember Norie's mother immediately getting up and angrily turning off the TV, pro-

ceeding to tell us stories about how she had to go out and steal food during WWII at great risk to her life.

It was our second day in this new and different country and I remembered this being a real eye-opener for me—a tiny peek at life outside my sheltered bubble of middle-class life in insulated America.

From Rotterdam we began to wind our way to Lausanne, Switzerland. Our first destination was Cologne, Germany. We stayed in a hotel right next to the beautiful and famous Cologne Cathedral, the largest Gothic church in Northern Europe; I had never seen anything like it. I remember thinking, "It took over 600 years to build, and the whole country of the United States isn't even 300 years old!" Mom was beside herself to be staying so close to this grand historic cathedral with its many ornate spires, beautiful stained glass windows and flying buttresses. She kept saying "It looks like a huge birthday cake," Unfortunately, it still showed scars from World War II bombings less than 20 years earlier.

Now, looking at our family pictures, I am in awe of this magnificent ancient masterpiece but as a thirteen-year-old I had other things to think about. This was not exactly an opportune time to start my period, but that's what my body chose to do on our first night in Cologne, and I was not prepared for it. Exhausted and feeling like a wet noodle, I curled up in bed just wanting to be "normal" again. Mom ventured into the streets of Cologne in search of my needed supplies. It was late, the night was dark, and stores were closed, the shop-owners having retired to their living quarters above. Luckily, she ran into a nice gentleman who opened his shop for her. Hooray for Mom!

The next morning I still felt unenthusiastic and sluggish and didn't want to leave the hotel. Steve was engrossed in playing with a small train Mom got him at the station. But Mom and Peter were dying to get out of the hotel and do some exploring. So they took off, challenging each other to climb the 533 ancient stone steps of the cathedral's spiral staircase. They came back excited about having seen the entire city and surrounding farmland from the viewing area at the top, 330 feet above the city. I had packed up our belongings as Mom had asked me to, so we were all ready to check out of the hotel. We needed to get to Lausanne in time to start school.

Once packed, checked out and ready to go, we headed to the boat launch for our trip down the Rhine River to Frankfurt. It was another beautiful, bright, sunny day as we floated past charming towns and villages, but this part of our long journey had taken on an undercurrent of anxiety. We were getting close to the end of our travels and the start of our life in a foreign country. I think we were all trying to hide our concerns about what lay ahead. What will it be like? What if we hate it? Will we have to stay anyway? Will we have friends? Will school be harder than back home? What will our house be like? Everything was an unknown. I couldn't find anything comforting to think about. I tried focusing on the scenery and the sounds of the riverboat, but my stomach was tied in knots. I remember Mom having some trouble with my brothers. Her tapes brought back the details.

I think they [Peter and Steve] thought that if they were naughty enough we'd turn around and go back. I think they were coming from deep, deep fear.

I remember they went to the bathroom and the guy in the bathroom who took tips came running out after them — they had seen the little dish of tip money and had taken it. So I had to be sure he got his money back. It was just a day trip so I hadn't reserved a cabin so we didn't have a private place to rest. I couldn't find a place for them to take a nap. I went to the captain and asked him if he had any cabins available, but he didn't. There was an old German man talking to the captain and he said, "I'm traveling with my two sons – your boys can come and use the cabin too." So the boys took a nap [or, I would guess, played] *with the German boys. It was such a nice gesture. The man figured that I was at my wits' end. I bought him a bottle of champagne and we had a nice little visit talking about what it's like to be parents.*

We were all feeling lost, anxious, and uncomfortable, but I don't remember circling our wagons as a family in support of each other. That was not the way we did things. We were each on our own, holding in our emotions. Since I always seemed, at least outwardly, to be in control of myself, Mom's attention was spent on dealing with her younger, very energetic children. I didn't think she had time to listen to my questions, and I didn't want to burden her even more with my worries. Being the oldest and a girl, I was given (or took on) a quasi-parental role — even before the divorce. That left me to cope on my own.

To make matters worse, after we docked and piled into the taxi, Mom accidently slammed Peter's finger in the car door. I cringed in sympathy for him, and took Steve's hand so Mom wouldn't have to worry about him while she comforted Peter. This seemed like a very bad start to the next leg of our trip, but a bright spot waited just ahead.

The next stop in what Mom called "our grand adventure" was with a family we had known in South Carolina who were stationed at a United States Army base in Frankfurt. Mom had kept in touch with them and they invited us to stay with them on our way to Lausanne. I was relieved to be around kids my own age who spoke English and Mom was able to relax for a bit with her friends and in familiar surroundings.

However, to my disappointment, we stayed only one night there. School was starting soon and we had to make our way to Lausanne and settle into our new home. This last leg of our journey was by train and then taxi — to a hotel! Mom had not arranged for a permanent place to live. I can't imagine making a move like that without accommodations waiting at the other end, but Mom, with characteristic trust in the Universe, had complete faith that the perfect place would materialize. In so many ways this was her philosophy — the way she went through life. And it didn't fail her at this moment. This is how she tells it:

I'll never forget waking up that morning — it must have been a Sunday morning and we were right in the middle of all these cathedrals and the bells were just bong, bong bonging. I rented a car to explore the city. I didn't know a soul in Lausanne but had been given the name of a couple who lived there. We had spent two days there before I got around to calling them, which was ridiculous — that's typical of me — not asking for help when it would be appropriate. We were living on my monthly child support, alimony and rent from the house. The exchange was very good and I could live on practically nothing, but staying in the hotel, I started worrying about running out of money. We had dinner with this couple. They had an old apartment building that was up the hill from Lake Geneva. It was in Pui, which was a wonderful lakeshore neighborhood of Lausanne. I told them we were looking for an apartment to rent. They said "There's an apartment empty right upstairs on the top floor of our building." So I was able to rent it that night. It was getting time for the kids to go to school. We got moved in just before school started.

The couple that owned our apartment building, Mr. and Mrs. Grosse, had seven children, all of who joined in welcoming us as if we were part of their own family. Their kindness made up for much of what we were missing from home.

The Grosse's youngest daughter, Lulu, was Steve's age and became his playmate. Balou, their son, made friends with Peter. Nono was the oldest — a boy three years older than I. Nono had a crush on me and his attention was just the distraction I needed. One of my favorite memories is sitting behind him on his Vespa motor scooter, arms around his waist, zipping through the streets and back alleys of Lausanne.

There's another Nono memory I'll never forget. One day he stopped me on the front steps of our building.

"Go upstairs to your apartment and look out your bedroom window"

"Why? What's up?" I asked. All I got was a sheepish grin and a nod. Too impatient to argue, I ran up the three flights of stairs and looked out my bedroom window as he'd instructed. There he stood in the dirt patch of the backyard, looking up at me still grinning.

"What are you doing?" I hollered down.

He moved aside so I could see a darkened part of the dirt in the shape of a big heart. In the middle were our initials with the plus sign between them. My heart melted.

"Oh, Nono, that's very sweet."

He held up a finger as if to say, "Wait, that's not all."

He lit a match against his jeans and tossed it to the ground. Suddenly there was a burst of flame that slowly followed the shape of the heart and finished up in the center, lighting up our initials. He had drawn it with kerosene.

My mouth dropped open.

"Oh my god, Nono, how did you do that? That's so cool!" I started laughing and clapping. I was giddy with delight, amazed at his cleverness and feeling pretty special at that point.

I don't know if I appreciated that family as much as they deserved, but I can see now what a gift they were to all of us.

....

Summer quickly faded into autumn, an amazing experience for us Californians. The brilliant colors of the leaves and the autumn flowers that by now were bursting from the window boxes were stunning and unexpected. This was something we didn't have at home that I truly enjoyed!

I cannot say the same about winter, which followed much too soon. Our first winter in Lausanne was one of the coldest ever. Our third-floor walk-up was heated by coal, supplied by poor Mr. Grosse. When he couldn't get strapping young Nono to do it, he himself hauled a wooden box of coal up three flights of stairs. To keep warm we would close the shutters over the windows, which made our rooms dark and a little depressing during the day. When we came home from school Mom would have some hot soup or cocoa for us and we would hunker down wearing several layers of clothes — including our mittens.

The apartment was furnished with run-down chairs, tables, lamps and eclectic pieces of art. The rugs were faded and threadbare. Mom was afraid they would fall apart if she tried cleaning them.

I enjoyed our "very Swiss" apartment, but there were times when I wanted something a little cleaner and more new. The living room had a fireplace, which is where we got a lot of our heat. The first caller, after we got moved in, knocked on the door and said in English "I am here to clean your chimney" He was a chimney sweep like the ones right out of Mary Poppins. Everybody had them in these old apartment buildings.

My room, next to the tiny kitchen, was much smaller than my room back home. There was barely space enough for a single bed, a small desk and an armoire for my clothes. Not feeling at all comfortable yet, I was trying my hardest to show the outside world that everything was okay, and so was glad to have my own retreat. Still, I was uneasy, which Mom could see even though I tried to act as if everything was okay. She suggested we perk up my room a little with a coat of paint. I was game and chose my favorite color — baby blue. We moved the furniture out into the living room and laid down old paint cloths that we borrowed from Mr. Grosse. He and Nono helped us paint the high places along the ceiling while Mom and I trimmed along the floor and around the door and window. The best part was rolling it on the walls. I'd never painted before, and it was a lot of messy fun. Doing it myself helped me make the room my own.

The walls had been covered in an old grayed and faded print wallpaper, and Mom and Mr. Grosse decided it would work just as well to paint over the wallpaper rather than go to all the time and trouble of pulling it off the walls before painting. That proved to be a mistake.

One weekend during that especially cold winter Mom took us all on an overnight trip to Les Diablerets, a picture-book village in the heart of the Alps. It was fun to be away and see a different part of the country. This was where I first attempted to ski, as a self-conscious thirteen year old I was trying my hardest to look super cool - like I had it all together. Our apartment seemed to always be cold so coming back to a warm cozy hotel room was a real treat.

When we got home I went to my room to unpack and couldn't believe what I saw. The wallpaper underneath my beautiful baby-blue walls was peeling and curling down like sad, wilting flower petals. We Californians, having no knowledge of cold-weather precautions, had neglected to leave the water dripping in the faucets so as to prevent the pipes from freezing. Why would that cross our minds? The worst had, indeed, happened. A pipe burst, and by the time we got home, water was seeping through the walls. All I could do was cry. I just wanted to go home.

....

The school that brought us to Lausanne, Switzerland was called École Nouvelle de la Suisse Romande. Its alumni included the eighth king of Thailand and Jacques Piccard. French, of course was the spoken language and I did not speak one word of it.

On my first day at École Nouvelle, Mom and I walked up to the old, three-story, red brick building. It smelled like a school — that is to say, like kids, books and floor wax. We found our way to the office of the principal, Madame DuPuy. Madame was an austere beauty, petite — about my height but bone-thin. She had curly auburn hair and piercing blue eyes that met ours from over wire-rimmed half-glasses. My first thought was those eyes didn't miss a thing around here. She shook hands with both of us, greeting us in English with a heavy French accent: "Very glad to meet you." She was warm but stern while explaining the basic rules of the school. She had Mom sign some paperwork, then invited her to leave and walked me to my classroom.

I entered a bit hesitantly and looked around. The room was quiet and dark, lined on two sides with blackboards. About fifteen girls and boys sat at individual wooden desks, bent silently over their work.

An older, distinguished-looking man with gray hair was standing in the middle aisle, tapping a lean forefinger on one little girl's paper, no doubt pointing out some error. When he saw us he stopped.

"Attention, tout le monde. Everyone, this is Patricia. She is from the United States and will be joining our class. Please welcome her."

They looked up, turned to me, in unison chanted "Bonjour Patricia" and went right back to work.

Madame DuPuy took my hand and walked me over to my new teacher. "Pat, allow me to introduce you to Monsieur Stein. Monsieur Stein, this is Patricia Vogl."

We shook hands. I managed to eke out a polite "Hello, Mr. Stein." He said, "How do you do, Patricia." His accent was German and those were the last English words I heard him speak all year.

Some of my classmates were from upper-class Swiss families; others were from elsewhere around the world. A few came from America but I was the only one who spoke only English. My classes in history, science, geography and math were all taught in French. I sat at a desk in the back of the room listening to my new teacher speak very fast in a foreign language, having no idea what he was saying. I thought; "How am I going to get through this?"

Depending on your perspective, it can be either good or bad to be in such a small class. The bad thing, according to me, was that I couldn't disappear in it. The good thing, according to Mom, was I could get some personal help. Unfortunately, Monsieur Stein wasn't so inclined.

Swiss schools had, and probably still have, higher academic standards than American public schools. Not being a good student in the States and not knowing any French combined to make my classroom experience pretty miserable. To say that I received extremely poor grades would be an understatement. Because of this experience I have true empathy for children, especially teenagers, from other countries entering American classrooms that don't know a word of English. Mom said:

My kids didn't do well at all, and I didn't expect them to do well. Of course, the teachers always thought I should expect them to. They're very much Swiss. Excellence. Excellence. Excellence. So my kids sort of slipped through; they didn't get very good grades, and I didn't care because they were learning so much.

Over the course of this once-in-a-lifetime opportunity to live as a family in Europe, Mom took every opportunity to travel and let us experience different countries and their people. She was right. Living in a foreign country, I learned much that would show itself later in my life. But not doing well in school plus not having her help and encouragement to do well took a toll on my self-confidence that took many years and many experiences to overcome.

As I listen to her talk on her tapes I can see she was proud of our strength, and even though we didn't talk about our feelings, she had some understanding of how tough it was for us that first year.

I just really, really admired the kids so much because they adjusted — talk about survival of the human spirit — that's what I was seeing. The kids knew that I wasn't going to turn back and go home, so they really pitched in and did the best they could.

To deal with this deficit, I did what I always did — I withdrew, at least in the classroom. But how I related with classmates in social situations was another story. I made friends easily with the girls and was a flirt with the boys. No one cared that I was a bad student and neither did I. Looking back at the shy, insecure thirteen year old I was then and knowing about the academic difficulties I faced, I see in hindsight that École Nouvelle was not my best option. It was beyond me to make things better for myself inside the classroom, but I did have the wherewithal to have some fun outside of it.

To get to school every day I rode the bus up the hill to the center of town, then switched to a trolley that let us off a couple blocks from the entrance. The trip to and from school gave me opportunities to get acquainted with other students.

One warm, sunny morning about a week after school started I met Suzi. She walked right up to me on the bus. Suzi was from Cape Town, South Africa. Her family was living across the street and up a way from our apartment house. She was my age and an only child, and was used to reaching out to make friends.

I scooted over so she could sit next to me and we started talking. We hit it off right away. With a little twinkle in her eye she blurted out, "Do you like boys?" My face lit up as I said emphatically "Yes I do!" Instantly, we were friends. We became inseparable. Either she was hanging out in my bedroom or I was in hers. She had been living in Lausanne for the past two years, spoke French fluently and became my own personal interpreter in social settings. That was probably a bad idea, because I made even less of an effort to learn to speak French myself. Suzi was fine with it and our friendship made life seem normal again.

. . . .

We survived the winter and made it to the end of spring, through a whole school year and a bone-chilling winter. Then summer arrived and thoughts of going back home popped in and out of my head. I didn't want to endure another year of school at École Nouvelle, but my friendship with Suzi was something I knew I would miss. Still, the plan was to be in Switzerland for just one year, so naturally I expected us to start making travel plans to go home.

When I brought it up to Mom one night at dinner, she admitted that she was seriously considering staying for another year. She had been in touch with the renters in Palo Alto and they wanted to stay in our house for another school year. I wasn't completely surprised, but my heart sank when I thought about going back to École Nouvelle.

Mom had another card up her sleeve and reading my mind she revealed some promising news. She'd been doing a little research on other schools in the area and found one within walking distance from our apartment.

My new school was just down the hill from where we lived. No more bus rides for me! Le Manoir was a girls' boarding school, but since we lived close by I wouldn't board. I was the only non-boarder, but that didn't seem to get in the way of my being accepted. Again, my classmates, aged fourteen to eighteen, came from all over the world: India, Venezuela, Thailand, Jamaica, Spain, Denmark, England and the U.S. The school was small — only about ten girls per class. We were housed in an old, white, three-story Victorian house with beautifully manicured grounds. With so few students, there was a close-knit environment. All the girls were friendly and open with each other, sharing stories of what it was like growing up in their respective countries. Even though we came from different parts of the world and from different cultures, we had much in common. We stood by each other – no games or backstabbing. We were all sisters together in this foreign country, which I especially loved since I had only brothers at home. A few of us shared our most intimate thoughts and feelings, and became quite close.

The teachers gave us all individual attention and, to my relief, classes (except for French) were taught in English. I have never been interested in math but because my algebra teacher was so good at engaging his students and did such a good job explaining everything, I actually enjoyed his class and did very well. As I approached my fifteenth birthday I was happy and thriving, doing much better academically, and starting to feel more confident and self-assured.

The first day of school I didn't want Mom to come along. We had already been there together to get me signed up, so I was comfortable going alone. When I arrived I went to the office of the head mistress. She smiled and said, "Hello, Barbara [my mom's name]. Welcome to Le Manoir. Let me show you around." I followed her, not really listening to what she was saying, but thinking about being called Barbara. I remembered my elementary school days back home when some kids teased me for a while, calling me "Fatty Patty". It affected my body image and my self-esteem. I had grown to dislike my name, and here was a perceived opportunity to change it to something I liked. What to do?

"Excuse me" I said to the headmistress, "My name isn't Barbara, its Sandy, Sandy Vogl. My mother's name is Barbara." Sandy had popped in my head because Sandra Dee and Bobby Darin were the teenage movie idols of the time.

"Oh, I apologize," she said. "I will make sure our records are corrected, Sandy." With no questions asked, that whole school year I was Sandy. All my school records listed me as Sandy Vogl. Even now it puts a smile on my face that in a spontaneous reaction I succeeded in changing my name for a year. I was finally putting Fatty Patty to rest.

The headmistress was responsible for the boarders, all day, every day – not just during class time. She had to keep a tight rein on their comings and goings. One of the most frequently broken rules was the one about not having any contact with boys. As hard as she tried, our hormones won out more often than not. To make it even harder, there was a boys' boarding school not far from Le Manoir. You could almost see the tension pulling the two schools together. One of the ways around that rule was for the boarders to spend weekends with the local girls.

I participated in that scheme several times. My friends had to get special permission to spend Friday night at our place, and the headmistress would always contact Mom directly, verifying that she would chaperone the entire time and that no boys would be included in our activities. Mom and I would joke about having to send Peter and Steve and all the Grosse boys away for the weekend. Of course, she agreed to enforce the rules so my friends could spend the night, but Mom was a bit of a rebel herself and not above bending the rules a little. She felt that we were typical, healthy teenagers and still young enough that our gatherings were innocent fun. So without the head-mistress knowing, my friends and I were able to hang out with a few of the dreaded opposite sex.

The banning of boy-girl co-mingling was a hard rule to main-tain. The year I was there, two sixteen-year-old American girls found a way to evade the system more extensively than most, managing to get romantically involved with a couple of Italian boys. With forged passports, they ran away with them to Italy, setting the whole school abuzz with the scandal. Eventually, they were found as their parents flew in from the States to take them home. I watched in amazement, impressed at their chutzpah and what they were able to pull off.

Suzi still attended my old school, École Nouvelle, but we re-mained close friends and constant after-school companions. One day, at a corner market we met a couple of boys from the nearby private boys' school. One of them was Peter Pasternak, an American from California, related to Boris Pasternak, the author of *Doctor Zhivago*. Our paths would cross later, in California. For many months Peter, his friend Rick, Suzi and I spent hours hanging out talking and laughing, walking along the lake holding hands, and innocently making out in the local movie theater.

What a difference a year made. I was coming into my own, not thinking at all about the friends and the life I had left back in California, feeling as if I was going to survive this grand adventure Mom had taken us on. Life was good.

It takes a year to cycle through the seasons and systems of a place in order to know what to expect, not always having to be tense and on guard. With that first year under my belt, gradually and without my noticing, things were actually becoming more enjoyable. I could relax and appreciate the beauty and excitement of my surroundings. Our second year in Switzerland made all the difference for me and completely changed my European experience.

....

Lausanne is a beautiful city on Lake Geneva, in the French-speaking region of Switzerland, boasting a dramatic panorama of the lake and the Alps. The promenade along the lake is a tourist attraction highlighted by the hilly medieval shop-lined streets and a twelfth-century Gothic cathedral in the center of town. We lived in the area just up from the lake called Pui. It had more character and a slower pace than California, although at my young age I didn't consciously appreciate those things. My focus was on boys.

On weekends we would pile into the Ford Taurus Mom bought when we arrived and take day trips to the nearby cities of Vevey and Montreux, and the famous Château de Chillon, located on an island just off the shore of Lake Geneva. Oftentimes Suzi came along, making those excursions much more fun for me, while Peter and Steve entertained each other.

During school breaks we'd take more time and travel farther into Switzerland and surrounding countries. Our time abroad truly did become the adventure Mom said it would be. My life was changing. I was coming into my own, feeling more comfortable in my skin with a sense of confidence that had evaded me all of my life. My memories of these vacations in Europe are filled with adventures young teenagers in the states could only see in movies.

Our first Christmas was spent at a picturesque, charming, snow-covered chalet Mom had rented sitting on top of a hill outside of Château d'Oex, near the ski resort of Gstaad. It looked like a chalet on a picture postcard. The snow was almost five feet deep on the sides of the road and nearly as high on the rooftops of cabins along the way with smoke rising from their chimneys. When we arrived we found the driveway was plowed, but steep and slippery with packed snow. Mom wasn't sure our car would make the grade so we gathered our belongings and started hiking up. When the front door opened a couple young women stepped out smiling and waving at us. I said, "Mom, who are those girls waving at us? Why are they in our house?"

Somehow Mom had neglected to tell us that she invited two young women, both in their early twenties, whom she had met in Lausanne.

"They're the ones who recommended this place to me," she said "They've been here before, and I thought it would be fun to have them join us."

Maria was a tall, striking woman from Cuba, with large brown eyes and shoulder-length dark hair. Her friend Sonny was shorter and one of those beautiful blonds you imagine when thinking of woman from Sweden.

This didn't surprise me at all. Mom had always made friends with people of all ages. I privately wondered if she was thinking they would be good babysitters for us. If she did, that is not how it worked out. Maria and Sonny were warm, friendly and a lot of fun. They adopted me as their little sister. Once, after a day of ski lessons, as we were all huddled around our rustic stone fireplace, Maria said to me, "Sonny and I are going into town. Do you want to come with us?" My face lit up. These two older, experienced women were asking me to tag along with them. "Yes, I would love to." I said, making a point of not looking too excited so Mom would let me go.

Getting dressed, I chose my most grownup outfit. I had no idea what we were going to do but I didn't want to look too much like the "little sister" tagging along. I picked out my most "mature" outfit, a green-and blue plaid wool mini kilt with a big brass pin, to go with a forest-green cable knit sweater and knee high boots. I dared to put on a little mascara and lipstick that Mom let pass with a knowing smile. When I came out of the bedroom ready to go I got a thumbs-up from Maria and Sonny and big smiles as Sonny tossed me my coat on our way out.

We went to a couple of bars and had a blast dancing to American rock 'n' roll. I even had a drink — I think a rum and coke, and was surprised I was able to get a cocktail without being carded. Europe is much looser about that than the U.S. Following Maria and Sonny's lead I found flirting with boys came naturally. This was probably not what Mom had in mind when she invited them to join us. It was 1963, and I felt as if I was living in one of the popular teen romance movies I loved so much. It was an amazing experience for a barely fourteen-year-old American girl. This was only the beginning of my adventures with the opposite sex. I was growing up fast and enjoying every minute of it.

Our next Christmas break, Mom went all out and reserved a condo in Zermatt, at the foot of the Matterhorn. The Matterhorn is, understandably, one of the most photographed and painted places in the world, and being in Zermatt, elevation of a little over 5,000 feet, was like being in a Christmas storybook. The snow, the lights and pine boughs, the shiny red ribbons and festive music, made for a holiday I had only seen on TV. Mom announced, "We all need to get to bed early tonight. I have us all scheduled for skiing lessons right after breakfast." Little did I know - the best was yet to come.

The sun was still behind the mountain as we got up and dressed, gathering our ski gear. We wouldn't be coming back to the condo before our lessons, so we clumsily traipsed down to the restaurant, bumping boots and skis along the way.

After breakfast, wearing the baby blue lace-up ski boots that matched my baby blue down jacket, I clumsily maneuvered my very long wooden skis to the foot of the mountain to join the others for my beginner ski class. A dozen or so beginner skiers of all ages awkwardly gathered around the instructor at the foot of the T-bar lift. I could make out French, Italian and German, but my ears perked up when I heard someone say, "Excuse me. My ski is caught up under yours." I looked up and saw where that English-speaking voice was coming from. I had inadvertently slid one of my skis atop the ski of a gorgeous blond British boy — Johnny.

He was on vacation with his dad. "Oh…this is going to be a good day," I thought, as I promptly lost my balance while my feet went out from under me. Johnny was laughing a little as he reached out a hand to help me up. "Are you all right?" I was too embarrassed to answer and just took his hand while he stepped on my skis to steady them while pulling me to my feet.

"Your first time?" He asked, trying to make light of our clumsy encounter.

"You would think so." I said, "but it is my second."

"Ah, an American. You didn't ski at home then?"

I was about to reply when the instructor called out for everyone to stop talking and pay attention. I was actually more curious and interested in getting better acquainted with the British boy, but we lost track of each other. We went in separate directions because he was not a beginner and was waiting for an advanced instructor. "Oh well, maybe I'll run into him again sometime," I thought.

Meanwhile, Mom had cut out of her lesson early and found a cozy spot in the lodge. She was enjoying the fireplace and a hot toddy when a handsome man introduced himself. Alone, beautiful, and the opposite of aloof, she readily invited him to join her. Bill was vacationing in Zermatt with his son Johnny. Yes, my Johnny. This chance meeting turned out to be as fortuitous for me as it was for Mom. She and Bill exchanged family backgrounds and discovered that they were both happily divorced with kids in tow.

Traipsing in from skiing, tired and happy, I found Mom chatting with Bill. "Kids, this is Bill. I would like you to meet him." Seconds later, Johnny strolled in, and over to our table. We had just settled in with hot chocolate when he joined us. About two years older than I, Johnny took after his father in the looks department — tall, well built, with sandy blond hair and a classic good-looking face. It didn't take any time for everyone to see that Johnny and I were going to get along nicely. After traveling with Mom and my two younger brothers, having someone my age to hang out with was great. A boy was even better.

"How did your lesson go?" he asked.

"I don't think I'll be ready for the next Olympics, but I improved a bit from my first time out. How was yours? You've been skiing quite a bit?"

And so it went. We talked and laughed and I could tell he was just as attracted to me as I was to him. We decided to have bratwurst sandwiches and cokes from the outdoor kiosk in the shopping area. We found a bench to sit on while we ate and watched skiers glide up and down on the chair lifts nearby. As we walked back to the lodge to rejoin the others I was hoping we would be able to get together at dinnertime and maybe find a place to be alone. I didn't know that Bill and Johnny had taken their last run on the slopes and were heading back to London after lunch. Disappointing for sure, but I still had so much to share with Suzi when were back home in Lausanne.

....

Not expecting to ever see Johnny again, I was thrilled when I heard he and Bill were going to spend Easter vacation with us in the south of Spain.

Mom, Peter, Steve, and I drove down through France to Spain in our Ford Taurus station wagon, meeting up with Bill and Johnny in Malaga, which sits on the Mediterranean Sea between Granada and Gibraltar. Malaga is one of the oldest cities in the world. Art and history are everywhere. It is famous for being the birthplace of Pablo Picasso. Our quaint, two-story hotel was right on the beach and couldn't have been more romantic and picturesque.

I was excited to see Johnny again and hoped he was feeling the same. By the time we got checked in Bill and Johnny were waiting for us in the dining room. I was feeling pretty road weary and rumpled from the trip, but seeing the look on Johnny's face when he saw me dissolved any anxiety I had about him still liking me.

I was now fifteen with just enough boy experience under my belt. I was no longer shy about getting affectionate and letting my hormones do the talking. Johnny picked up on signals that triggered his own natural responses, and we excused ourselves to take a walk on the beach.

The full moon was reflected in the shimmering waves. Johnny took my hand as we walked to a spot where we took off our shoes to wade in the surf. Lying on the warm sand, making out, we were suddenly startled. Looking up, a flashlight was aimed in my eyes and the stern voice of a man was saying something in Spanish that sounded like we were in trouble.

Johnny understood Spanish and said, "Pat, it's a bobby. We have to go." He apologized in Spanish as we brushed off the sand before bolting off toward the hotel. Once out of earshot we started laughing uncontrollably and went back to wading in the surf.

The James Bond movie *Goldfinger* had just come out, featuring an Aston Martin with ejection seats and machinegun taillights. Bill had driven down to Spain from London in his own sexy, brand-new Aston Martin. I felt so grown up as he drove Mom, Johnny and me away in it one night, off to dinner in the nearby little town of Rincon De La Victoria — leaving Peter and Steve behind at the hotel. As we sped along the windy coastal road of southern Spain, Johnny and I cuddled in the small back seat of Bill's glamor machine, stealing kisses. Looking up at the starlit sky through the sunroof was dizzyingly romantic. It was another amazing experience for a young American girl who was totally star-struck and boy-crazy.

Despite my innocent teen adventures with Nono, Peter and Johnny, Robbie was my first true love. I had met him for the first time before we left the States for Switzerland and didn't expect to ever see him again. Our mothers had been friends for years. He and his mom, Jan, moved to Hong Kong for a year, and were now heading home. I'm sure my face turned bright red when Mom remarked nonchalantly, without knowing how I felt about him, "We are going to pick up Jan and her son Robbie in Genoa next weekend." I had not thought about him for the longest time. Now all my old emotions were flooding back.

Robbie was a year older than I, but having lived in many foreign countries he felt like a "man of the world." He was tall, dark and handsome and carried an aura of aloofness.

As we greeted them in the Italian port of Genoa, my palms were sweating and my heart pounded out of my chest. He had changed a lot — we both had. I instantly fell madly in love with him all over again, and the attraction felt mutual. I couldn't get enough of his eyes, his smile with those perfect white teeth and his thick, dark chocolate hair. But it was his laugh that relaxed and endeared him to me. He actually thought I was funny and we never ran out of conversation — no awkward moments of silence.

Taking it slow, on our way back to Lausanne, we stopped for the night in Avignon, France, a romantic ancient hillside town on the banks of the Rhone River with narrow brick walkways winding through the city. We checked into a beautiful old world hotel overlooking the river. The dining room of the hotel was crowded, so Mom and Jan decided it was best to get room service and make an early night of it. Robbie had other plans.

Leaning close to my ear, he asked if I wanted to go exploring with him. The warmth of his breath on my neck sent sensations through me that made me weak in the knees. "Mom," I said "Robbie asked me to go for a walk with him. I'm not hungry anyway. Would it be okay if we went out — just us — without Steve and Peter?"

She looked a little surprised and then glanced over at Robbie, probably noticing for the first time how good-looking he was, and got it immediately. Then in a stern motherly tone she said; "Okay, but it's getting late and you don't know the area. Don't go far and be back by ten — no later."

Finally by ourselves, we went off excitedly to explore the city. The air was warm and the moon was full as he took my hand. We walked toward the bridge across the river to the top of a hill surmounted by the Abbaye St. André — ancient ruins with a history reaching back a thousand years, up through the era of the Holy Roman Empire and occupation of the papacy in Avignon. Finding a spot where we could sit together, our chatter gradually faded. He put his arm around my shoulder and asked if I was cold. As I turned to answer we locked in a cocoon of passion, lust and young raging hormones. We kissed under the stars. Wrapped in his arms I felt safe and at home.

Our innocent romance continued as we drove back to Lausanne. In the back seat, with my brothers between us, Robbie's arm reached along the back seat of the car, gently caressing my neck. My heart was racing. I was in ecstasy and agony at the same time, wanting more.

Back in Lausanne, Robbie and I reveled in the dance of young love, kidding around, exploring the city, talking, laughing and kissing with some touching but not going any further. I wasn't ready for intercourse, but I definitely wanted more than kissing. Robbie's mom was not the usual mother. On their way through the Middle East to Genoa she had arranged for him to have an early education in sex. She paid for him to have sex with a prostitute. I suppose if it had been at his father's encouragement it wouldn't seem so surprising. I don't remember his experience shocking me. It was probably because of who he was — a kind, attentive and sweet guy — and wanting to focus more on what was happening between us.

I didn't think twice about what he was telling me as he shared this information with me along with his feelings about the experience. His young brain thought of women in one of two ways: Either he treats her with respect and dignity, puts her on a pedestal and brings her home to meet his mom, or she is someone to just have sex with to satisfy his hormonal needs. Later I would come to understand this as the Madonna/whore syndrome, in which some men stereotype women as one way or the other without seeing women in all their dimensions.

For good or bad, I was in Robbie's first category. He was good at holding back. I was not at all experienced and probably would not have been able to stop his advances. He told me he respected me too much to go any further physically. I didn't understand it but in hindsight I appreciate Robbie's restraint. At the time, I was just getting a taste of sexual arousal and could only want more of it.

A few weeks later, as Robbie and his mom boarded a plane for the States, my heart was aching. But as time passed I became more focused on what it was going to be like for me when I got back home.

I had mixed emotions: sadness for leaving and excitement for returning. By that time I had a best friend, a school I liked, neighbors who were like family, and a whole new level of self-confidence. My experiences abroad had a positive effect on the self-conscious, insecure, uncomfortable thirteen-year old girl who first landed in Rotterdam. Living in Europe at that vulnerable age was challenging to say the least. But my experiences were helping me come out of my shell, feel comfortable in my body and confident as the young woman I was becoming. Mom had given my brothers and me an invaluable experience, despite the rough start. It had done a lot to expand my horizons and help me become a more secure person.

Thinking about returning to Palo Alto felt good. I wanted to get back into my old room and see my friends and feel the California sunshine on my face. I imagined slipping back into the groove I'd left behind two years prior and hanging out with my old friends.

Mr. Brown, my 4th and 5th grade teacher

My 7th grade class picture

With Mom, Peter, Steve (on the floor) in our Palo Alto living room just before we left for Europe. I can feel my uneasiness seeping out of my body and hurt for the shy and self-conscious thirteen year old I was.

Mom with Bob Seese enjoying dinner on our balcony in Lausanne, Switzerland

Our landlords son Nono Grosse and his Vespa

My friend Suzi and I with a few other classmates (one from the U.S. and the other from Sweden) at Ecole Novelle, my first year in Lausanne

CHAPTER 3

FUELING MY PASSION

We have to begin with the understanding that a woman's right to her own body is a fundamental human right.

~ Bettina Aptheker, Author and Professor,
University of California, Santa Cruz

When I returned home to California after spending the eighth and ninth grades in Switzerland, I attended Palo Alto High School. Palo Alto is a pretentiously upscale town, home of Stanford University, and "Paly" is an equally pretentious high school. It was a larger school than I was used to, with about five hundred kids in my graduating class. It was easy to get lost in the crowd, and I did. I had just come from a school of about thirty-five girls where I knew everyone, classes were held in a relaxed environment and I could have one-on-one conversations with my teachers. At Paly I had no teachers I liked or who took any interest in me, or any subjects that struck a chord. Returning to my old groove that I had looked forward to was not to be.

In the middle of my sophomore year, I worked at Dad's clinic. He had a small practice with just himself and one nurse, Millie, who ran the office. A friendly older woman with a warm, loving smile, she took me under her wing. My job was to take the kids' temperatures, measure and weigh them and do some lab work. I was good with patients, and felt as if I was learning a skill, which helped me feel good about myself. Working there also enabled me to see firsthand how much my dad's patients liked him. He had a good bedside manner, loved small children and was most comfortable with them. He was a good pediatrician even though he wasn't such a good father —especially as I got older.

One day at work I got a call from Peter Pasternak, the boy I had met in Switzerland. He was now home in Los Angeles.

"Hey…I know it's been a long time but I am coming to San Francisco in a couple of weeks. Think you can meet me there?"

That sounded pretty good — and it got even better.

"Dad is going to be interviewed on the *Gypsy Rose Lee* show. We would be part of the live TV audience. Can you? It would be so great."

It would, indeed be great! Joseph Pasternak was an Oscar-winning Hollywood film and TV producer. At sixteen, I saw this as something like a chance in a lifetime.

"Of course! I'd love to go. I'll just need to tell my dad I need the day off, but that won't be a problem."

Was I ever wrong! I could not have been less prepared for his reply.

"No, Pat, I can't give you the day off. I need you here. You have committed to this work and it is your responsibility."

I was furious. I had never asked for any time off. He clearly didn't understand how important this was to me. But I could see he had made up his mind, and there was no point in trying to have a conversation. Indignant, I shouted back at him. "

"I am going anyway. No matter what you say."

"Well, if you do you are fired," he replied evenly.

Wow! That was harsh.

"Well then I quit." And that was that.

The sad fact about my father is that in so many instances he didn't stop to try to understand what a sixteen-year old was like, or later what a twenty-five-year-old or a thirty-five-year-old was like. Everything was all about him. He didn't have any idea how to communicate at the right age level. He didn't seem to realize that he was the adult and I was the child; had it been otherwise, he could have been such a better teacher.

I am sure his decision not to let me have the day off was intended to teach me a lesson in responsibility, but the lesson was not successful. I could only see him being arbitrary, rigid and controlling. What he did that day didn't just leave me without a job I was enjoying and learning from. It put distance between us. Was it worth it?

....

Though I considered myself to be back home, the kids at school didn't. They saw me as a new girl in town — this at an age when being part of the in-crowd is paramount. I was as much a new girl as someone who had never lived there before. There was no penetrating the established circles of friends; their cliques were shut and bolted to me, a newcomer. A group of girls had even titled themselves the Top 12, given they had now reached junior high. On one level I was intimidated by them, because I saw them as pretty and popular, but on the other hand I saw them as small and shallow. Except for an old friend I had first known in the fifth grade, I was out in the cold.

My friend's name was Linda but I called her Cass for her last name, Cassineri. Cass was the only person who cared about what I had experienced in Europe. She saved me just as Suzi had a few years earlier. Without her, high school would have been a much different place. Cass had her own set of challenges at home and I became her confidant. She lived down the street with her dad; her mother had left one day and never returned; her older sister, with whom she was not close, had moved out and was on her own. I think Cass's dad did his best to raise a teenager all by himself, but there always seemed to be conflicts between the two of them.

School bored both of us, so by our senior year we were forging our parents' signatures in order to cut school. We would sneak wine out of Mom's liquor cabinet and buy cheese and French bread at the local market. Then we would head over the hill and down Highway 1, along the beautiful California coast to San Gregorio Beach, where we would sit for hours on a blanket on the beach having wonderful, easy conversations. We unloaded our deepest thoughts and feelings about our lives and dreams and what we thought about the state of affairs in the world. I think it was as good as any professional therapy and it helped keep us both sane, and able to enter young adulthood a little stronger. Eventually getting caught and being suspended for just a day didn't seem like a big deal to either of us.

Disliking high school, I did the bare minimum to get by, graduating in 1967 with no sense of my strengths or interests and no knowledge of how a good education would affect me later on in life. Adrift and lacking anything to do, with Dad's help my friend Janice and I got an apartment — in, of all places — the same apartment complex he lived in, although he and I never spent time together. I took a few classes at nearby Foothill Junior College. It felt a lot like high school.

. . . .

In the mid-1960s, at least in my world, girls were not encouraged to figure out what they wanted to do with their lives. High school counselors were no help in giving direction. My parents neither tried to guide me toward an education that would lead to a subsequent career, nor counsel me about the emotional side of life. It was simply assumed I would somehow get married and have children, and my husband would take care of me. So in some pretty important respects, I was on my own during my teen years. Of all my challenges, my scholastic difficulties were perhaps the least critical.

I had just turned 19 with one semester of junior college under my belt when my world fell out from under me. I lost my virginity to a boy I was dating — the result of letting my hormones take over and not knowing how to say no. I didn't have the wherewithal to get birth control pills and was embarrassed to insist on protection from a partner who didn't see the need for it.

In my own defense, I must point out that this was 1968, and it wasn't until 1972, four years later, that the Supreme Court (in Baird v. Eisenstadt) legalized birth control for unmarried women. In fact, the Supreme Court had only given married couples the right to use birth control in 1965 (in Griswold v. Connecticut).

True, I lived in progressive California and perhaps could have gotten the pill somehow, but information was not readily available.

And although the sexual revolution was in full swing, safe sex wasn't part of it. I managed to believe that somehow pregnancy wasn't going to happen to me. I wasn't really interested in the boy I'd had sex with, and certainly wasn't interested in any of my classes, so when Janice suggested we take a road trip back to her hometown of Wichita, Kansas, I was totally on board. A little adventure was just what I needed.

A couple of weeks into our stay there I got this terrible, nagging feeling: I should have had my period when we arrived, but there were still no signs of it. My young mind couldn't even imagine being pregnant. That happened to other girls, not to me. Surely my period would start soon. I didn't want to face what was happening to me.

As the truth became impossible to avoid, I had no idea what to do or whom to turn to. Janice and I hadn't known each other long, so we weren't close, and as soon as we had arrived in Wichita she hooked up with her old boyfriend and was staying at his place. I ended up staying with a young couple, old friends of Janice's to whom she'd introduced me. I was a long way from home with no one to talk to. No one who cared about me even knew I was pregnant or that I needed help —and I didn't want them to know. I didn't want to disappoint my mother, and I didn't need my father's demeaning judgment. I walked through the hours and days in a haze, completely overwhelmed.

Thanks to rearranging hormones and being scared to death, I wasn't the most reasonable person. One night I got into a heated argument with the couple I was staying with. I don't remember what it was about — probably not a big deal. I angrily I stomped out slamming the door behind me. Not knowing the city, I just walked through the dark, rainy night, tears streaming down my face, without thinking about where I was going. My anger soon turned to fear and desperation. I felt completely alone. What was I going to do?

After what seemed like hours of walking aimlessly I somehow found my way to the apartment of another couple I'd met through Janice's friends. They looked surprised at my miserable, bedraggled appearance, and kindly invited me in. Shivering, I shed my sopping wet jacket and sat at their kitchen table. They offered me tea, asked me what was wrong, and I told them. Since these people hardly knew me, it seemed easier to confide in them. They told me about a place just outside of town where I could get help. It was what used to be called a home for unwed mothers. Strangely it hadn't crossed my mind to go to a doctor even though I desperately needed help.

We talked until I was warm and dry and figured I should get back to the place where I was staying. My helpful new acquaintances were kind enough to give me a ride back.

As I got out of their car I said, "I am really scared. I never ever thought this kind of thing would happen to me. You both have been wonderful. Thanks so much."

I was still scared, but because of their comforting words and advice I felt a bit of relief. I felt for the first time that there were people who cared about me — even if I hardly knew them. I was just going through the motions, feeling shaken and petrified inside while on the outside trying to put a good face on my situation.

Not having any idea what the future held for me, a few days later, with their help, I got myself to the unwed mothers' home.

A pleasant older woman welcomed me into her office and began explaining how their services worked for "girls like me." But I was in a daze. This was not happening to me. My clearest memory was of me saying to her, "I do *not* want my parents to know I am here."

"Everyone eventually always tells one or both parents," she replied.

My mind was in slow gear as I tried to formulate what to say next. Finally I blurted out, "I understand what you are saying, but I really want to do this without either of my parents knowing. I can do that."

She gave me a warm, knowing smile as if she had heard this many times before but wasn't convinced.

"I am not everyone. I can do this," I insisted, even though I was terrified and had no idea what the next many months were going to be like for me.

Finally, after what seemed like a really long time, I gathered myself together. Trying to look in total control, I left with a pamphlet outlining the house rules and what I could expect while I lived there — and what to expect when I delivered my baby.

It's all I thought about for days: imagining myself with a baby in my arms, handing her over to a nurse who would never bring her back again. I knew I couldn't go through nine months of pregnancy followed by hours of labor, hear my child's first cry and then give her away to a complete stranger. I had no doubt that this was the wrong option for me.

Waking up that night, I found my sheets and pajamas soaked in blood. Terrified, silently crying, trying not to wake anyone, I cleaned up the blood while trying to figure out what to do next. I had no idea what was happening. It never occurred to me that I might be having a miscarriage.

Luckily the bleeding stopped on its own. It was then that I realized it was time to call the only person I felt I could talk to — my dad. Looking back I think I decided to reach out to him because I knew subconsciously that we had no relationship to destroy. Mom and I were close and I didn't want to disappoint her. Full of dread, all I could do was just spit out to him what had happened. I said I was pregnant, gave no details, and he didn't ask for any. Without emotion or hesitation, he told me he would book me a flight back to California.

Letting Mom believe I was still in Kansas, I stayed with Dad at his apartment. We had no heart-to-heart conversations and there was no display of emotion on his part. He was helping me, but warm and loving was never what I felt from my father. I know now that he cared — his actions told me that, but at the time I sensed his unspoken judgment. It was all business when we discussed options and logistics. Dad's cousin, Uncle Joe, said I could stay with him and his family up in Tiburon, north of San Francisco, have the baby and give it up for adoption. It was a generous offer, but I knew I could not do that.

In California, legislation had just passed requiring a woman wanting an abortion to be seen by two psychotherapists. With luck, the therapists would report back to a board that she was mentally unstable and unable to carry the pregnancy to term. This was before *Roe v. Wade*, the 1973 Supreme Court ruling legalizing abortion. This was the only way a woman in California could obtain a legal abortion: place her fate in the hands of two therapists, most likely both men.

Thankfully, Dad said it was *my* decision and he went about arranging for me to see the two psychotherapists required by law. For this I will be forever grateful to him.

As one of the "good ol' boys" in the Palo Alto medical circles, my dad was able to grease the skids so I could be considered mentally unstable and, therefore, obtain legal permission to undergo an abortion. When I talked to the two requisite therapists, I was as calm and composed as possible under the circumstances, so to call me "unstable" must have been a stretch for them. As humiliating as it felt to be declared mentally unstable when I was perfectly sane, to relinquish control over my own body would have been even worse.

I checked into Stanford Medical Hospital in late March of 1968, with my pregnancy about 12 weeks along. Alone in a small, stark, windowless room about the size of a large closet, I was visited only by Dad and my good friend Cass. Mom didn't know and I had no idea that she had gone through her own, much more traumatic abortion only a few years earlier.

The nurses did their job, but they were not friendly. I sensed they were judging me. It must have been obvious I wasn't too insane to have a baby and that I was beating the system. Nobody at the hospital told me anything, and I wasn't comfortable or confident enough to ask questions. The not knowing was scaring the hell out of me. With my anxiety level off the charts, I was given intravenous Pitocin, then left alone, not knowing what to expect. The Pitocin was supposed to induce labor and cause expulsion of the fetus. Nothing happened. Looking back I think my fear was preventing my body from responding.

I hadn't told anyone about the bleeding incident in Kansas, so all of us, including me, were acting on the assumption that I was still pregnant. Because I wasn't responding to the drug, I was taken into surgery for a D&C. The D&C must have revealed that I'd had a miscarriage, but no one told me anything during or after my procedure. With this level of incompetence offered at a prestigious hospital, I can only imagine the horrors women experienced seeking an abortion from the hacks operating out of dirty backrooms.

After the D&C I got an infection and had to stay in the hospital for eight days. During that time, Dad called Mom. She immediately came to be with me. I was glad to see her and feel her warmth and loving concern for my welfare.

In hindsight, I realize that having access to a medical facility for the purpose of ending my pregnancy at that time would not have been possible if: I hadn't been a white middle-class woman living in California; if my dad had not been a doctor with his connections to the gatekeepers; or if he'd had moral objections to abortion. I may have been only nineteen at the time, but I was clear and at peace with my decision to terminate this unplanned and unwanted pregnancy.

....

I would eventually learn that Mom had an abortion story of her own. On a warm, sunny summer morning almost twenty years later, she and I and two other women were on our way to San Jose to attend a pro-choice rally. As we drove the winding, four-lane highway over the hill from Santa Cruz to Silicon Valley, excited to have the opportunity to put our bodies on the line for what we believed in, we all started talking about our own personal experiences.

"Pat," Mom blurted out, "I have never told you, but I had an abortion." Stunned, I looked around at our traveling companions, who did not seem at all surprised. I guess Mom knew she could count on the comforting support of the women in the car that day and finally felt free, all these years later, to share the secret she had carried for such a long time.

Mom's abortion took place in 1964—just four years earlier than mine. But because abortion was completely illegal in California at the time, what she experienced was far worse.

She discovered her pregnancy on the way home from our two years in Europe, onboard the ship with my two brothers and me. In her taped description, I could feel the panic of her desperate situation:

When I arrived in the U.S. I was getting along in the pregnancy, and I had never in my life thought I would have to deal with something like this, and that was when it was illegal. The first person I went to was my psychiatrist. He told me, "I'm sorry, I can't help you, I don't believe in abortion." I was so amazed that a guy who had been my savior and had helped me and had been such a good psychiatrist — I was really stunned. But I had used him as my father, my savior, my everything, and I think that he was doing the right thing for himself because he couldn't risk it. And maybe he didn't know any others, but I can't imagine there weren't some doctors who were performing abortions. Maybe not, because everyone had to go down to Mexico. So I started getting really panicked because, my ex-husband, being a doctor could hear about it.

So while it was on that sunny summer morning in 1988, driving to San Jose, that I learned about Mom's illegal abortion, it wasn't until four years later that I would really appreciate what she went through. Her fear was not for herself or how she would manage with a newborn, but how she would keep her ex-husband — my dad — from taking us kids away from her.

Abortion has long been shrouded in shame, hidden and private. Unable to discuss their experiences, many women have been forced to feel isolated and alone. In 1992, to help counter this, a group in Santa Cruz, called the Action Alliance for Reproductive Rights, published a booklet of women's personal abortion stories. Mom's was one of them; she called it "A Horror Story." And even though it was twenty-eight years later, she signed it "Anonymous."

A Horror Story

This is a horror story. Because it is true I will not spare any details. Only now, as the Supreme Court is deliberating whether a woman has the right to a safe and legal abortion, do I feel the need to share my experiences.

In 1964, I was 40 years old. My three children and I had just returned from Europe where we had lived for two years following a divorce from a man who had used every legal tactic in the book in an attempt to deny my right to leave a destructive marriage. It seemed impossible that I could be one month pregnant. Getting the children settled back into school kept me busy while I wondered what to do. Marriage to the father of this fetus was impossible. I feared going to a local doctor for help as my ex-husband was one of them. I knew that if I had a baby out-of-wedlock he would use that to take custody of our children. He was still vindictive and I knew I was the better parent. I did talk in a roundabout way with a psychiatrist friend who indicated he was against abortion... No help there. Illegal abortion was something that happened to other women, but now I was faced with finding someone who could help me.

I went to San Francisco and picked a doctor out of the phone book. (Looking back on it now I realize it had not even occurred to me to seek out a woman doctor.) I made up a name for myself. Anonymity was important. He was cruel, telling me of all the bloody abortions he had been called in on at the point of death. He seemed to enjoy my pain and fear... No help there.

I went to Los Angeles where, through a friend, I met a man who knew a technician in a hospital who would be able to "arrange something." It would cost me $1,000 [equivalent to over $8,000 in 2019]. I had to trust this man because I knew no one else and I was in my second month of pregnancy. We met at the hospital. I produced the money and was told to go home and wait for their call. The man was solicitous, but insultingly insinuating. I have never felt so powerless in my life. The call came as I was in my third month of pregnancy. I was told that the technician had "cold feet" but the man had found a doctor who would perform the abortion in his office. It would cost another $1,000 [now a total of over $16,000 in 2019]. I felt trapped and desperate and completely vulnerable. I had confided in only two friends and they were feeling uncomfortable... wanting, yet not wanting, to distance themselves from the "problem." We all felt like soon-to-be-exposed criminals.

On the doctor's examining table I had what I thought to be a D&C (dilation and curettage). Because the doctor did not want to risk complications in case there was a reaction to anesthesia, I was fully conscious and feeling every bit of it. I can even today recall the pain. The nurse had blindfolded my eyes so I would not be able to recognize the doctor in case of his arrest. My procurer was present with more than consoling caresses. It's amazing to me now to remember how grateful I felt to these two men who had "delivered me from evil." The doctor wanted me to return the next day for more antibiotics. I was pleased that he was so concerned.

The doctor's "clinic" was in a house in the black ghetto and I felt very white and obvious. I knew everyone knew I was having an abortion. I tightened at the sight of policemen. Again my eyes were covered. When the doctor arrived he had me on the table again, explaining that because by then I was so far along in my pregnancy he had not been able to abort me. I was to take some pills he gave me and come back in a week if I did not abort.

Again I was back home, lying to my children and friends about my frequent trips to Los Angeles, praying desperately that the pills would work and knowing that precious time was passing. The pills did not work. My return to the "doctor" of whom I knew nothing filled me with terror. His only recourse was to insert a catheter and send me home again with it in place. He was washing his hands of me. At this point I must have gone numb... My survival system went into automatic.

I returned home, sent the housekeeper away, did the grocery shopping, fixed dinner for the children, and while they watched television in the family room I silently aborted a formed fetus in the toilet. The bathroom was covered with blood, but I carefully cleaned all the traces before I crawled into bed.

In that bed, 26 years ago, I experienced a deep, compassionate, loving, forgiveness of myself, which can only be attributed to the spiritual realm of the loving Jesus or the compassionate Buddha, an experience of grace, which allowed me to go on. When I hear the anti-abortionists rave about killing children I force myself to see that formed fetus *floating in the toilet bowl to see if I feel guilty. I see only the sneeringly righteous face of the doctor in San Francisco, the power-hungry face of my manipulating procurer. If legal abortion had been available to me as it is now I would have destroyed some cell tissue in my first month of pregnancy. I would not have been forced to struggle for over three months to find an "abortionist". The delay itself forced me, in the view of these vehement anti-abortionists, to "kill a child." For there was never any question in my mind that, whatever it took, I would not risk the loss of my children and what I felt was their well-being.*

Every time I read my mother's story, even all these years later, I cry for her. I can see myself and my two brothers sitting in the living room watching TV. I see my mom too. I see her in the bathroom tearfully manipulating a catheter between her legs and painfully delivering a fully-formed tiny fetus, frantically staunching the flow of blood and swallowing her heartbreaking sorrow to clean away all evidence of anything "untoward" in her children's home.

Though there were profound differences between my mother's abortion experience and mine, plenty of women in 1964 were having experiences like hers and worse. Looking back many years later, I realize that I could easily have had an experience like my mother's, or could have been forced to seek an abortion in Mexico and ended up dying there. I was able to procure a safe abortion only because my dad was a part of the medical community. It was still inaccessible to Californians with fewer resources than I had. Still, while Mom's experience was threatened by dangers from which I was protected, we both endured judgment, humiliation, isolation, fear and confusion.

I believe strongly that women's reproductive freedom is a basic human right. Having the choice to keep or end a pregnancy is the right of every woman, no matter her age, race, economic or marital status. It is up to women to decide if and when they are going to bear a child. The exercise of my right to control my own fertility and wait to have children until I was ready for them affected everything in my life and has fueled my lifelong passion to work for a world in which women are treated with dignity and respect and are equal in every way.

CHAPTER 4

SOULMATE

You have half our gifts. I the other. Together we make a
whole. Together we are much more powerful.

~ Joss Stirling, British novelist

In the summer of 1968, Mom and I moved from Palo Alto to Santa Cruz, about an hour away on the north end of Monterey Bay. Mom had gone back to school, to San Jose State University, and was now transferring to the University of California at Santa Cruz (UCSC). I started classes at Cabrillo, the local junior college in the nearby town of Aptos. Peter and Steve were in high school and lived with Dad, and of course Susie was still living in the home for mentally disabled.

Mom and I were growing up together. I spent my teen years becoming an adult at the same time she was breaking away from her destructive marriage and finding out who she really was. Mom would say of that time that she was going through her second adolescence. She rented a duplex; she lived upstairs and I lived downstairs. It was nice to live only a few steps from the beach, but Mom started to drive me crazy; walking into my apartment without knocking, as if it was okay to just barge in on me. I needed some space.

I had a new friend, Carol, whom I met in one of my classes at Cabrillo. We decided to move in together, into an old Victorian house in Santa Cruz within walking distance of downtown. Like Mom's place, it held two apartments, one up one down. We rented the downstairs one and proceeded to make it our own by painting the bathroom bright green and purple, hanging posters on the walls and making huge, wildly colorful pillows that served as our living room couch. It was a carefree period of enjoying my independence without a thought as to what I wanted to do with my life. Little did I know that it was about to change forever.

One sunny July afternoon I was visiting my upstairs neighbor, Mary, when there was a knock at the door. It was her friend Jim. She let him in, another guy followed — and my heart stopped. I saw an Adonis. I watched him step into the sunlight that streamed in through the window. He became radiant. His face was tan, surrounded by long chestnut ringlets. He had a grown-up mustache and bedroom eyes. He wore tight, white, hip-hugger bell-bottoms and a holey tattered t-shirt. His name was John. I was a goner.

My whole being was captured by his presence. We were introduced, but I didn't hear a word of it.

For me, it was love at first sight. I later learned that he thought I was "a cute blonde who kept looking at me, so I kept looking back." He had been attending college in Hawaii and was spending the summer with his sister Joan and her husband Jim in nearby Aptos, recovering from "island fever."

This encounter was way too brief. There was no doubt I needed to get some time alone with this man, so I set out to make that happen. Together Carol and I hatched the idea of a barbecue on the beach.

It's hard to mess up a warm summer night, the sun setting across the bay, a grill smoking under charred burgers and hotdogs, and a bonfire for roasting marshmallows. We invited my mom, Joan and Jim, their two kids Maury and Melissa, a few friends — and of course John. I could hardly eat, fixated on trying to get him all to myself. Then it happened so naturally.

"Wanna take a walk?" he said.

"Um, sure." I faked nonchalance while wiping marshmallow goo off my fingers onto the paper tablecloth.

And that was that, we were strolling down the beach. It didn't even matter that Maury, the annoying nine-year old was running circles around us. John spent that night with me in my apartment, and for the next couple of months we were inseparable. It was 1969, and for me, *that* was the summer of love.

John was not like any man I had ever met. He was smart and interesting. He paid close attention to world affairs. He had a sincere love for our fellow human beings and understood we are all connected on this planet. He was ahead of his time in his global consciousness and compassion. He was funny, creative and unconventional in his thoughts and ideas. He recognized a depth of character in me, and loved and appreciated it. I had found my soul mate.

We spent the summer connected at the hip, then decided it was time to get a place of our own. We rented an upstairs apartment in another old Victorian house – very funky and probably not more than six hundred square feet. The living room stepped up on one side to a tiny, one-fanny kitchen made even more intimate by a low ceiling. On the other side it stepped up to a bathroom with no door, a half-wall separating it from the living room, and a row of windows that offered an expansive view of the neighbor's rooftop. For John and me this was fine, but guests found it a bit uncomfortable. Another step up off the living room led to the cozy bedroom where we spent most of our time.

We lived simply, completely absorbed in being together, responding day-to-day to whatever came into our lives. It was a rare gift to be able to discover each other without the distractions of jobs or school and thus establish the foundation of our relationship based on deep mutual understanding.

Although we were just a few blocks from the beach, we rarely went there, choosing to spend most of our time smoking marijuana, making love, sharing ideas, opinions and our feelings about life and each other. We lived mostly on the $265 monthly stipend that the divorce decree required my dad to send me as long as I was a full-time student. John received a small monthly check from his sister and brother-in-law to repay a loan he had made to them.

Our downstairs neighbors, Marcy and David, were a little older than we were. Every so often David would knock on our door with a few samples of good "Jamaican Red." If we liked it he would get us some. He was our dope-delivery service and an artist who used the back yard as his studio, creating huge oil paintings commissioned by hotels. His wife Marcy was an elementary school teacher. She often told David, "Go see if they want any weed. That might keep them quiet" — referring to the noise we made when we made love.

Richard, another friendly neighbor, baked wonderful bread in a hole-in-the-wall bakery off the alley behind our house. We'd get our bread from him and share a joint. He was an enterprising young entrepreneur, who, with a lot of hard work, turned his little bakery into Staff of Life - a large and very successful health food grocery store in Santa Cruz.

On my first visit to Fresno to meet John's parents, I was greeted with warm loving hugs and total acceptance. It didn't seem to matter to them that we were living together without being married, which was not common back then. Dinner that night, to my surprise, wasn't a quiet affair with just his parents. The whole extended family was there to meet me: grandparents, aunts, uncles, cousins and distant cousins. We met at a Basque restaurant in downtown Fresno, and occupied the whole middle part of the restaurant. The long table was covered with bowls and platters of home-style dishes. Cousin Jimmy was yelling across the table at Uncle Johnny and Cousin Charlie was laughing with Auntie Armen. It was like a scene out of the movie *My Big Fat Greek Wedding*, and I loved it. John's family was loud, emotional, warm and loving. They instantly made me feel like one of their own.

John was the first male baby born to his large, extended Armenian family, which included three older girl cousins and a sister nine years his senior. He grew up in a modest household surrounded by women — his grandmother, mother and older sister, all of whom doted on him, wrapping him in unconditional love. Amazingly, John didn't turn out to be jerk, given the degree of indulgence he enjoyed when growing up. Instead, he grew up helping these women clean, cook and even sew. I believe his genuine love of women comes from growing up cloaked in that feminine affection and energy.

He could so easily have developed an attitude of entitlement and superiority, but to this day there's not a condescending or demanding bone in his body. He was treasured as a child, which gave him the self-confidence and self-esteem that enabled him to love the world. He brought an expansiveness to *my* world, a desire to embrace life and the people we encountered along the way. I'd always had that ability but never had the nurturing required to bring it forth. Living with John brought it out naturally in me.

The contrast between John's family and mine couldn't have been starker. His father was a warm, loving, generous man who would give you the shirt off his back. You could see and feel the love he had for his family. And now, there being no hesitation on his part, that family included me.

....

In January 1970, I turned twenty-one and received $20,000 from a trust fund set up by my Grandpa Vogl. The trust money was an amazing gift for me at such a young age, but it didn't change our way of life. We honestly weren't looking for ways to accumulate possessions or more money. I do remember being excited to buy a cute little brown dress, and the feeling of pride and a bit of astonishment talking to the teller at the bank when I deposited all that money in my savings account.

Meanwhile, the Vietnam War was raging. Young men were being drafted to fill the voracious need for American soldiers day after day, month after month and year after year. John was eligible for the draft. We were both aware of the political and historical background of our country's involvement in Vietnam and were committed to non-violence. John also thought it possible that President Nixon would shut the border to Canada for men of draft age. He had argued against induction in every legal way he knew, but none of it worked. So after a lot of talking, thinking, soul-searching and investigating the options for avoiding the draft, we made the decision to move to Canada.

John and I and my younger brother Peter, along with John's cousin Martin, piled into Martin's cramped two-door Javelin and headed for Vancouver, Canada. We camped our way up the coasts of Oregon and Washington State. Pulling into one campsite, we were directed to the back of the campground. The attendant had taken one look at the four of us with our long hair and hippie attire and sent us to the back to be with the other hippie types. Not bothered by this, we had a great time meeting other young campers, sharing our stash of pot around the campfire. We had no overall plan and took each day as it came.

With no hassle, we crossed the border into Vancouver on a beautiful sunny August day. What a relief to be on "the other side"! The four of us immediately drove to the ferry to Vancouver Island. Onboard, John and I ventured onto the deck to watch the mountains sail by. After a while, a young woman came over and introduced herself. Her name was Daisy. She was Canadian, but to me looked straight out of Haight-Ashbury — swishy long skirt, beads, droopy fedora. She bore a slight herbal scent.

I'm sure she could tell we were Americans.

After a meandering, politically seasoned conversation about why we were in Canada she blurted out, "I have a house you guys can stay in. It's on the beach — an A-frame. You can use it rent-free."

Taken aback, I looked to John, who was nodding vigorously. Of course we would accept. The prospect of cozying into a cute little rustic cabin on the seashore was too romantic to pass up. Plus, we had no specific plans and of course "free" was pure providence.

"Wow! Thanks! That is so nice of you." I said, overwhelmed by Daisy's generosity.

"Yeah," she shrugged. "I haven't been there for a while, and I like it when people are there to watch my stuff."

Of course. A beach cabin would need watching.

"It's not far. Drive to the other side of the island and leave your car next to the beach. It's another half a mile along the shore. You'll see it."

"Cool! I don't suppose you have the key on you?" John asked.

"You don't need a key," Daisy said. "It's open." That sounded easy enough, but the "no key" thing should have been a big red flag.

The narrow, winding road over the mountains to the beach seemed like it would never end. I actually got to the "what have we gotten ourselves into" stage but didn't say anything. And then the road did end at the beach just as Daisy said. We got out of the car just as daylight was waning. Bending into a strong wind, we passed at least a dozen makeshift driftwood shelters scattered randomly on the desolate beach.

Our Canadian benefactor was right — we wouldn't miss the A-frame cabin. It was the one with a deflated red air mattress door flapping in the wind — no need for a key. It may have been one of the most elaborate driftwood shelters on the beach but certainly not what we expected.

Nevertheless, we decided to settle in for the night and see what happened the next day, Martin and Peter volunteered to go back to the car for food and other supplies while John and I checked the place out. When it got dark and they hadn't returned, we started to worry. Then we got hungry, and then irritated. We just knew they'd stopped to hang out with those two cute young women we'd passed on the beach and decided to spend the night with them.

But we were wrong. Peter and Martin had taken what they thought was a shortcut to the car, through a dense rainforest that lined the beach. As it got darker they got worried they wouldn't get back while it was light. They started to run, but soon realized they were lost and needed to stay put. They would wait for daylight to find their way out.

It was a cold Canadian night so they found some twigs and small branches to burn, and huddled together around it to stay warm. Sleep was futile, since what they considered hair-raising sounds of wild animals kept them awake. But the real scare came at dawn, when they discovered their campsite was on the edge of a cliff above a deep ravine. A few more feet of sprinting through the woods would have pitched them over the cliff, possibly to their death.

Affecting some bravado, they sauntered back to our cabin next morning and told us about their grand adventure. We were all so shaken that we decided to pack up and head back over the hill to the more populated east side of Vancouver Island. We were not great campers. But the Universe seemed to be helping us.

Our next stop was Hornby Island, a tiny island about twelve square miles tucked between Vancouver Island and the British Columbia mainland. Reaching it by a short ferry ride, we set up camp, but this time built our very own house from the plentiful driftwood on the beach. We spent three joyous, relaxing days there, playing in the water and exploring the surrounding area until the owner of a nearby lodge threatened to bulldoze our very comfortable make-shift home.

Not having a lot of material needs and desires, we lived frugally on what I had inherited, with the idea of making it last as long as we could. We put ourselves on a strict food budget of a dollar a day per person, and did pretty well except for eighteen-year old Peter, who seemed to be starving most of the time.

The Canadians we met welcomed us with open arms and were extremely generous and helpful. Daryl and Maureen and their two young sons were outdoorsy, free spirited, gun-toting Canadians who hunted and fished. They shared the fresh salmon they caught and invited us to their home for dinner up the island. That kind of generosity and open-heartedness was repeated many times as we traveled around Vancouver Island.

At Dick and Di's Campground we met a large Canadian family, the Lazmans, who took pity on us. They noticed that our camping skills were minimal. The father could only watch us chop firewood for so long before he had to jump in and teach us the correct way to do it — and how to start a fire, too. One night it rained really hard. We had pitched our tiny tent on a downslope and of course the rain came pouring down, washing us out. The Lazmans kindly invited us into one of their tents—much to Martin's delight, as he was developing a crush on one of their teenaged daughters. A departing couple from West Germany gave us a big tarp, chuckling, "We won't need this anymore, but we think you will."

Indeed. As campers we were pathetic. It wasn't until the summer had come and gone and it was getting cold at night that we discovered our sleeping bags were actually sleeping bag *liners*. Camping was definitely starting to lose its appeal. It was time to find indoor shelter.

Peter decided to go back to the States to work on a dairy farm in northeastern Washington State. Having no itinerary, the three of us stumbled into Kye Bay Guest Lodge in the little coastal town of Comox, British Colombia. This became our new home. Fred and Mary Luck, a friendly older couple, owned the place. They were closing it down after the summer tourist season, but agreed to rent a unit to us for the winter at a much-reduced rate. The Universe was working again! Fred and Mary felt like caring, comfortable grandparents who adopted John, Martin and me as their long-lost grandchildren. Mary told her friends that they had some nice young Americans staying at their lodge and the word spread; we soon were the beneficiaries of small-town good will.

The lodge was a beautiful, rustic, L-shaped two-story building with a huge grassy lawn sloping down to a white sandy beach along the water. There were about twenty small apartments. Ours was a simply furnished two-bedroom, one-bathroom unit with a small kitchen, dining area and living room combined.

Two schoolteachers, the only other tenants, soon became our good friends. We often caught sight of a tall, thin man riding a bicycle, noticeable for his long red beard, which flapped in the freezing cold wind. Bill was his name, and he and his wife, June, also became friends. They were from Scotland. June was a teacher in town and Bill was an architect who worked out of the little cabin they lived in down the street from us.

We were living a laid-back, slow and stress-free life. It was a relief to be out of the worry and turmoil of a country that was making war. We explored the nearby town and walked on the beach, keeping tabs on a family of bald eagles whose nest far up in the trees looked like an upside-down Volkswagen bug. John and Martin went fishing—although John never caught a single fish; I think we all knew he actually didn't want to kill anything.

We had entered Canada as tourists, but didn't want to leave. In order to stay and work legally in those days, we would have to gain Landed Immigrant status. We would need to appear before a Canadian Immigration board that would question our intentions for residing and working in Canada. If we were approved, we could, after five years as Landed Immigrants, apply for full citizenship, but only if we had not voted in any U.S. election during that time. We had no long-term plans, but knew we'd eventually need to get jobs, so decided to try for Landed Immigrant status.

Off we drove to Nanaimo, a city some ninety miles south, to obtain the necessary paperwork and instructions. That's when it hit me that part of the process was a one-on-one personal interview with an officer of the Immigration Department. True to form, I was terrified at the prospect of going through the interview by myself. What would happen if I failed the interview? Our future in Canada would be doomed. We'd have to return to the States, and John would be drafted. It's hard for me now to believe how shy and insecure I was then. Finally, reading through our paperwork, we discovered a workaround: we'd get married. If we applied for Landed Immigrant status as a married couple, John could be interviewed on behalf of both of us. This was in 1970, when married women were often not seen as separate human beings from their husbands. We could get married and my worries would be over.

John and I were in love, and even though we hadn't really talked about it, there was no doubt we would get married at some point.

There was no formal wedding proposal. We had been living together for about a year and a half, so why not get married now? Once the decision was made and we started making plans, we got excited. Instead of a quick civil service followed by a champagne toast, we would make it a real celebration.

I hand-lettered formal announcements and mailed them to our families. I thought I was being quite counter-culture when I asked the local seamstress to make me a deep-purple velvet wedding dress, but at the last minute I chickened out and asked her to make a very short white velvet number with a plunging neckline instead - not at all conservative, but in keeping with the traditional bridal white. John wore a white shirt with embroidered trim and brown corduroy hip hugger bellbottoms—pure hippie style. Thanks to John's mop of long, dark curly hair and full beard, and me looking sweet and very young (I was twenty-two and he was twenty-six), our wedding picture has been called "Beauty and the Beast" ever since. Mary made us a traditional three-tiered Canadian wedding cake (fruitcake with white frosting). We hired an officiator and planned a formal ceremony to be followed by drinks, food and toasts.

On the morning of our wedding, December 19, 1970, it started to snow. Among our thirty guests were our parents, my two younger brothers, John's older sister Joan and her husband Jim, and their two kids Maury and Melissa. Also there to help us celebrate were our adopted grandparents Fred and Mary, along with an assortment of our new Canadian friends. None of us had snow tires, so we were all crossing our fingers as our caravan of cars drove slowly and carefully up the highway from Kye Bay to Painter's Lodge.

The Lucks were friends with the owners of this lodge — a famous rustic fishing destination for Hollywood stars and heads of state. It, too, was closed for the winter, but once again that generous Canadian spirit opened it up for our wedding. And because it was off-season we had the whole place to ourselves.

We gathered in the main room, which had a large elegantly decorated Christmas tree in the corner between a huge stone fireplace with a roaring fire and a massive window overlooking the water and falling snow. Our family happily sipped their drinks and got to know our Canadian friends. As the time for the ceremony approached our family and friends formed a loving circle around us. We'd found the preacher in the yellow pages of the phone book. He was in his 60s, only about five feet tall, had a fringe of graying hair and an endearing British accent. When he pronounced us husband and wife it felt like something out of a storybook. It was the perfect wedding for us.

Before the wedding I had been concerned about having my mom and dad in the same room together. Ten years earlier they had gone through an extremely nasty divorce and since then had rarely talked, let alone occupied the same room. Who knew what disaster scenes could materialize at the wedding dinner? But John and I figured out that we would seat my dad with John's mom and John's dad with my mother. It was like we were melding our two families, and as it turned out, they were civil to each other. I was relieved. Except for my dad, our families stayed with us at the Kye Bay Lodge for a week to continue celebrating and spend Christmas together.

Life was good but about two months after everyone went home from the wedding, cabin fever and maybe a little homesickness started creeping up on us. Twenty-six was the age limit on drafting men into the armed forces, and John had reached that magical age the month before our wedding. We had Landed Immigrant status, loved our life in Canada and had every intention of staying indefinitely. But faced with the prospect of a long cold winter, warmer weather was pulling us soft Californians home. Just as spring was hinting at its arrival, we packed it up and headed back to California and to our next great adventure.

John and I hanging out in the driftwood A-frame house we built on Hornby Island (an island tucked away between Vancouver Island and the mainland of British Columbia). There was a plentiful amount of driftwood on the beach.

Our official wedding picture taken with our 11 year old nephew's instamatic camera on our wedding day, December 19, 1970 at Painter's Lodge in Campbell River, British Columbia

CHAPTER 5

AND THEY SAID IT
COULDN'T BE DONE

We criticize and separate ourselves from the process.
We've got to jump right in there with both feet.
~ Dolores Huerta
Labor leader, civil rights activist and co-founder of the United Farm Workers

Santa Cruz County paints a swath of land along the northern end of the Monterey Bay. Redwood-forested mountains overlook the Pacific. Twenty-nine miles of curving beaches attract surfers and sunbathers. South of the city of Santa Cruz along the coast are several smaller towns lined up back-to-back. One of them is Capitola, a square mile of commercial and residential diversity.

The portion of Capitola that a visitor sees immediately after exiting California's Route 1 looks much like the commercial strip of almost any other town in the country. You drive down 41st Avenue with its four lanes of traffic flowing past strip malls, chain restaurants, gas stations and the only enclosed shopping mall in the county. Then, as it nears the shores of the Monterey Bay, 41st Avenue gradually narrows to two lanes and heads toward Pleasure Point, a semi-funky neighborhood of homes and homegrown businesses, famous for surfing.

Not far from Pleasure Point is a quaint commercial area known as Capitola-by-the-Sea. Locals call it the Village. There, along the shoreline where Soquel Creek flows into the Monterey Bay, a hundred yards of sand stretch from the Esplanade to waves that roll in from the bay. This little enclave of bayside shops, restaurants and beach is a magnet for tourists of all ages.

Aries Arts was a big store on the corner of Capitola Avenue and San Jose Avenue owned by a couple named Tom and Joanne. They sold an assortment of hippie paraphernalia—pipes, incense, clothes, madras bedspreads, pillows, alternative books and magazines. Across the street Carin sold handmade crafts, mostly from local artisans at the Craft Gallery. On the other corner stood Geyer's Gallery. It was run by Gary Geyer and featured his paintings of maritime ships. What became a popular Mexican restaurant and watering hole called Margaritaville was Joe's Pool Hall back then. Joe's wife, Alice, a seventy-year old, platinum blonde, cigarette-smoking bartender, served the best liverwurst sandwiches and potato salad ever.

The Village was picturesque and charming, but that was for the tourists to enjoy. We took it for granted, because it was simply where we lived. And we needed to make a living. When we returned from Canada we stayed with John's sister Joan and her family in Aptos, the next town south of Capitola. I don't remember exactly where the idea came from, but we soon found ourselves in the throes of opening our own restaurant. The fact that neither of us had ever owned a restaurant before did not deter us; it never even entered our minds. Our combined restaurant experience was the three years John spent working his way up the ladder in a restaurant in Hawaii, starting out below the bottom rung of dishwasher as a scrubber of pots and pans. Later he filled in as prep cook and eventually worked as the relief manager on slow days. But his real training came from a childhood spent in his mother's kitchen. He learned how to make delicious Armenian dishes from his mother and grandmother, while gaining the confidence that he could do anything he set his mind to.

John and I worked easily together; it came naturally. I loved the way he energized my life with a continuous stream of creative ideas and I got behind our new project one hundred percent. We were a team no matter what, having a great time, free spirits flowing with whatever presented itself. I don't remember ever thinking that we couldn't do something or worrying about where money was going to come from to pay the bills. I always felt that if we wanted to do something, the money would come. We were young, without kids, able and willing to live on almost nothing in order to do what we wanted to do.

We found the perfect property for rent at the south end of the main street, at the bottom of Monterey Avenue next to the theater parking lot. The landlord was happy to have us convert his apartment into a restaurant, and I was happy to use the last of my inheritance as the seed money to get our restaurant off the ground. It was less expensive and easier to start a new business in those days. Excitedly, we began mapping out what needed to be done. We enlisted the help of our families and friends, and set about designing, furnishing and unveiling Dikran's Armenian Restaurant. We named it after John's paternal grandfather, Dikran — "Richard" in Armenian.

The older buildings around the Esplanade and side streets had a lot of character, but they were fifty years old and needed some sprucing up. In the early 70's young entrepreneurs like us were excitedly rolling up their sleeves and injecting new life into the Village. In some circles we were referred to as hippies. We did have a laid-back lifestyle, but also a traditional work ethic, creativity and business sense. Our appearance, however, troubled the old guard. They were paranoid about the area being taken over by people they considered pot-smoking ne'er-do-wells.

Bill Clarke was the City of Capitola's building inspector we dealt with when we applied for our business license. A staunch conservative, he didn't hide his dislike for our kind, and threw down every possible roadblock he could come up with. He made us add extra sheet rock to the ceiling when it was already adequate by law. We did. He required that we have four extra parking spaces – more than any other Village business had to provide. We did — by asking the owner of the bowling alley to rent us four parking spaces. After about a month that particular requirement mysteriously went away. I am not sure why. Then, to get our business license, we had to apply for a use permit and go through a public hearing with the Capitola Planning Commission.

Undaunted, we eventually procured a lease and business license for our 1,200-square foot-apartment and immediately began retrofitting it to meet government code regulations for a restaurant. John and cousin Martin were the resident carpenters and gatherers, purchasing kitchen equipment and a hodgepodge of dining room furniture. My mom, Joan and I covered the old chairs they found, made cloth napkins and quasi-Armenian costumes for the wait staff, which was comprised of Linda and me. Linda, a young Lebanese-American woman, noticed what we were doing and came by looking for work. She was the only one working at Dikran's who was not related to us. My brother Peter washed dishes and did general food prep, Martin was the master pilaf chef, and John was the main cook. Occasionally our niece Melissa and nephew Maury bussed tables after school. We had seating for twenty-eight people in the main dining room, and a separate banquet room that seated twelve to fourteen for private parties.

John and I lived in the restaurant—not above it, but *in* it. Since it had all of the amenities of an apartment, we made it work. Every night we pushed aside the table in the banquet room and replaced it with a thin mattress we'd stashed in the closet. We showered in the apartment-now-restaurant bathroom. As business picked up, we worked longer hours, made a little more money, got tired of sleeping on the floor — and were able to move out. We found a tiny, rather funky apartment across the street on the ground floor of a historic Victorian building owned by our landlord Jim Redding.

We were a good team. I made the sign for the new Dikran's Armenian Restaurant out of an old weathered door, which we had hung above the front window. It was also my job to hand-letter menus and duplicate them at the local copy shop and place ads in local newspapers. John and Martin made lists of what we needed each day. They spent their mornings shopping for the food while I set up the dining room and prepped the kitchen.

Our grand opening in the summer of 1971 was well attended by locals as well as family members from Fresno happy to celebrate with us.

Six nights a week, in our cozy hole-in-the-wall restaurant we served authentic, homemade Armenian food. It had no rival. Word spread and the business grew. To add to the ambience on slow nights, John and Martin set up a small wooden table out front and played backgammon, yelling and screaming at each other (because that's what you do when you're Armenian and play backgammon). It was like a live show advertising our restaurant to passers-by.

One summer night after closing, John and Martin were washing dishes when they heard a ruckus outside. Looking up to the open window above the sink they found themselves nose-to-nose with two big, burly guys with long, scraggly hair. They were on Harleys.

"Two Big Macs to go," growled the one in the "Wanna F---k?" t-shirt.

I was standing just to John's side and could see his hand, immersed in dishwater, slowly closing in on a knife. He glanced at Martin, who tipped his head forward and raised his eyebrows as if to say "Do whatever they want." I did not disagree.

"Yeah, man, like we're closed, but lemme see what we can do."

Believe me when I say it didn't take us long to make up two plates of dolma and pilaf and hand it through the kitchen window.

Ten minutes later t-shirt guy stepped up to the window with their empty plates.

"Great food. Anytime you guys need your house painted or protection or anything of that order let us know." Whereupon he and his pal gunned their motors and thundered off.

A few weeks later I was working hostess when a pre-booked party of twelve arrived. One glance and I recognized our biker friends, now in sports coats, accompanied by their wives and young children. I guess they knew where to find great food! Just shows — you never know.

This episode may have been responsible for our becoming so quickly embraced by the other young so-called hippie business owners in the Village. We were making friends and having the time of our lives.

. . . .

Since 1952, Capitola had been home to the annual Begonia Festival and Arts and Crafts Fair. It attracted thousands of locals and tourists every September and was a huge boon to the Village shop owners. Folks would meander down the Esplanade to find that perfect piece of pottery or have their caricature drawn. Outdoor grills sent up aromatic smoke signals, local wineries and artists presented their best offerings, and live bands played near a dance floor on the beach. The highpoint was undoubtedly the Nautical Parade of begonia-bedecked floats down Soquel Creek into the bay. John and I enjoyed this time of year, and depended on the revenue it brought to our restaurant.

But this year, 1972, the Chamber of Commerce, which ran the festival, decided to call it off — both the parade and the whole festival. We believed they were trying to run the hippie business owners out of town; indeed, our livelihoods depended on it. Outraged, a few of us went to the next Chamber meeting and said we want to take over the festival.

The city manager, who was at the meeting, countered that what we proposed was a physical impossibility. If the creek was to be deep enough to accommodate the floats by September, he said, the city would have had to dam it by July — and it was already August. There just wasn't time.

It was true: the floats were room-sized — ten-by-twelve plywood sheets mounted on empty fifty-gallon drums. Loaded up, they needed several feet of water. Since we couldn't increase the water depth, the only remaining solution would be to build floats that could navigate a shallower channel. We had not a clue as to how to do that.

One day as we were getting ready to open for dinner, Kevin showed up in the Dikran's doorway. Our friend Kevin — with the long, stringy hair, faded jeans and open shirt that perpetually flapped in the breeze — had hitchhiked into town. His jeans had lost the top button, exposing his navel. On one shoulder he carried a large wooden crate that, it turned out, was filled to the brim with fresh peyote buttons.

He said, "I need a sunny area — a secluded one — where my buttons can be laid out to dry without being disturbed. Do you know any place?"

Mom had just bought a house on a couple of acres on Glen Haven Road, about a mile up in the Soquel Mountains — it would be the perfect place, and when I asked her she had no problem giving her consent.

Up at Mom's we hung out on the porch, catching up on the couple of years since we'd seen each other while John and I filled Kevin in on the intractable festival problem.

"You know," he said, "my dad was the mayor of my home town." He stopped and looked at us as if that was supposed to mean something to us. It didn't.

"Mmm-hmm," I said after a while, to sort of decorate the silence.

"So I've been there, and I've seen what they do. They've got this river, where the docks float because they're made of ..." and he stopped again, midsentence. He could see John and I were leaning eagerly into what he was saying. What fun. He nodded and looked off into the mountains.

"Oh, yeah, those floating docks. They're something."

With a little research we discovered the docks they used were made of Styrofoam billets, which could support a lot of weight and only needed about two feet of water. Nearby in South San Francisco — "The Industrial City" — was the place to get them. John and Kevin drove there the next day and picked up enough billets to make a trial float. It worked like a charm.

Good news traveled fast, followed by a call for volunteers to build the Styrofoam flotillas. The next challenge was to pick begonias, mainly from the nearby Antonelli Begonia Gardens and a few of the smaller growers. People worked feverishly picking by day in the fields of flowers and by night creating the floats on the docks along the creek - cool nights kept the flowers from wilting. There were three nights of partying along the creek as hundreds of people from all walks of life (and political persuasions) came together. The docks outside people's houses were lit up with lanterns of every size and shape as parade participants ate, drank and merrily created their annual Begonia Festival floats.

The newspapers had already announced that the Begonia Festival was dead. We knew better and asked John Mallot, a local Village artist, to make a huge canvas banner about fifty feet long saying *And They Said It Couldn't Be Done*, which became the official theme of the festival that year. What normally took many months to plan and produce came together in two weeks. We pulled it off, and just as the floats reached their final destination and were being judged, the banner was unfurled from the railroad trestle above the creek — our declaration of victory. How sweet it was. The locals cheered, yelled and jumped up and down. We had saved the twentieth annual Begonia Festival—and, as a result, many of our fledging businesses.

We became members of the Capitola Chamber of Commerce along with other hippie business owners. At the annual meeting John unexpectedly was elected Chamber vice-president. Friends of the president accused him of being in cahoots with the hippies and pressured him to resign. John then moved up into his seat as the new president of the Chamber.

The local paper came out with the headline: "Long hairs take over Chamber of Commerce." In fact, we just wanted to join so we could help promote our Village businesses. I'm not sure what the conservative town leaders were afraid we would do, but I don't think we met any of their low expectations of us.

Though John and I didn't realize it at the time, the Begonia Festival affair launched our social activism. This community victory ignited a fire in us that has burned brightly throughout our lives. We came to understand that you don't have to accept the status quo. People can make change happen if they come together for a cause they believe in.

It never occurred to us that we wouldn't be successful. We just barreled ahead knowing we had to do something, believing that someone or something would appear to help us.

We were just a little surprised that it was Kevin.

. . . .

The county and city of Santa Cruz were politically conservative in the early 70s. And in Capitola, city council members and the more conservative business owners were used to calling the shots. Capitola was booming, and people were opening up new businesses left and right. The Village was changing and growing, which attracted real estate developers to our little seaside town. They were building new houses to take advantage of the boom as fast as they could. It seemed that every empty lot was being developed, which in turn overtaxed the infrastructure. The authors of the building boom had no concern for the impact it would have on this small coastal town, but we were getting a firsthand look.

The ongoing development was straining the sewage system, and awful stuff began bubbling up through the manhole in front of our restaurant, carrying an unappetizing stench. During a busy summer season, it was chasing customers away from our fledgling eatery. John and I reported the problem to city hall, telling them "We have a business to run and nobody wants to eat with the rotten smell of an overflowing sewer system in the air."

In a typical city response, they passed the buck to the Santa Cruz County Public Works Department. At the county, we were told that the sewer lines in Capitola were only three inches in diameter, five inches smaller than they were required to be. New development was being allowed to hook into these three-inch pipes, burdening them beyond their capacity. The Capitola Planning Commission issued building permits and the City Council approved them without regard to the added strain on the outdated infrastructure.

John's approach to a problem like this was to learn as much about it as he could. He spent the next few days at the County Public Works Department library, where he discovered the tools we needed to start fixing the problem. He learned that Capitola's wastewater drained into the East Cliff Sanitation District, which had been using an outdated and inadequate water treatment system for years. Nine years prior, to stop the flow of pollution into the ocean, the State Regional Water Quality Control Board had ordered the County Public Works Department to cease and desist until they updated their facility. No new sewer hook-ups, no new buildings, were to be allowed until that happened. Not only was the order being ignored, but no one on the Capitola City Council or Planning Commission even knew anything about it. Building permits never stopped being issued and the system had become a ticking time bomb.

We talked to everyone who would listen and many who wouldn't. With no one taking responsibility or making a single move to stop the growing problem, John and I knew it was going to take more than our two voices. Not being the only ones on the receiving end of this foul smell, we started talking to our fellow business owners and neighbors. It became obvious that we needed to organize in order to harness enough people-power to be heard. We called ourselves the Capitola Survival Committee. Our goal was to slow down the incessant development taking over our small seaside community by out-of-town developers who did not care about the environmental damage they left in their wake.

John and I were a team. He was a natural spokesperson and I began educating, organizing and activating our community behind the scenes. I found I had natural organizing skills that kicked into gear the same way my mom's organizing skills had revealed themselves when she helped start a school for her disabled daughter. To get the word out about what was happening, we published a monthly newspaper called *The Capitolian*. I mapped out the city—not difficult in a city of one square mile and about seven thousand residents—and enlisted the help of our friends' kids to deliver *The Capitolian* to the doorsteps of every house in town. To cover the expenses, I reached out to businesses to place advertisements in the paper and even drew their ads myself. (How funky that seems in today's Internet age.) We had the *Capitolian* printed at Jim and Katie Heth's *People's Press*; an alternative newspaper and print shop that supported the local community.

People from all political persuasions—from American Independents and Democrats to Socialists and Republicans—joined the cause. We shocked the mayor and city council members by turning people out by the hundreds to attend council meetings. Many times the meetings had to be held in the city hall parking lot to accommodate the crowd. John, armed with sewer system maps and existing regulations that were being ignored, addressed our elected officials.

We had educated ourselves. We had educated our community. We got organized and we were united. And we spoke up. People who cared deeply about Capitola, most with more conventional lifestyles and conservative opinions than ours, joined the Capitola Survival Committee. This put enough "people-powered" pressure on the council to result in a two-year ban on all new building in Capitola and the surrounding areas until the East Cliff Sanitation District (which included Capitola) could obtain funding for a new regional sewage treatment plant.

But a few developers slipped through. A builder from Tennessee arrived in town before we were able to get the ban to apply to new housing units. Pulling up in their big black limousine, stepping out in their expensive suits, Stetson hats and cowboy boots, they were expecting to build a seven-story office building on 41st Avenue. It would be the tallest building in the county and completely out of character in Capitola. We saw it as an eyesore, and even worse as an invitation for more and bigger buildings over time. We took them on. The Capitola Survival Committee, with the help of many citizen activists, stopped it.

There was a proposed apartment building on the cliff above the Village that was grossly oversized for the surrounding neighborhood. The Capitola Survival Committee got it scaled down.

Another huge housing project was proposed for the last remaining large parcel of land in Capitola. It was adjacent to a neighborhood of single-family homes. The proposal came from the McKeon Construction Company, which was the fifth-largest construction firm in the U.S. and used to getting its way. In Sacramento, where they were based, local headlines read: "McKeon Firm Bulldozes Nature Preserve," "McKeon Sues County for $40 Million for Land Uses Loss," and "McKeon Sues Conservationist for $80 Million over Stonelake." Again, the Capitola Survival Committee got the McKeon development scaled down to fit the neighborhood. Our local papers told the story of "How Little Guys Defeat Giants."

Never knowing whether our actions would be successful, we had to try—and we were having a great time doing it. Community activism was now in our blood and the successes under our belt proved that citizen activism was possible.

John was learning environmental law and land-use policies and I was learning the art of coalition building, helping to bring people together who had nothing else in common but to fight for the future of their shared community. Spurred on by our many successes, this was my university—my on-the-ground training in empowering people to make change. I enjoyed working alongside John, getting to know and work with people in our community; I felt empowered by the skills I discovered I'd always had.

As we grew more involved outside the restaurant, our focus changed. We gradually discontinued serving dinners on weeknights. The last year we were open we served dinner only on Friday and Saturday nights. Eventually, three years after we had opened, we sold Dikran's to a new owner who converted it to a soup-and-salad restaurant. The money from the sale now fueled our social activism. And the next big giant was rumbling into town.

....

In the early 1970s, Santa Cruz County was one of the fastest grow-ing counties in the state. The Moroto Investment Company, based in Canada, had a plan that would have doubled the size of the city of Santa Cruz and created a myriad of stressors on the city and county's infrastructures and social services. The developer's intent was to build ten thousand homes on four thousand acres of farmland, including the Wilder Ranch, adjacent to the northern Santa Cruz city limits. The projected population was forty thousand people.

This was the kind of unbridled growth that changes the face of a community in ways no one can predict. It seemed developers just wanted to come into our community, make their money and leave without any thought to the impact. We were not opposed to careful-ly-planned, well-supported development on a reasonable scale that the city and county services could handle. This development was not that—it would have eventually doubled the population of the city.

Because of our work in Capitola, John and I were invited to join a group of nine other community leaders to address this threat. Called the Ombudsmen, the group hired Shirley Zimmerman from Saul Alinsky's Industrial Areas Foundation in Chicago; home base for his cadre of professional community organizers. Each of us contrib-uted one hundred dollars a month to pay her $1,000 monthly salary. As John and I were living on very little, each month we collected ten dollars apiece from nine other people for our share.

The other nine Ombudsmen were a little older than John and I and had established careers and families. We were young, had no family responsibilities, and were willing to live on very little in order to work full time to stop this development. Helping us to survive and sustain our community activism, many of our Capitola friends, who were older and more politically conservative, invited us into their homes for dinner. This was a huge help and they got to hear firsthand about our work to save the North Coast.

Again, I was a part of educating and getting people to join in opposition to this massive development. We worked with Shirley every day with John on strategic moves and me on tactics to organize the county. Making phone calls, meeting with people and distributing materials were just some of the things I did. This was a time of great social activism in all parts of the county. Grassroots groups with names like Aptos Action, Save Soquel, the Frederick Street Irregulars, Save San Lorenzo River and Save Lighthouse Field Association were springing up to control pockets of undesirable development. Shirley helped us build a coalition of these established groups in order to work together and combine forces on this single issue.

The umbrella group created by the Ombudsmen was called Operation Wilder. Even though the Wilder Ranch and Beaches development was on the North Coast of Santa Cruz, it was important for people countywide to understand that this enormous expansion of the City of Santa Cruz would affect everyone in the county. Working together would send a message to developers and city and county officials that we were united in our concerns.

Spokespeople were designated and trained, and committees were formed to deal with the press and issue press releases, do research, decide on strategy and coordinate volunteers. We agreed upon our leadership and held regular meetings. I was just 23 and learning directly from Shirley Zimmerman, a well-known professional organizer. This was an amazing opportunity, one that you can never get in college, at least not back then.

We believed the people needed to be involved in any development that could have an effect on the quality of life in our community. We studied the impact on the city's infrastructure: roads, water, air quality, schools, police and fire departments and medical services, and began formulating our arguments. At the same time, the development company was distributing an eighty-page, glossy four-color booklet filled with beautiful artist's renditions of an idyllic seaside residential community. In response, an Operation Wilder newspaper was distributed to about fourteen thousand homes, describing in detail the devastating effects this development would have on the infrastructure and social fabric of the community. A puppet show was created to dramatize the conflict. The show was a wonderful creative way to communicate with the public and draw attention to what the developers were proposing. It provided an avenue for people with a creative streak to help, and was an entertaining tool to raise awareness. It was played all over the county, including on the university campus, which was a huge voting bloc in city council elections. Taking advantage of current city council elections, we sent people to the candidate forums to ask questions about the issue. We kept it constantly before the public. A speakers' bureau was developed along with a slide show that was shown to churches, senior groups, and civic and service organizations.

To educate, inform and gather more supporters, we distributed a survey, not only to the candidates for the Santa Cruz City Council and the current council members, but also to county residents. The survey covered topics such as the cost to taxpayers for building and maintaining the additional infrastructure and public services to serve a greater population, whether the citizens should be able to vote on the matter, and the yet unaddressed need to upgrade the North Coast Sewage Treatment Facility. The survey results gave us the ammunition we needed. We used it to let the public know how their elected officials stood on this issue, and to tell council members how the people felt. It also enabled us to gather hundreds of new supporters.

Operation Wilder issued a press release describing the many ways the development would destroy the city of Santa Cruz. The developers fought back, filing a suit against Operation Wilder for libel to the tune of one hundred and twenty-one million dollars. This legal tactic was designed to stop us and enable them to get their development approved. It was one of the country's first harassment lawsuits filed by a developer in order to try to intimidate concerned citizens and prevent a community from opposing a project.

Intimidated? What were they thinking? The ridiculous amount named in the suit only served to galvanize the community against the developer even more. Our answer to their outrageous lawsuit was to announce "The Committee of 121 Million." Local attorney, Robert Blake brought ten other attorneys together to defend us. They created a way for community members to sign on as defendants to the lawsuit as a John or Jane Doe. Thousands of people did.

The lawsuit was eventually dropped. Because the community was engaged and involved the development was defeated. Our local state senator, Donald Grunsky, introduced a bill asking the state of California to purchase the property as a state park. With the help of political connections, the bill passed and the property became the Wilder Ranch State Park, integrated into California's state parks system in 1974.

Our success did more than stop a terrible development project. It resulted in a wonderful new resource for California. Back in the 1850s, farming at Wilder Ranch involved a creamery, dairy barn and a variety of farm animals. Restored, along with the original 1897 Victorian home and water-powered machine shop, many people of all ages have been able to see what it was like to live back then. There is a Wilder Ranch historical education program highlighting the Ohlone Indians, who made this land their home for hundreds of years. And the park has more than thirty-five miles of scenic hiking, biking and riding trails which thousands of people enjoy every year. All because people united, got organized, and spoke up.

It felt extra-exhilarating to have been a part of this success because it contributed to a local political sea change. In 1973 the seven-member Santa Cruz City Council had been in favor of the proposed development. The pressure of a united front, citizens making their demands known to their public servants, made it impossible for them to approve it and stay in office. A year later, two of the community activists who had worked to defeat this proposed development were elected to the city council, and in another year there were two more. In a two-year span the majority on the council had changed. The council's attitude became one of inclusion and solicitation of ideas and opinions of the residents and business owners. These two elections were a turning point for the city and county of Santa Cruz.

The developers had the money, but we had the people power. Truly a David and Goliath story, our community organizing experiences reveal how much is possible when people are united in speaking out. For me, this was a beginning. I was just getting my feet wet. John and I were a part of our community's mounting momentum of effective citizen involvement. Because of these experiences I saw firsthand not only that change is possible, but that it can also be a lot of fun.

My insecurities from childhood had not disappeared. I was still not comfortable leading the charge, preferring and feeling more comfortable working behind the scenes, one-on-one. But I was finding my strengths for the first time in my life. It was exciting, rewarding, frustrating, exhausting, ridiculous, perfectly logical, meaningful and almost better than sex.

. . . .

Both John and I were happily committed to our political activism. It was our focus and our values all rolled into one, revolving around who was running for office and what community projects we could support. Because of it we paid as little attention to money matters as we could get away with. We were the antithesis of Yuppies. We never talked about buying new furniture or cars or socking away a stash of money for the future, and our health care costs were covered by the standard American health insurance policy of the time (i.e., "just don't get sick").

We lived for a while with friends in Bonny Doon, an area in the mountains just north of Santa Cruz. One day John asked me how much money I had. I checked my purse and came up with $7. That was it—I literally had $7 to my name. This, unbelievably, did not seem to bother me. Looking back, I wonder: Who lives like that? How could we have paid so little attention to making a living, working so hard on what we believed in for no compensation? Once we started having children, I hasten to add, we became a little more financially responsible.

As Mom always said, "The Universe works." And during our time in Bonny Doon it was indeed working for us. John had even less money than I did, a quarter in his pocket, to be specific, the day I dropped him at Babe's Bandstand burger joint on the Esplanade in the Village. Babe, the owner, was a friend and longtime Capitola Survival Committee member. With his quarter, John was enjoying a cup of coffee at the counter when Babe came in from the kitchen looking frustrated.

Exasperated, Babe said, "I should have hired you, Johnny."

"What for?"

"What for? You can't miss it — the fence! Guy next door put it up. You can't see the ocean from here anymore, but you sure can from his place."

Of course John had noticed it. It was six feet tall and ugly.

"Guy is totally unreasonable, won't take it down. I even offered to pay for it. I had a buyer on the line for this place and now he's dropped out. Can you help me with this one, Johnny?"

Of course he would. Babe handed him $150 to get started, promised another $850 when his property sold.

Back home, John threw the cash on the bed. We hugged, laughed like fools, and carried on as if we'd just won a million bucks. Yes, John did get the fence reduced in size by pointing out city policies setting maximum fence height. This was all Babe needed to sell his property. He had a done deal in about two months. And we were $850 richer.

Because John had become an expert in land-use issues he was appointed to the newly established California Coastal Commission by then California Assembly Speaker Leo McCarthy. And it was a natural progression from there to start his own land-use consulting business. Partnering with Robert Blake and John Gammon, they called it Community and Land Use Consulting, and it allowed John to continue working on the kinds of projects and problems that he loved, and make a living as well. Babe turned out to be John's first paid land-use client.

John and I in front of our restaurant in Capitola, California in 1971 before I made the permanent sign. I was wearing the "kind of" Armenian costume I wore as a waitress.

John and I enjoying the Capitola Begonia Festival in 1972

CHAPTER 6

SEARCHING

*If you hear a voice within you say 'you cannot paint,'
then by all means paint, and that voice will be silenced.*
~ Vincent Van Gogh

By January of 1976, I was three months pregnant with our first child. That's when John decided to run in the Democratic primary for a seat in the United States House of Representatives. His opponent would be Leon Panetta.

Our congressional district stretched hundreds of miles along the beautiful Central Coast of California, from liberal Santa Cruz County south to the wealthier, more politically moderate Monterey County that included posh Carmel and Pebble Beach, and further south to San Luis Obispo County. For as long as I could remember, conservative Republican Bert Talcott had represented the district. Both John and I believed that a Democrat who stood for more liberal ideas than Panetta should run in the Democratic primary, but no one was stepping up.

Panetta had recently switched his affiliation from Republican to Democrat. He had been working in Nixon's White House when we were in the streets protesting the war in Viet Nam. He had rather moderate views, at least in our opinion. John wanted to cut the Defense budget while Panetta did not. John and I worked against the opening of the Diablo Canyon Nuclear Power Plant in San Luis Obispo. Panetta was for it.

Most of the district's voters lived in Monterey County, where Panetta was an established figure. His campaign had a head start and much more money than ours. Not only was John getting into the race late, he was skipping several rungs of the political ladder that candidates usually climb before running for a national position. Never having been elected even to a local office, John faced an uphill battle, but he was nevertheless determined to present his ideas to the voters.

Because my pregnancy was an easy one, I was able to engage fully in the campaign, organizing activities from the second bedroom of our house. I was the field organizer, lining up friends and supporters to call voters, stuffing campaign mailers, walking door to door, attending public events and fundraisers and rallying our supporters to get out the vote. I was involved in campaign strategy and press meetings, and traveled with John up and down the district talking to as many voters as I could. We talked, ate, slept and breathed the campaign.

However, as my mid-July due date approached, the changes in my pregnant body and the hormones that went with it started to dominate my life and my perspective. Just moving around and trying to sleep with a gigantic belly was exhausting. I did not get the attention I deserved during this monumental time in my life and in our life as a couple, and had bouts of feeling sorry for myself. Everyone, including John, was so caught up in the campaign they had no energy left for me.

Even Mom was focused on her community activism, despite the fact that this was her first grandchild. She was a teacher at the Santa Cruz Community Free School, which she had helped create; a board member of the Homeless Garden Project; and involved with a group called CALM - Citizens Against Legalized Militarism who were working to bring attention to local police becoming a militarized force. Both my husband and my mother were creative, adventurous, free thinkers who jumped into the activities they cared deeply about. Mom certainly got no special treatment when she was pregnant with her children, so it probably didn't cross her mind that her attentiveness would be important to me. And it didn't help that I had grown up not learning how to express my feelings.

We lost the primary in June. Although we won Santa Cruz County, Panetta's support in, the much more populated, Monterey County put him over the top. But the experience yielded some great contacts and exposure. People from all over the congressional district had become aware of John, his background and what he believed in. I believe that because John challenged him in the primary campaign, Panetta moved more to the left on many issues in the general. John wound up helping Panetta by taking him around the University and introducing him to key people. Panetta won, and as our congressman, he represented our district very well. Years later, my relationship with him helped when I recruited a number of his larger donors to meet with him, one after another one day at his district office, to ask him to vote against a restrictive abortion bill. He ended up voting against it. We also became friends with Sam Farr, who was running for a seat on the Monterey County Board of Supervisors. I later worked for Farr —when he ran for Congress in 1993 after Panetta left to become the Director of the Office of Management and Budget.

The impulse toward social activism, stimulated by my work with the Capitola Survival Committee, Operation Wilder and John's cam-

paign for Congress, now ran deep in my blood; the political projects
I'd been involved in so far would become the foundation and training
ground for my future work. But now John and I were starting a different chapter in our life together. On July 30, 1976, about six weeks after
John's campaign ended, I gave birth to a beautiful baby girl, Kelly,
and the second bedroom in our two-bedroom home was transformed
from a campaign headquarters to a nursery.

John opened an office in downtown Santa Cruz, and was busy
building up his land-use clientele as I started my life as a stay-at-
home mother. Initially, I didn't think twice about this familial division of labor. I found it easy to slide into my new role as Kelly's mom.
I didn't have any specific career in mind. By then John's land-use
business was paying the bills and we didn't need a second income.
We had kept our campaign expenses reasonable, so luckily didn't
have a debt to pay off.

We didn't have a lot of money, but we also didn't have a lot of
needs or desires. Times then were simpler than they are for new parents today—a cliché, perhaps, but true. This was before parents felt
the commercial pressure to spend lots of money on all the latest and
greatest baby gear, before the advent of website registries and corporate big-box stores like Babies R Us. And it didn't even occur to us to
start thinking about buying a house or saving toward future college
expenses. John, being self-employed, was able to take some time here
and there to help me with Kelly, changing her diapers, feeding her,
bathing and playing with her. We were happily coming together as a
new family.

Our family grew quickly. Kelly was about two-and-a-half when
Sara was born. By the time Sara was eight months old, I was back to
my pre-pregnancy weight and feeling pretty hot. I can still see the cute
flowing flowered skirt, soft mesh blouse and yellow-orange platform
heels I bought myself to celebrate my slimmed-down body. (Years

later the kids would use them for dress-up.) I was still nursing Sara—mistakenly assuming this made birth control unnecessary — when I got pregnant with Lesha. John was planning to have a vasectomy but hadn't gotten around to it. A third pregnancy was not in our plans. Yet the Universe was working again: this unplanned event was meant to be and very happily received.

So now I found myself chasing three little kids around, trying to keep up with their energies and their messes. In those days there were few opportunities to meet other mothers at moms' groups or baby-oriented activities like baby yoga or music classes. With little access to social interaction or mental stimulation, I kept myself busy ripping out the four-foot-tall weeds in our back yard, building a sandbox and covering old pieces of furniture. John was fully engaged in building his business, having adult conversations and using his brain. I was reading *Green Eggs and Ham* until I had it memorized, watching Sesame Street, changing diapers and doing household chores. I felt as if I had lost myself. My identity seemed reduced to mom and wife. From the outside I looked happy, but inside I was shriveling up, feeling as if my brain was going dead and my energies were wasted. I was bored and starved for adult interaction, yet couldn't seem to make any moves to change my situation. The three kids kept me endlessly busy, and the amount of physical or mental energy left to do something just for myself was zero.

You might say I had it easy, just as my mom had years earlier. Unlike mothers who worked outside the home, I didn't have the compounded stress of childcare and household tasks on top of a paying job. Nor was I carrying the work of parenting all by myself. John was a great help with the girls from day one. After all, he was their father and unlike earlier generations when fathers didn't do any of the childcare duties. Still, I envied women who had a direction, who knew what interested them and what made them happy outside of their family. Not having a clue what kind of job I could do or wanted to do, I only knew I needed something more to stimulate my mind.

After Lesha was born, our two-bedroom, one-thousand-square-foot house felt cramped. We moved to a bigger house with a large, fenced, grassy back yard, next door to a family with two little girls whose mother was an attorney. I watched as she left for work each day in her power suit, ready to tackle the world. I envied her for having launched a career before she had kids. Her life seemed nicely balanced between her family and her work outside the home. We didn't talk much, so I could only speculate, looking in from the outside. For all I know, she may have even been envious of me. In any case, to fill my own creative urges, I focused my energy on becoming the perfect "Martha Stewart" mother and wife. I made the kids Halloween costumes and simple dresses, Christmas stockings and decorations for our tree. I even painted a huge mural on the wall at Kelly's daycare.

Each of the girls, on turning two-and-a-half, started attending the Santa Cruz Montessori School. John and I believed that a good preschool was important for their mental and emotional development, and we scraped by financially to be able to give them that experience. This enabled me to develop friendships with other moms who didn't have outside-the-home jobs either — finally real adult people I could talk to! We took our kids to the beach and the park and traded off having all the kids at our house to give each of us time for ourselves. Having these women in my life was a great help to my sanity, but I still needed something to sink my teeth into.

I have always found it natural to find a way to take action when I see a need — no doubt a result of my mom's influence. When Mom saw a problem she jumped in to figure out how to solve it, just as she had in creating a preschool for her disabled child in South Carolina. In 1981, when the kids were five, two-and-a-half and one, I met Gladys Anderson, who worked for the County Social Services Department. She was starting The Christmas Project to collect gently used toys and clothes to distribute to migrant labor camps, not far from us in the southern part of the county. On Christmas and their birthdays, our girls received tons of gifts from family and friends — way more than they needed. The other Montessori kids were just as blessed as ours, while the children of poorly paid parents who toiled in the fields had far too little. The organizer in me went to work getting the word out, helping Gladys expand The Christmas Project by organizing Montessori parents and kids to donate toys and clothes, and wrap and deliver them on Christmas Day. Together my kids and I witnessed the extremely poor living conditions in which these people lived — the dirt floors, light seeping through the walls of their shacks, makeshift roofs and the poor plumbing. It made a big impression on us. These were the people who worked hard in the local fields so we could have food on our table. The girls learned about the existence of poverty, inequality and the value of giving to others, while the kids at the migrant labor camps enjoyed a brighter Christmas. The project continued for many years after our girls left Montessori to enter public kindergarten.

Using my community organizing skills in this way gave me tremendous satisfaction and helped me feel less trapped in "kidland" — but it still wasn't the answer. I didn't feel I was using my skills and energy to my full ability. What John and I had done together before the girls were born was exciting. I was fully engaged, even though many times it felt like I was following him in a supportive role. Now I needed something of my own. Like my mother before me, I still didn't know my strengths or what I was really capable of. Growing up in the 50s and 60s did nothing to encourage most young girls to become fully equal members of society.

Some forty years later, in *A Strange Stirring: The Feminine Mystique and American Women at the Dawn of the 1960s*, Stephanie

Coontz wrote brilliantly about what life was like for many women in that era. My mother was an adult then, so probably a more susceptible target than I was for the media messages Coontz described in her book. But I'm sure they influenced me as well. Coontz wrote:

> On December 22, 1962, one month before [feminist Betty Friedan's] *The Feminist Mystique* hit the book stores, the Saturday Evening Post published a cover article purporting to offer a portrait of the typical American woman. The opening page featured a photo of "Mrs. Charles Johnson," surrounded by her husband and children. "I just want to take care of Charlie and the children," the caption explained, summing up what the reader soon learned was the collective attitude of "American women, in toto."
>
> ...Advice books for girls and women hammered home the idea that a woman's greatest goal should be to get married and that she should bury her own interests and impulses in order to please and flatter a man into proposing.

I can't remember being told specifically that my role in life was *only* to be a wife and mother, but I know that the messages being spoon-fed to girls during this time had an influence on me. Again Coontz writes:

> In 1963, Helen Andelin self-published Fascinating Womanhood, which became a runaway best seller when it was picked up by a mainstream publishing house in 1965. Andelin counseled women that the way to a happy marriage was to become "the perfect follower." She urges them to cultivate a "girlish trust" in their man and never to "appear to know more than he does." A woman should never let her

voice exhibit such qualities as "loudness, firmness, efficiency, boldness." While it was ok to be angry, she told them, you should be sure to display only "childlike anger," which included "stomping your feet" and scolding your man in terms that flattered his sense of masculinity, such as "you big hairy beast."

I can't help but laugh in amazement when I read this now, not so many years later. It's impossible to know exactly how this kind of talk influences a person, but I do remember holding myself back, not speaking up in front of boys when I had an idea or a thought for fear it wouldn't be a good one — and by whose measure? As a girl and even as a young woman I recall being conscious of the need to avoid upstaging the boys or to be seen as smarter than they were. I grew up with the underlying feeling that boys, and later men, knew more than I did. It's no wonder I was struggling with discovering what I wanted to do with my life, what my passions were and what I could do well.

I was in my twenties, and married when the so-called second wave of the women's liberation movement was in full swing. Women of my generation were going to college in greater numbers, graduating, starting careers of their own —challenging the notion that a woman should be restricted to the roles of wife and mother. I felt caught between generations. While I had been strongly influenced by the ideals of my mother's generation, I yearned for something more.

The feminist ideas I was being exposed to were becoming increasingly influential on me as the seeds of my awakening found fertile soil in 1972, when I bought the preview issue of *Ms.* Magazine. *Ms.* was the first major magazine owned and operated entirely by women. Unlike *McCall's, Redbook,* and other conventional "women's" magazines, *Ms.* addressed taboo issues such as reproductive rights and domestic violence. The front cover of that issue featured a woman with a baby in her belly and eight arms radiating out from her body, Hindu goddess-style, each hand holding a different object: an iron, clock, phone, typewriter, mirror, steering wheel and frying pan — all representing "women's work." John and I didn't yet have children but the image struck a chord in me. Subconsciously, I was still buying into the patriarchal system that put women in charge of any and all household chores. After all, John didn't do half the housework. This contradicted my conscious ideas of marriage being a fifty-fifty equal partnership.

Another article that was very risky for the times was "We Have Had Abortions." This was before *Roe v. Wade*, when abortion was still illegal. The article included a petition to the federal government signed by more than fifty well-known women who acknowledged having had an abortion and who invited readers to join them in signing on to the "campaign for honesty and freedom." I signed immediately.

At that time, both women and their experiences were sorely underrepresented in the academic world. It was rare to study about women scientists in a science class, and history pretty much focused on the exploits of men. In the late 1960s and early 1970s, women's studies courses started popping up in colleges around the country.

In 1973 I excitedly enrolled in a women's history class at Cabrillo College, and was fascinated by the assigned book, *Century of Struggle: The Women's Rights Movement in the United States*, by Eleanor Flexner. It covered the one hundred years (1820-1920) that it took for women to gain the right to vote. For the first time I understood what my foremothers' lives were like and what they had gone through so I could have this fundamental human right. I was able to better understand how physically courageous and politically ingenious our foremothers were. Not only was the right to vote prohibited; they couldn't go to college, they didn't have the right to own property, nor any legal right of guardianship over their children. If they did work outside the home they were restricted to teaching or factory or farm labor, and they had no control over or right to the household income. A woman's position and struggles were considered a private affair. There was no organized women's movement until the first Women's Rights Convention at Seneca Falls, New York, in 1848. Many of the leaders of this movement worked against slavery before becoming suffragists. Traveling long distances by horse and buggy under harsh conditions to communicate their message, they were publically ridiculed by both men — and women. Women's rights advocates in those days showed great courage as they struggled to make sure their hopes overcame their fears, facing jail, forced-feeding, and even violent mobs. I felt then and will always feel a great debt of gratitude to these courageous women.

Learning this history gave me a whole new sense of myself, and a way of being in the world I had never felt before. I felt connected to sisters who had fought for and won the many rights that I took for granted. I came to see the cause of women's equal rights in America in the context of a big picture stretching back hundreds of years.

For me it didn't matter whether I was personally affected by an injustice. I felt that the violent or inequitable treatment of any woman or girl on this planet affected me too. Feminism was less a personal issue than one of social equality and justice. With this new awareness I felt an obligation to the women who would come after me to do what I could to continue the fight for full equality. At the same time, 1970's feminism and its media coverage seemed to focus on "women having it all" — being both a mom and a career woman. It was a message that made me feel that because I was *just* a stay-at-home mom I was not fulfilling my potential.

It was a very confusing and conflicting time for women like me. I was both increasingly aware and feeling increasingly trapped at home with three small children and no direction. My boredom reached a critical point, motivating me to take another look at my life. I realized my lack of education wasn't helping me. Thinking back on my school years, I wondered if I'd had a better experience then, would things be different now?

My brain felt stagnant. It took my good friend Cass to point out the obvious; I could go back to Cabrillo College and take a class or two just to get my mind cranked up again. Cass and I had remained friends since high school. We were now in our early thirties and she was still there giving me the emotional support I needed.

In 1969, when I first met John, I was enrolled in classes at Cabrillo. In 1973 I took the women's history class. Now, in 1982, with three young children, I was going back to school. It would get me out of the house and thinking about something other than what to fix for dinner. The kids were thriving at Montessori, so there was time in the day to concentrate on something that would stimulate my mind.

Navigating through the list of classes, I decided to try my hand at mechanical drafting. To this day I am not sure why. I had absolutely no experience with this kind of drawing and it was not a class girls would have been allowed to take just a few years earlier in high school. Fortunately times had changed. The teacher was excellent — a man who loved his subject and loved teaching. There were only three women in the class, all of us a little older than the other students. We sat next to each other, supported each other and had a great time. I did so well, the next semester I dove into architectural drafting. I loved the challenge and enjoyed what I was learning. But I had no plan or direction, no conscious path toward a degree or career. I neither knew myself well enough, nor had the outside pressure or encouragement to make those kinds of decisions.

After taking all the classes that were offered in that department my architectural drafting teacher said, "You are really good, Pat. You should be drawing plans for a living."

That was all I needed to hear. Characteristically, I didn't say to myself, "Okay, I will go to work for an architect." Interviewing for a job still felt too scary. Instead, I designed and printed my own business cards. It wasn't long before news of my services spread by word of mouth and clients were calling – mostly for drawing plans for remodels. I even designed a new solar house (which a licensed architect had to sign off on). Another job had me drawing plans for a building that was already under construction. The project had a building permit but it was not being built according to the approved plans. The onsite crew was all men. I was a real curiosity to them and could tell they were uncomfortable — I was invading their space and interfering with their free flow of crude jokes and swear words.

There wasn't much money in it, but for the first time in my life I was collecting checks written out to me for work I had performed. Interacting with clients and the county planning department staff was fun. I was good at asking the right questions and listening to my clients, so was able to understand their lifestyles and needs. I knew how to schmooze the county planning department staff so I could usually get what I wanted. Being with people was what I loved. Sitting at the drafting table all by myself was a lot less rewarding. As in my early Capitola days, it was becoming more fun and gratifying to interact with people.

I also eventually realized that work that was less rigid and more creative than architectural drafting was more to my liking. So I approached real estate offices and was commissioned to draw houses that were hard to photograph. My creative and entrepreneurial juices were flowing when I drew a series of twelve historic Santa Cruz homes, then sold them to a local bank, which sent prints to their customers as thank-you gifts. The eighteen-by-twenty-four inch framed original pencil drawings hung in the bank lobby and then in the business office for a number of years. Maybe I should have launched an architectural drawing career at this point, but I knew deep down that wasn't what I wanted to do for the long haul.

. . . .

In 1984, New York Congresswoman Geraldine Ferraro became the first woman nominated for vice-president by a major American political party. She was the running mate of former Vice President Walter Mondale. Excited by this historic moment, I wanted to help support Ferraro's bid any way I could. The most fun and comfortable thing for me to do was to organize a fundraising event. In that pre-Internet era, I didn't ask the campaign or even let them know what I was doing. I knew they would be grateful for the money I raised —and they were.

Before my event, Ferraro came to nearby San Jose for a campaign appearance, and of course I was there. Determined to give her a copy of my fundraising invitation, without thinking I made a mad dash for her car as she was leaving the event. I told her how much I admired her and handed her the invitation. This all happened in seconds. Afterwards I was a more than a bit mortified as the Secret Service firmly ushered me away, but happy that I had the wherewithal and guts to approach her.

Reagan was expected to win reelection, but ever the optimist, I called my event the Mondale-Ferraro Victory Party. Hundreds of supporters turned out at the old Catalyst bar and music venue (later the home of Bookshop Santa Cruz) on Pacific Avenue downtown. Through a friend, I was able to get Los Angeles County Supervisor Gloria Molina to be our keynote speaker. Mondale and Ferraro lost that election to President Reagan, but the fundraiser I organized was a great success —and it got me out of the house.

Soundly defeated with the re-election of Ronald Reagan, Santa Cruz County Democratic Party regulars got together to lick their wounds and figure out how to move forward. Because my fundraiser had been a major success, I was asked to address the group at a forum billed as *Strategies for Victory Going Forward*. Stepping out of my comfort zone big time, I accepted.

Up until then I had rarely spoken publically. Just introducing myself to a group as we'd go around a room got my heart pounding out of my chest. But something inside of me was saying I needed to take this next step. I wrote about what I thought the Democratic Party should be doing. I sweated over my speech for weeks, practicing it endlessly in front of a video camera we had bought to film the kids. When the date of the forum arrived, I was petrified. I felt I didn't speak as effectively as I'd have liked to, and didn't feel a satisfying connection with the audience. In fact, I felt I had made a fool of myself. But I had done it and to me that's what mattered!

My speech to the Democratic forum could have opened up new "career" possibilities through involvement with local political groups. But I didn't jump in and run with it. The timing wasn't quite right. Even though my interest in drafting and architectural drawing was waning, my three little girls were keeping me very busy.

Kelly in her "A Woman's place is in the House and the Senate t-shirt" and Sara in the high chair

I had my hands full! Feeding Lesha as Kelly and Sara look on

*My girls – Kelly 6, Sara 3 and a half and Lesha 2 in their "The ERA is for my Future" t-shirts in our back yard in Rio del Mar, CA in 1982
(as of 2019 the ERA has still not passed)*

CHAPTER 7

70 LETTERS

> When fathers don't take their daughters'
> achievements and plans seriously, girls sometimes have
> trouble taking themselves seriously.
>
> ~ Stella Chess, an American child psychiatrist

Both John and I were involved parents, but I did the majority of the work by far. John's relationship with the girls was solid, strong, loving and caring. He was an integral part of their lives, so much so that when the girls wanted something they would call out "Mommy-Daddy" and see which of us answered their call. The kids were our joy.

This was quite different from the way I grew up. During the 1950s it was fairly typical for fathers to do little child-care. But my dad was hardly ever at home — first because he was a doctor, and then because my parents divorced when I was eleven. He was absent during most of my childhood.

My relationship with Dad always felt like an emotional rollercoaster ride. In the absence of broken bones or bloody lips, it's hard for outsiders to see abuse, but anyone who has been emotionally tossed around will recognize what existed between my dad and me.

As unusual as it is for me to have twenty-four audiotapes of my mother talking about her life, it is probably even stranger that I still have seventy letters from my dad (and a few I wrote to him) spanning seventeen years. I have read them many times, trying to figure out what made our relationship so distant and dysfunctional. I've wanted to understand what effect he had on the person I was and the choices I made in my life.

Almost all of the letters were but a few lines long and included the mention of an enclosed check. Money was a tool he used to control me. It was the only glue he had to hold us together. True, he had been my lifesaver, helping me deal with my unwanted pregnancy. But throughout my life our relationship was generally strained and centered on money. With no feelings of love or caring about who I was as a person forthcoming, money was the one thing I could get from him. But once I was exposed to the love of John's family, I realized I would exchange the money for love like that any day of the week.

Dad rarely called me, and when he did I would grip the phone so hard my hand would turn red, and my heart would pound out of my chest. Anytime I had to see him I would be a nervous wreck.

The first letter I have from him was written when I was nineteen, about seven months after my abortion. I was living in Santa Cruz. He was in Palo Alto, just forty-five minutes away. On its face, the letter looks fairly innocuous. But there's much between the lines, and there were many letters like this that got worse over the years.

October 23, 1968

Dear Pat,

Thanks very much for your letter. It's always good to hear from you. [This always sucked me in and made me feel just for an instant that he cared.]

I can't write a long answer - because I have to leave in just a few minutes to go on a house call and I want to mail this on the way.

I want you to have good reliable transportation — safe too. And I'll help you get it. What I would like you to do is come to Palo Alto some Saturday soon — and we'll help you find the right car for yourself — and help you make sure that the same kind of <u>silly business</u> [his underlining] *doesn't happen again as is happening to your present car.*

This coming Saturday (Oct. 26) would be just fine for me. Drive your car here if you can.

On one of the two following Saturdays (Nov. 2nd or 9th) I'll be on call. I don't know which one yet. But Oct 26 is OK for sure. Let me know. Gotta run now. Sorry I can't write anymore.

Love,
Dad

P.S. Pat, <u>please learn how to spell.</u> [His underlining]

The P.S. was an unnecessary jab and it hurt, aimed at my insecurity about not being the greatest student as I was growing up. From a loving father who could tease, play, hug and laugh with his daughter, this comment could be taken as a joke and given right back with light-hearted banter, but there was never of any of that between us.

The cut was subtle, but I knew it was intentional. I never knew what Dad was going to say, except that it would be some version of disapproval. He made me nervous and on edge waiting for the other shoe to drop. And then he would put me down. My emotions would swing wildly — from good to bad — when I read his letters. First he would say something nice, and I would be hopeful ("I want you to have good reliable transportation — safe too. And I'll help you get it"). Then came the put-down ("...and help you make sure that same kind of <u>silly business</u> doesn't happen again" or "P.S Pat, <u>please learn how to spell</u>").

I had no idea what he meant by "silly business," and I didn't ask him. I can only guess that since my mom and I bought my car together, it was a jab at our decision-making abilities. He always felt he knew best.

There is so much I will never know about my dad and his childhood. What were his father and mother like together? How were they as parents?

When he closed his letters with *Love, Dad* it felt like a formality, and indeed, over time it became *From, Dad* or *Yours, Dad*. His next letter was short and to the point.

May 4, 1969

Dear Pat,

Please try to improve your manners. You have had some recent communications from me, and some sort of answer is in order. As I have said before, this is more for your own benefit than for anyone else's. These words are meant well. Read them over again.

Yours with love,
Dad

Later on as an adult, when he would summon me to his house (and it did feel like a summons), it was never to just hang out together and have fun. There was always some reason, which proved to be unpleasant for me. I didn't know what kind of behavior or words to expect from him. I got nervous every time I had to go see him, so I avoided it as much as possible.

This was how our relationship went on for years. It felt like what relationship we had was hanging on by life-support. A few incidents stood out.

In 1978, I was almost 30 years old. John and I had been married for eight years; Kelly was two and I was pregnant with Sara. I was summoned up to my dad's home in Marin County, not knowing what he wanted, which made me nervous. And because I grew up not knowing how to "speak" I didn't ask. Driving the two hours from Santa Cruz to his house, I was trying not to feel anxious. When I arrived he was cordial. As we chatted about this and that I thought, "Not bad so far."

Then the hammer dropped.

As I sat next to him on the couch, he announced he had decided to give my two brothers and me each an annual gift of $3,000. Up went my antennae. Was he doing this for tax purposes? "There must be a catch somewhere," I thought, because there always was. Of course I was right. This time it arose from a grudge he'd been nursing for many years.

The year I met John I was taking classes at Cabrillo Junior College, trying to figure out what I wanted to do with my life. Alas, distracted by love, I failed to motivate myself to attend classes that didn't interest me, and dropped out of several of them. I did know that my parents' 1962 divorce agreement stipulated that Dad was required to give me a modest monthly stipend of $265.00 after I finished high school, — but only if I was taking a full college course load. I didn't tell him I wasn't.

He found out soon enough when he asked for and received a copy of my transcripts. For nine full years he said nothing while his anger at my "fraudulent behavior" festered. Finally he figured out how to punish me. I was, he said, to deduct the amount I had "stolen" from him from his gift of $3,000.

Our discussion was painful, confusing and humiliating. That time in my life had long since passed. Talking about a choice I made so long ago made my head spin. I felt chastised, as if I were a small child. I told him I was a much different person now, but that made no difference to him. I wanted to know why it had taken so long for him to figure out how to punish me and why was he using his money to do so?

He coldly and matter-of-factly told me to figure out how much I owed him and to let him know what it was — though I'm sure he already knew it to the penny. Was he hoping to catch me in trying to cheat him again? Not thinking clearly at the time, in my state of disbelief, I said okay and tried to get out of there as quickly as I could. This was what he had summoned me to his house to tell me. Fun father/daughter time was not a part of the day.

Later, I methodically figured out the math and sent him this letter.

March 28, 1978

Dear Dad,

After thinking more about our conversation I decided to send away for my transcripts from so long ago. As you probably already know I didn't complete 12 units or more of any of the 4 semesters that I attended. Those were the days I was sowing my wild oats and I would much rather have done it then and gotten it out of my system than still have the desire.

Dad, I want you to know that if it were now and I decided to drop classes for whatever reason, I would let you

know and not accept your money. I hope you can accept this
and go on from here.

You have decided to give me $3,000 a year, which I
thank you for very much. It will come in handy and will
make things easier. The way I figure it is like this:

1 semester = 18 wks = 4 ½ mo. x $265.00 per mo. =
$1,193.00. And $1,193.00 x 4 semesters = $4,772.00 which
is what I owe you. So next year you can give me $1,228.00 of
the $3,000 and I will have paid you back and we will be able
to start with a clean slate and can become friends, adult to
adult. I hope that is possible.

When we had our visit and you told me about your
offer to give each of us some money each year I don't know
if I thanked you. If not — thank you very much. Write and
let me know what you think of my analysis.

I gave Kelly a hug & kiss from you.
Love,
Pat

Ever the optimist, I was still trying and wishing and hoping. I do
have a tendency to beat my head against a brick wall for way too long.
Dad accepted my accounting and sent me a check the following year
for $1,228.00, and that was it. He stopped giving his annual gift — at
least to me. I am not sure if he continued with my brothers. This was
a bizarre conflict, but not our last.

. . . .

Three years later we were living in Rio Del Mar, just south of Santa
Cruz, in a sprawling ranch-style home well suited to entertaining. I

was a busy stay-at-home mom of three now. Kelly was five, Sara two and Lesha almost one.

It was Easter, and we were hosting the entire family. In an Armenian household, that means everyone: aunts, uncles, distant cousins, friends — including a few who had come to be designated as aunts and uncles — plus anyone else who didn't have a place to go. This is not what I grew up with, and I loved it. I loved our big Armenian family gatherings and was grateful that my girls were experiencing the kind of warm and loving extended family that I didn't have growing up.

We invited John's dad, sister Joan, and brother-in-law Jim and their two teenage kids. Cousin Martin, Aunt Alice and Uncle Caesar. And Mom. She lived only ten miles away, and always spent Easter with us since my two brothers lived far away. I even invited Dad. The girls were beyond excited that the Easter Bunny was coming and they would have a house full of family to play with.

It seems strange to me now that I invited both parents. They didn't get along, never talked if they could help it. I am not sure what I *was* thinking. Actually I don't think I was thinking, which is why I had no trepidation or even thoughts about how it might be with them in the same room. Let's just say I was oblivious.

I actually felt jubilant at the thought of Dad enjoying Easter with us. After all, the girls were his only grandchildren. Happy to be invited, he took the bus down from his home in Marin. He was quite conscientious about protecting the environment and rarely drove his car if he didn't have to. I picked him up at the bus station the day before Easter. We drove up to the house and the kids ran to greet him with big hugs. Their energy was off the charts as they escorted him to their rooms and showed him all their special things. They didn't know him, he hadn't been a part of their lives, but they were nevertheless excited to see their "other" grandpa.

We took a trip to the nearby park. Dad pushed the kids on the swings and caught them as they slid down the slides, enjoying every minute. He was a pediatrician and loved children, so he was in his element. I watched with pleasure as he had fun with my girls, and let myself imagine the possibility of a better relationship with him. For that moment, all was good.

By late afternoon most of the gang had arrived. We gathered in the kitchen to prepare traditional Armenian foods — *dolma, pilaf* and *cheoreg* Easter bread. I remember standing over John and the kids as they sat at the table painting hard-boiled eggs in rainbow colors when the phone rang — it was my brother Steve calling from Vermont to wish everyone a happy Easter. Dad eventually got on the line with him, and after they'd talked for a while, I could see that something was going terribly wrong. Dad got tense, his face turned white. I could hear barely restrained anger bubbling up in his voice. The moment he hung up he turned on me.

"Take me to the bus station," he snarled. "Right now."

"My god, Dad, what's the matter?"

"You know damn well what's the matter. There's no way I am going to be in the same room with your mother. You, you…." He paused, locked eyes with me and turned up his lip in a display of disgust that was like a blow to my midsection. "You tricked me."

I hadn't remembered that Mom would be joining us for dinner — as she always had — until Steve somehow mentioned it. He continued in a rant: I, Pat, had done this to him on purpose. I always had been deceptive. I was doing him great emotional harm. I was out to hurt him. As always, it was all about him. No amount of explaining would mollify him. No matter what I said, his finger remained pointed at me, the bad guy.

As I stood there gored by his wrath in front of my shocked family, years melted away and I felt again like the admonished and traumatized child. At the same time, it dawned on my adult self that the loving father who would enjoy spending time with my family — his grandchildren — was a phantom that would never materialize. I felt traumatized. My hopes of a loving father enjoying time with my family, his grandchildren were crumbling away.

A couple of days later I called to apologize, tell him I had meant no harm and had simply made an innocent mistake. It was to no avail.

"You did this on purpose. To hurt me. You're a conniver. A manipulator."

He hung up. There was something indefinably familiar about this awful conversation and I found myself wondering if this was the way he regarded Mom. Was this the basis of his vast anger toward her — the anger that he couldn't overcome even for a few hours to enjoy his grandchildren, and our family's Easter feast?

Now, looking back, I wonder what possessed me to think that my mom and dad could enjoy their grandchildren and a holiday meal together. Was I subconsciously trying to put my parents back together after twenty years of barely having spoken to each other? Why would I think this could work? Or maybe the normalcy of John's family made more sense and I expected the passing years to allow some sense to penetrate my family too.

After that Easter, Dad and I didn't speak or see each other for fourteen years. My three daughters — his grandchildren — never saw him again.

On that day, watching him with the girls, I had for the first time felt hopeful that he would be in my life and theirs as a loving father and grandfather. I didn't know, or didn't want to see, what kind of person he actually was. Two years later I was still trying hard to see him as I wanted him to be. I reached out to him, suggesting a visit with the girls, but he would have nothing to do with us.

April 28, 1983

Dear Dad,

I had been wondering how you were, and whether or not the kids and I could make a trip up there soon to see you. I talk about you but they haven't seen you for two years and really don't know you, and you don't know them. They are great kids, and everyone concerned is missing out a lot.

I have always felt it doesn't matter what I say to you, because I have the impression that you never believe what I say. I feel that you think I say one thing and feel another. It isn't like that. This makes it very difficult for us to communicate.

Maybe if we got rid of all these money matters between us, we could start our relationship. It seems all through this letter I am guessing at what you think, when it would be nice to know what you think. What do you think a father-daughter relationship should be like? I am an adult and would like to be your friend — you have qualities that I like and we might even be able to have fun together. I am not my mother, or my brother — I am me and my actions are mine alone. It seems like you connect all of us and are very bitter. What are you bitter about? What have I done or not done?

Dad, I don't understand your reactions sometimes but I truly don't have any hatred for you. We have to accept each other's differences and have a little give and take in this relationship. It seems to me you have to give up trying to have power over me like I was your little child and accept the fact that I have grown up and have my own thoughts and ways of doing things that are different from yours.

With love that is waiting to flower — your friend,
Pat

P.S. Enclosed is a picture of the kids and my business card [my architectural drafting business] — my business is growing! If you care to know more about my new life, just ask and I'd love to tell you all about it - I'm really excited about it.

Ever the caretaker, in this letter I was trying yet again to make him feel better. I wanted so badly to have a warm loving relationship with him. Then a few weeks later I got this.

May 11, 1983

Dear Pat,

   This letter will be a short one, because there is little need for it to be long. In your letter there was no mention at all of the terrible black, black Easter of about two years ago — which I will never forget as long as I live. It is late. I am growing weary of it all, and have come to a point where I have very nearly ceased to care.

   You grew up virtually without a father — and have done quite well nevertheless. Certainly a grandfather is not as important in one's life as a father. I am sure that your daughters will do quite well too.

   Sincerely,

   Dad

I never knew what to expect when I got a letter from him but this one was over the top. I was in shock. Rereading my dad's words, I realize now how little he knew of the value of a father's love and for that matter the value of family. If I'd had more clarity then, my response would have been much different. I didn't address what really mattered in his letter; instead was sucked into responding to his childish whining about what he called "the black, black Easter"—still trying to explain myself and comfort him.

August 8, 1983

Dear Dad,

Your last letter was very sad and I am truly sorry for all the hurt you have felt because of that Easter over two years ago. It was never meant to happen — I assumed (wrongly so) that you knew Mom was going to be there and that it was all right with you. I am sorry. I would never want to hurt you.

We are all doing fine — kids are healthy and happy and growing by leaps and bounds. Hope you are having a nice summer.

Love,
Pat

His response took over two months and was short and to the point.

October 14, 1983

Dear Pat,

It may or may not be true that you didn't mean to hurt. But you did nevertheless.

It is unlikely ever to happen again.

Yours,
Dad

In view of his childish, narcissistic behavior I decided to let things go for a while and focus on my family and my life. Then, out of the blue, he sent this letter.

May 11, 1985

Dear Pat,

This isn't going to be an easy letter to write, but I'll try anyway. Everything is so much subject to <u>manipulation and scheming</u>, as for example that last very Black Easter in your home. This instance is, by no means, the only reason for thinking as I do; it is just the last in a series, the weary last. I am really very tired and weary of it all. I've lost interest, and also any desire even to attempt to change anything. As I've said before, all feeling is gone, and I just don't care anymore.

This letter could go on and on. But it might as well end here and now, because there is little else to say.

Yours,

Dad

Over the years, his letters were traumatizing for me in one way or another, but this one took the cake. I was devastated, but this time, also numb. It was strange and confusing to feel both emotions at the same time. On the one hand, I could feel the heartlessness and cruelty, and well understood how his behavior had stunted my growth. And even though I was a thirty-six-year-old adult, I still felt like a child chastised and abandoned by her father. But at the time, it just felt like *this was him* — the way he was. I had learned to expect this from him. I somehow coldly assessed that, of course, since I hadn't responded to the cruelty in his last letter, he decided it wasn't cruel enough and needed to thrust the knife as deeply as it could go - one last time.

Seven years later, on her own initiative, Lesha, our youngest, who was then eight years old, wrote a letter to her grandfather asking if she could come see him. He did her the courtesy of writing back, but let her know that such a visit would have to wait until she was old enough to not have to rely on me for transportation. It was impossible for her to understand why her grandfather would reject her — why he didn't want to see her, when in fact it was me, his daughter, he wanted nothing to do with ever again.

I spent many years uselessly reaching out to my dad. Rereading his letters has made me realize how he never looked at himself to try to understand our lack of relationship. Bizarrely, he made me feel guilty in an effort to try to draw me closer. Then he would either back away or else treat me like a broken toy needing to be fixed. The cycle was never-ending, until I realized there was no way I was going to get the love from him I always craved.

I can understand Mom saying on her tapes, *"He would treat me real nice and then pull the rug out from under me."* He was treating me the same way. He had no idea what unconditional love was. His help always had strings attached.

Years ago, if I had been able to see more clearly and understand the dynamics, I would have saved myself a lot of emotional ups and downs. But my dad was not physically abusive, and his subtle and manipulative behavior was hard for me to see clearly.

It was around this time that I stumbled onto the book *What You Think of Me is None of My Business*, by Terry Cole-Whittaker. The title spoke directly to me, and believing that others could relate to it as well, I bought 20 copies and gave them to everyone I knew. Being more of a spiritual as opposed to a traditionally religious person, I didn't relate particularly to the author's frequent references to a formal God, so I looked beyond that and focused on her essential points about self-awareness and personal growth.

The message I had received in childhood was to seek the approval of others, to try to please others — including my endless attempts to secure my dad's approval. Cole-Whittaker helped me see that I shouldn't focus so much on what other people thought of me. I needed first to love and accept myself. I learned that it doesn't matter whether other people approve of me or not: I needed to live my life for myself. If I could love myself I would have more love for others. She talked about the power each one of us already has within ourselves, and the need to find that power rather than relying on others. Her words were like a candle glowing in a dark room where something precious and exciting had been hidden away. Feeling an untapped power deep inside of me, I wanted to allow myself to have access to it, trying to incorporate this growing consciousness into my day-to-day life. I wanted to catch myself before I fell back into my old ways of thinking and acting, and instead make choices and decisions based on what I liked and wanted. Old habits die hard, but the good feelings I felt when I succeeded motivated me to keep trying.

Even so, while I could see the person I was trying to become, I wasn't yet fully able to embody her. My mind was split between two personas: the shy woman who thought she had nothing to offer, and the extrovert who was fighting to come out. To blossom into that fully expressive self, I would have to learn how to let go of my need for external love and approval — a journey that would require a lot of small steps, some forward and a few back.

CHAPTER 8

"IT'S BIGGER THAN YOU"

The Nature of This Flower is to Bloom
~ Alice Walker, an American novelist, poet, and activist

Over the years our income was erratic, fluctuating with John's ability to sign new clients. Between land-use clients, he worked on various other projects. I loved his creativity and entrepreneurial spirit, and learned to live with the fact that some of his projects came to fruition and some didn't. But while I found the uncertainty exciting, it was also stressful. We never knew from month to month if a client or project was going to pay off; a weekly or even monthly paycheck was not part of our world. Whatever income we had always came in big chunks, which we then used to pay overdue bills.

John always felt he could come through in a pinch, but there came a time when our unpredictable income cycle wasn't working. It was the mid-80s and the economy was sliding into a recession. His land-use clients started to dry up, and the income from my architectural drafting and rendering work was never enough to cover our expenses. We had always lived on a financial rollercoaster. Now we were too long on the downside, and our lifestyle was slow to catch up with the reality of our dwindling resources.

John seemed paralyzed and wasn't facing our financial crisis. The year 1986 stands out in my mind. As usual, we went to a Christmas tree farm to cut down our own tree and wound up selecting the most humongous Douglas Fir we could find, an extravagance we must have figured would make us momentarily forget our dire situation. But underneath the bravado I was stressed. How were we going to live? How were we going to pay the bills? I was angry with John for getting us into this mess and his inability to get us out of it. I wasn't bringing in enough money myself for us to survive. I felt I had no control and I was scared.

A private man by nature, John became increasingly cut off from me emotionally. Neither of us shared our feelings; we just went through the motions of normal life. But I knew he was scared too. Bill collectors were calling, so instead of trying to work out payments, we screened out their phone calls with an answering machine. I had thoughts of leaving John, and tried to figure out where I would go with three small children and no income. A friend said the children and I could stay with her, but I didn't pursue it. I didn't really want out of our marriage; I just wanted John to wake up.

The final straw was the sheriff arriving at the door with an eviction notice. He'd barely made it out the door when I let John have it.

"Damn it!" I screamed. "I won't live like this!" I was panicked, terrified.

"You think I like it any better than you do?" he roared back. "What am I supposed to do? You got a great idea you're not telling me?"

"No, but I'd sure like it if you figured out how to support your family like a normal husband."

He flinched and of course I didn't mean it. I took a deep breath and delivered what I knew would be another blow.

"We should move in with your sister Joan. Into her barn. It's got living quarters. I already talked to her and she said we can stay there until we get back on our feet."

He shut his eyes, crumpled into a chair. After a long minute he dropped his chin in almost imperceptible agreement.

Perhaps he knew that moment was important, but he didn't know how important: I decided I didn't have to leave him.

It was November 1987. Kelly was eleven, Sara almost nine and Lesha seven. They were my biggest concern. We were moving them from our comfortable four-bedroom home in a great neighborhood close to their friends. Not wanting to burden them with our desperate financial situation, I chose to treat the move as a grand adventure; much as my mom had characterized our move to Switzerland. I am my mother's daughter in so many ways. Taking a page from her book, I had always dealt with difficult situations by putting them in the best possible light. I was always good at pushing down my feelings and trying to make the best of any situation, and I didn't see a need to shift gears now. In hindsight, I'm not sure this was the best way to handle our move to the barn. Was projecting such jaunty optimism the right thing to do, or was it a failure to speak the truth that needed to be acknowledged? Were the children old enough to understand what was really going on? Should we have shared more with them?

Joan's property was in the farming belt outside the town of Watsonville, in the southern part of Santa Cruz County. To get to our new home we drove toward Monterey on Highway 1 past Watsonville, then up a hill, turning left down a two-lane road with few houses. After parking at the end of a dirt driveway, we walked around a large weathered barn to the back, where the front door was located. Surrounded by endless strawberry fields, I felt isolated, as if we were in Nowhere Land. But drawing on my experiences in Europe, where I had learned how to be flexible and flow with whatever came my way, I was determined to make a cozy home.

The kids got the bedroom and bathroom just to the left of the front door, furnished with bunk beds and a single bed. The girls were already sharing a bedroom so that was not a problem. Upstairs was a kitchen with just enough room for a small dining table, a compact living area with a large picture window, and a small bedroom and bathroom for John and me. It was all carpeted in pieced-together gold-toned shag carpet remnants. Every day before the girls came home from school, I made sure to dispose of the huge potato bugs that had died on the floor of their bedroom.

Years later, Kelly told me that she was initially excited to move to the barn because she and her sisters had always had fun there, visiting their aunt and uncle at Easter and Christmas time. But after moving in and experiencing the spiders and bugs that lived in the barn, she said, it was no longer fun.

We made things as normal as we could. There were a few attempts at playing baseball on the bumpy field of weeds and brush just outside our front door. Meanwhile, our resources were stretched to the limit. Opening the refrigerator, I would say to the kids, "Oh, I forgot to go to the grocery store today," when the truth was I hadn't gone because I didn't have the money.

Our station wagon seemed to break down every time I got behind the wheel, so on school days I made the twenty-minute trip with the girls back to Rio del Mar Elementary School in my mom's rickety, rusty pickup truck, all four of us piled into the front seat. When we rumbled into the school parking lot, the girls would jump out as quickly as they could, pretending they didn't know me. Years later they told me they were teased and bullied about the truck and their distinctly untrendy clothes.

Living with the daily undercurrent of uncertainty, isolation and lack of money was wearing me down. I tried to hold us all together, put a good face on things, maintain something of a normal life, but the stress and trauma left me exhausted most of the time. After more than a year of not knowing if we would be able to pay the monthly bills, John found a regular nine-to-five job. It was in Redwood City; a two-hour drive each way. He worked for a development company as the head of the "real estate owned," department, which involved reclaiming property in foreclosure, fixing it up and reselling it. This job was our lifesaver.

Although we didn't see much of John except for the weekends, I was grateful for the income. The company even gave him a new car. It was strange but wonderful to see him tooling down the pot-holed dirt driveway to the barn in a brand-new Acura. To our amazement, we had gone, relatively speaking, from rags to riches. Our goal now was to pay off old bills and stash away everything we could in order to move back into town as soon as possible. The girls missed their friends, and living so far out of town was a big change for them.

As another Christmas approached, I wanted to make things as nice as I could, without being extravagant. I splurged a little on three sets of matching bedspreads, sheets, pillowcases and dust ruffles, white with tiny pink roses for the girls. I could just imagine their faces light up at the sight of their sweet, cozy new beds. As it turned out, their Christmas gift triggered a more significant event than I was anticipating.

Joan and her husband Jim lived in the main house on the property. She enjoyed having us around, especially her three little nieces, whom she adored. Jim, not so much. He had a workshop downstairs in the front of the barn. Since the girls never ventured there, I thought it would be the perfect place to hide their Christmas presents. Big mistake.

One afternoon I'd just returned from running some errands and was getting out of the truck when Jim came charging toward me like a bull after red pajamas, yelling at the top of his lungs and dragging one of the packages of bedding behind him in the dirt.

"What is this crap? Who the hell gave you permission to enter my space?" Except he didn't say "hell."

"Joan and I have gone out of our way to let you live here, and what do we get? Gratitude? One bit of gratitude for what we've gone through for you?"

By now he was in my face. I felt humiliated. I was grateful, had been grateful from the moment we arrived. I tried mightily to show it, almost kowtowing to him on a daily basis, knowing he didn't particularly like us. But it wasn't enough.

"What you've been through," I screamed back, "my god, do you have any idea what we are going through? If you want us out of here, all you have to do is say so!"

We screamed at each other until I couldn't anymore. I got in the truck, careened off as fast as I could, crying hysterically.

By the time I got to Santa Cruz, my tears had dried up and my anger subsided. I headed straight for the nearest drug store and bought a newspaper so I could check out the rental listings. We had been living in the barn for about a year, and I was angry — angry with John and angry with myself for having no control over our situation, and for not being able to contribute to our family income. I was determined to find some other place to live as soon as possible, and was sure we had scraped together enough money enough to do so.

In a month we had moved into a townhouse in Soquel, just south of Santa Cruz, in a small neighborhood where the girls had kids their own age to play with. The school bus to their junior high and elementary schools stopped on our street corner. They got to ride their bikes down to the nearby 7-Eleven and the corner grocery store.

It was better for them, and a tremendous relief for me to be away from Jim and the isolation of the barn.

Moving back to town into a clean new townhouse felt luxurious to all of us. The girls had friends nearby, and being able to walk to their houses gave them the freedom they needed. Being back in town was liberating for me, too. Moreover, we were now able to buy our very first new car — a Dodge Caravan. The days of taking the kids to school in our old station wagon and having it break down more often than I want to remember, and of having to borrow my mom's dirty, old, rickety truck — those days were over!

The helplessness I had felt made me realize for the first time that I needed to be financially independent rather than just sitting back and relying on John to be the sole breadwinner. For the sake of my own growth and confidence, and in case something should happen to John, I needed to be able to take care of myself and my family. Without an income of my own, if we were to divorce, or if John were to die or become unable to work, the kids and I would have been stranded.

Financial gain had never been a big motivator for either John or me. Our erratic income had never bothered us, and it helped that every so often we received an infusion of cash. When I turned 30, 35 and 40 I received fairly large sums of money from a trust set up by my grandfather Otto Vogl. We used it to pay off bills and buy much-needed household items. A couple of times I splurged on new clothes, going to the store and buying anything I wanted without concern for how much I was spending.

But by this time, having experienced both that indulgence and the need to watch every penny, I had learned that being able to spend as much as I want doesn't make me any happier or feel any more satisfied. This periodic influx of trust money gave me the luxury of doing things that were meaningful to me, without needing them to generate income. I now realize how freeing that was, but also how it kept me from feeling a sense of urgency, or recognizing a need to push myself.

That's what I learned from the barn experience; that I had no excuses. We were living in town again. The kids were getting older and didn't need me at home as much. Now I was ready and able to act. I started to move cautiously out of my insecurity and dependence to challenge my biggest fear — entering the job market.

At that time, there were some young women climbing corporate ladders, achieving great career and financial gains, but many more were stay-at-home moms like me. Without any "real work" experience, I was terrified of interviewing for a job. I was afraid I wasn't good enough, afraid I wouldn't know how to answer a question correctly, afraid I would make a fool of myself. I thought I needed to already know how to do whatever job I was applying for.

This fear of being exposed as inadequate played out even when I was a child living in Palo Alto. At nine I got my favorite Christmas present, a purple velvet ice-skating outfit with red and white stripes under the short skirt and matching red-and-white-striped panties. I spent hours at Palo Alto's small local outdoor rink, teaching myself how to skate, repeatedly picking myself up off the ice in my determination to learn. Shy and self-conscious, I didn't want to take lessons where I would be seen as less than a perfect skater. Though I had confidence in my learning ability, I was unwilling to make myself vulnerable to a critical teacher. I appreciate now how undaunted and persistent I was, but also how frightened - shunning the very help I needed to succeed.

With John's total support and encouragement, I checked the job postings in the local paper and found one for a medical assistant at an abortion clinic. Perfect! I'd had my own experience with abortion (as had my mother) and believed passionately that a woman's ability to control her own body was a basic human right. Now this job would not only give me a regular paycheck, it would also enable me to understand abortion services from a provider's standpoint. I applied for the job and was called in for an interview. The Universe was working.

At almost forty years of age, I went to my first job interview. My maturity and years of experience as an activist and a mom paid off, as I found myself much more comfortable than I had expected. In fact, I felt so good about the experience that when the clinic called a few days later to say I was not being offered the job, I just brushed it off without any feelings of failure. About a week later, before I'd had time to regroup and restart my job search, they called again. They had another position to fill, and offered me the job.

Working at Choice Medical Clinic as a medical assistant, I was part of a team for the first time in my life. I felt a genuine camaraderie with everyone on the staff. I had always been organized and efficient and liked working in my dad's medical office as a teenager. I was comfortable with the functional aspects of the job — checking women in, doing pregnancy tests and getting blood samples. But my job also involved the personal — talking with women, listening to their concerns, understanding their emotional state and being able to counsel them in an intimate way. My maturity and my own personal experience helped a lot. I knew what it was like to be pregnant and not be able or ready to take the pregnancy to term. I could offer sincere empathy to the women coming into the clinic.

Once a week I assisted the doctor and anesthesiologist in the surgery room. About eighty percent of the time women were under anesthesia. It was the twenty percent who opted to be awake that I was able to help the most. I took their minds off of the procedure and helped them breathe through it. Having had three natural childbirths, I knew the technique of breathing through the pain. I could see the sense of comfort I was providing and it felt good. One woman was so appreciative of my support that she gave me a crystal necklace, which

I still have today. When I look at it all these years later, I think about her. It was immensely rewarding to be able to give these women the comfort I had not received.

Patients represented a wide spectrum of backgrounds at the clinic. They were rich and poor, white, black and brown, academics and laborers, politically right and left. It became clear that men and women sometimes have sex irresponsibly, and that sometimes birth control fails, and then there's rape. Whatever the cause of an unwanted pregnancy, we were there to help our clients work safely through the consequences.

One day a father brought his young daughter to the clinic. She was about fourteen, withdrawn, and hardly said a word. Because of the way her father was acting — on edge, pushy and controlling, many of the staff began to suspect that he was the one who had impregnated her. But we had no way of knowing. At the time, protocols for investigating or reporting such cases did not exist. So we simply treated the young girl without judgment. This was very hard.

Another teenager, the homecoming queen at a local Christian high school, came in. Her mother had been an anti-choice protester. Now she was sitting in our waiting room with her daughter. There is no way of telling what long-term effect the girl's abortion had on her or her mother, but I do know that we gave this young woman excellent medical care in a warm, loving, non-judgmental environment. Afterwards she thanked us and said, "My experience was so different and so much better than what my mother and I expected."

Abortion clinics were then and still are targeted for violent protest in all forms, from graffiti to bombs to murder. At my clinic we were luckier than most, but not totally immune. Well aware of the attacks by anti-choice forces around the country, we had installed a strong security system. One morning I was first to arrive at the clinic, punched in the security code, entered, and was shocked to see a large swastika painted on the wall just outside the surgery room door. How had the perpetrators gotten in? What else had they done? Would they strike again? We called the police, who searched the clinic thoroughly and filed a report. But, as is often the case, the perpetrator was not found. We felt shaken and violated, but were not deterred.

My job was to counsel patients, do prep and follow-up and once a week assist the doctor in performing abortions. But I occasionally got other assignments that were fun and challenging. One day, the clinic's nurse practitioner asked me if I could take her place at an annual health fair. I was to wear a full-length "Broken Condom" costume that she had made, complete with a broken tip that included spurts of fake semen coming out. How could I pass up a chance to give out birth control information dressed as a broken condom, my face peeking through the front and "semen" spurting out of my head? Not a chance! Needless to say, I got a lot of attention, gave out more information than expected and had a great time.

Another interesting job popped up when my daughter's teacher asked me to speak to her high school class about what it was like to have an abortion. She wanted to impress on her students the importance of using either safe sex or abstinence. I loved talking to these young kids, who were so receptive and asked a lot of good questions. And the cherry on the cake was that Sara told me afterward that I hadn't embarrassed her too much.

Extra activities like these made my first real job more interesting and boosted my sense of confidence and self-worth. I felt passionate about what I was doing. It felt meaningful to help women in their time of need. I wasn't making enough money to support my family on my own yet, but it was a good first step.

My daughters could see the passion I had for helping women at this difficult time in their lives. Sara says she remembers me talking about my work at the dinner table and giving them an after-hours tour of the clinic. I wanted to impress upon them the importance of safe sex, telling them I hoped they would never have to experience an unwanted pregnancy. But they were teenagers, preoccupied —appropriately — with boys, clothes and friends. They didn't yet have the experience to fully understand why a clinic that gives women the freedom to control their own bodies was critical to women's autonomy — and so politically fragile. They were just too young to realize the implications.

But years later, I could see my influence when Lesha volunteered at a Planned Parenthood clinic in San Diego, checking in patients. "I sat behind a glass partition with these pictures of a few creepy men on the wall," she told me. "If I saw one of them I was to not let them in and to call someone."

. . . .

In 1989 my friend Shana Ross and I traveled to Washington, D.C. for a massive and historic pro-choice march. The United States Supreme Court had just decided the case of *Webster v. Reproductive Health Services* imposing restrictions on the use of state funds for facilities and employees performing, assisting with, or counseling on abortions. In *Webster*, the court allowed states to legislate against the freedoms it had awarded to women when *Roe v. Wade* was decided in 1973. It's one of many ways in which anti-abortion forces have chipped away at women's legal health care rights since *Roe*. Just in the first six months of 2019 alone, 378 abortion restrictions were introduced across the United States. Among them was a surge in bans on abortion as early as six weeks, before most women even know they are pregnant. In addition, Alabama enacted a near-total abortion ban and Missouri enacted a ban at eight weeks of gestation. This has been done with the intent to set up a legal showdown at the U.S. Supreme Court to overturn *Roe v. Wade*.

I was thrilled to be among the over half-million women (and some wonderful men) who felt passionately enough to leave their homes, their families and their work and travel hundreds of miles to make their voices heard. The energy was out of this world. In support of our foremothers, we dressed in white and purple, the colors of the suffragists. We stood for hours, packed shoulder-to-shoulder, surrounding the Washington Monument, waiting to march toward the Capitol steps.

"Shana" I said, "We aren't moving at all. Anti-choice protesters must be blocking our way."

But the truth was there were so many of us we couldn't move. It's a scene and a feeling I will never forget.

Once home, Shana and I were so energized that we had to do something. Given our experience as organizers, a fundraiser was a logical choice, so we got together to lay out our plan of action. Where would the fundraiser be held? Would we serve food or just have a reception? How would we fill the room? And most importantly; who did we want to be the recipients of the money we raised? There were so many things to decide and to do.

Deciding we would call it "A Choice Dinner" we approached the California Abortion Rights Action League (CARAL) and the local Santa Cruz Reproductive Rights Network with the idea to raise money for them. They were thrilled.

One of the highlights of the night would be the keynote speaker, whom CARAL helped us recruit. It was Norma McCorvey — the real Jane Roe in the *Roe v. Wade* Supreme Court decision legalizing abortion. A well-known speaker always helps get good attendance and press coverage, and in fact, Norma, Shana and I were all interviewed in advance by the local newspapers.

Shana and I started getting threatening phone calls, but that did not stop us. One caller threatened harm to my family if I continued with the event. Another said he knew I had three children and asked how a woman with children could behave like this. Despite these calls, I couldn't back down and John was in complete support of my continuing.

Networking fools in the pre-Internet era, we knew how to create excitement about the event. We developed a master contact list that grew exponentially. We sent postcards and made phone calls. We identified twenty highly influential people who had their own networks, and asked each of them to sponsor a table at the dinner and fill it with their friends. We got a local artist to create a beautiful poster that hung in stores and businesses all over the county.

I was confident in my role as an event organizer and had no problem engaging people from all over the county and from all walks of life, including the movers and shakers. My problem would rear its head the night of the event, when I would have to speak in front of them all. I was able to put my apprehension out of my mind while having fun with the preliminaries, but as the date drew closer I started feeling that clenching feeling in my gut. Imagining myself at the podium made me weak in the knees.

The answer to my panic was to reach out to Shana's friend Clare, who taught public speaking at Cabrillo Junior College. I met with her one evening in an empty classroom. Facing her camera, I rehearsed in front of an audience of one as she critiqued my fledgling public speaking skills and gave me helpful tips.

Putting together a large-scale fundraiser felt something like planning a wedding — on steroids. We secured a date at the Cocoanut Grove. We arranged for "stems" of red, white and blue helium balloon bouquets to be anchored on each large round banquet table with the "flowers" blooming high above. A balloon arch would curve over the raised stage. Meeting with the caterer, we tasted samples of delectable salads, main dishes and desserts. All the details were coming together.

Then, on a clear, starlit Indian summer evening in October of 1989, Shana and I welcomed over five hundred people to A Choice Dinner. I was in my element; schmoozing one-on-one was something I was good at. I tried to ignore the panic rising in my stomach at the thought of having to speak in front of hundreds of people.

The room was buzzing wall-to-wall with people enjoying themselves — seeing old friends and meeting new ones. Slipping into the bathroom unnoticed to freshen up and try to calm my nerves, I accidentally let the sleeve of my black one-piece jumpsuit plop squarely in the toilet. "OMG! – What the fuck!" I said out loud, fortunately to an empty ladies room. With only a few minutes until my big moment, I desperately blotted the dripping sleeve with paper towels, waved it under the hot air hand dryer, and then made my way to the stage, hoping the evidence of my mishap wouldn't show. My heart was pounding out of my chest. Scared to death, I mustered my faculties into a display of total control, stepped up to the podium and, to my own amazement, proceeded to graciously welcome a ballroom full of allies to our gala evening.

Clare had taught me to keep looking from one side of the room to the other and to speak much more slowly than I normally would. "Pause between thoughts", she advised, "longer than you would normally, so that people can understand you better." Grateful for her help, I did just fine.

Shana and I wanted to show that women's reproductive rights affect both women *and* men, so we had asked my longtime friend, County Supervisor Gary Patton, to be master of ceremonies. Before starting to speak, he spontaneously lifted Lesha, my eight-year-old daughter, up to the microphone so that she could say, in her cute little-girl voice, "May I please have your attention?" What a thrill! Then later in the program, Susan Kennedy, the head of CARAL who would eventually serve as California Governor Schwarzenegger's chief of staff, announced to the crowd, "This blows me away – we've never even had anything like this in San Francisco!"

There was no denying it: The evening was a great success. In the three short months since the *Webster* decision, we had managed to organize a major, successful fundraiser. At the time, it was the largest fundraising event ever held in Santa Cruz County.

Our initiative and hard work garnered lots of press coverage and raised thousands of dollars. Totally gratified, I was doing what I was good at to make a difference in the lives of other women and their families.

....

I was slowly overcoming my insecurity and lack of self-confidence. When I told Mom about my fear of public speaking, she had wise advice: "You have to remember that it's not about you. It's bigger than you." Her words made a difference. They helped me to deliver my remarks focused on what I was saying instead of on myself. I also felt energized by knowing I was doing my part for a cause I believed in.

A few years later, spurred on by our success, I organized another fundraiser, called Voices for Choice. Janet Benshoff, director of the ACLU's Reproductive Freedom Project, and actress Susan Ruttan, who starred in the popular TV series *L.A. Law*, eloquently inspired the audience to open their checkbooks for the great work that the Santa Cruz Reproductive Rights Network was doing. This time, as the organizer, I had decided early on I was going to stay behind the scenes. I invited Carol Fuller, a well-known reproductive rights activist in our community, to emcee the event. It felt good to be relieved of the pressure of public speaking and concentrate on what I loved to do; organize. A year later I was honored to be singled out, along with

Carol Fuller, by the local People's Democratic Club to receive its annual award for my reproductive rights work.

Then, because I had put myself out there for what I believed in, my county supervisor, who was aware of my pro-choice activities, asked me to serve on the Santa Cruz County Commission on the Status of Women. The commission was comprised of ten commissioners, two appointed by each of the five county supervisors. Although I had never been on a commission or county board before, I didn't hesitate. I was excited to have a chance to positively affect the lives of women throughout my community.

This was all new for me, and a real testament that one thing leads to another. At my first commission meeting, I felt nervous and intimidated by the other women who seemed so together and knowledgeable. After sitting quietly for a while trying to absorb and understand the process I asked, "What do I do?" In response the chairwoman asked, "What issue are you interested in?"

Women's physical safety, specifically domestic violence, had been another passion of mine and since none of the commissioners were working on this issue I decided to take it on.

I had a lot to learn. First, I needed to find out what city and county organizations were already doing to help domestic violence survivors. The obvious focus was on helping the survivors, but there was a lot that needed to be done to prevent the violence in the first place.

I met with and interviewed everyone I could and formed a working group. Santa Clara County, home of the City of San Jose, had an effective Domestic Violence Commission from which our group drew inspiration and knowledge. After several months of research, many meetings, and a lot of hard work, the Santa Cruz County Domestic Violence Commission was created.

The opportunity to help establish this commission benefited me as well. It was another step toward finding my voice, my strengths, my personal power and myself. Each opportunity that came along since my first job at the clinic increased my self-confidence. I was being recognized and appreciated and was feeling valued for the contributions I was making. Working on issues to help make women's lives everywhere safe, free, and in their control had been a passion of mine since the time of my own abortion in 1968. My work was now pulling me forward to more and more challenging and exciting possibilities. The flower in me was starting to blossom.

Kelly playing baseball on the field in front of the barn

Shana Ross and I with Norma McCorvey (aka Jane Roe) before our "Choice Dinner" a fundraiser for the California Abortion Rights Action League (CARAL) and the Santa Cruz County Reproductive Rights Network

Speaking – trying to hide my fear – in front of 550 people at the Choice Dinner that Shana and I organized

So happy! Counting the money we made from the Choice Dinner at home on my bed

With Susan Ruttan (Actress in the LA Law TV series) at gathering after the Voices for Choice fundraiser that I organized

At the 4th of July parade for Planned Parenthood with my
daughter Sara in Aptos, California

600,000 women and men (gathered around the reflecting pond) during
the 1989 March for Women's Equality in Washington DC

CHAPTER 9

FINDING MY GROOVE

Far and away the best prize that life offers is the
chance to work hard at work worth doing.
~ Theodore Roosevelt, 26th President of the United States

One day in the fall of 1991 I saw an article in the newspaper: "California Congresswoman Barbara Boxer announces plan to run for U.S. Senate." I thought, "Oh, my god, we have never had a woman senator in California! It's about time. This would really shake things up."

Boxer caught my attention for the first time in the early 1980's when, as a member of Congress, she exposed egregious overspending at the Pentagon. She made it public that $7,600 had been appropriated for a single coffee maker, $640 for a toilet seat and $436 for a hammer. This was possible because the Pentagon didn't require competitive bids for spare parts. As Boxer says in her book, *The Art of Tough*: "Large defense contractors were making these parts in-house and charging a fortune." She introduced a bill, the Small Business and Federal Procurement Competition Enhancement Act to correct this abuse of taxpayer money. Her actions led to several procurement reforms that have saved taxpayers millions of dollars. I saw Barbara's picture in the *Washington Post* holding a photo of the $7,600 coffee pot with the caption, "It might as well be made of gold". I thought, "I like her knack for gaining public attention and fighting for what's right."

In 1991 President George H. W. Bush nominated Clarence Thomas to the Supreme Court. Many women's rights and civil rights supporters opposed his nomination. He had expressed opposition to abortion, and it was feared he would vote to overturn *Roe v. Wade*. He was also against affirmative action policies, even though as an African American he had benefited from them himself. The Senate Judiciary Committee hearings on Thomas's nomination were stalled when a leaked Judiciary Committee/FBI report came out saying that Anita Hill, a professor at the University of Oklahoma College of Law, had been interviewed in connection with the Thomas nomination. Hill said that Thomas made inappropriate sexual comments to her when they worked together at the Department of Education. She described his remarks in detail. They included telling her about pornographic films he watched showing women having sex with animals, group sex and rape scenes, and graphically describing his own sexual prowess.

Accompanied by the press, Congresswomen Barbara Boxer, Pat Schroeder, Eleanor Holmes-Norton, Louise Slaughter, Jolene Unsoeld, Nita Lowey and Patsy Mink marched to the Senate to present their case against Thomas. They said Hill's charges were serious and demanded that the stalled hearings be reopened and that Hill be heard. The iconic picture of the seven congresswomen walking up the stairs to the Senate chambers chronicled that watershed moment in history and got my attention.

In response to their demand, a new hearing was scheduled. The whole country was riveted to the television as Hill spoke calmly and with great dignity, even as the all-white, all-male committee treated her with distain and disrespect. Thomas "played the race card," accusing Hill and the media of a "high-tech lynching." Despite Hill's testimony, the Senate voted 52-48 in Thomas' favor, and four days later he was confirmed as a Supreme Court Justice — a lifetime position.

I hung a large framed poster on my wall with a picture of the all-male, all-white Judiciary Committee members that said "Remember this when you vote." It was there for many years.

Women around the country could relate to Anita Hill. They had themselves experienced sexual harassment and the negative impact on their careers and their lives. Fortunately, I was never exposed to sexual harassment in my work experiences, but many of my friends have told me their stories.

What Anita Hill did, and the bravery she showed, was not in vain. The issue of sexual harassment came "out of the closet" and was written about in the press as never before. It became more real in the minds of the public and for the first time workplaces were forced to address it. Federal laws were passed requiring employers to hold informational meetings with all employees to clearly define the meaning and parameters of sexual harassment, and they set new policies and procedures to protect women and allow safe recourse for violations. That's not to say sexual harassment has gone away, as proven by the #MeToo and #TimesUp movements, but it finally started to register as an issue that demanded legal attention.

Another issue surfaced by the Anita Hill hearings was the glaring absence of women in legislative seats. Women were not represented in the government on local or national levels. Barbara Boxer says in her book, "The pull of this issue of respect for women was tugging at me. It was one more reason to try to get into the Senate…."

Boxer was a fighter; a fearless champion for women, and an outspoken supporter of women's reproductive rights. I was glad when she decided to run for the United States Senate in 1992 and wanted to get involved in her campaign. Excitedly and without thinking much about it, I wrote her a letter that said, in essence, "I have followed your work and would be thrilled to help you get elected to the U.S. Senate. I want to be on your campaign staff."

I imagine that few people, sending off a message like the one I sent to Boxer would actually expect a positive response. It's easy to think, "Who am I, and why would this person even answer a letter from me?" I had certainly thought that way most of my life. In the not-too-distant past, paralyzing fear had kept me from job interviews. But now I was asking for the job I wanted. Barbara Boxer's Senate run was a historic moment as far as I was concerned, and I felt my inner chutzpah being released.

I sent the letter and gave it no further thought. But a few weeks later, to my great surprise, Boxer's campaign manager wrote back with a job offer. They wanted me to be her California Central Coast field director. Shocked and over-the-top excited, but to my amazement not at all nervous, I accepted. This represented a huge change in my life, but I felt totally up for the challenge. John and I had been active in local politics for the past twenty years, so I knew my community. This would be my first paid political campaign job. I was offered $2,000 a month, almost twice as much as I was making at Choice Medical Clinic.

Up until then, all of my campaign work had been local. I was accustomed to being a volunteer, stuffing thousands of envelopes for Suzanne Paizis' unsuccessful 1972 state Senate campaign and organizing a fundraiser for Julian Camacho for Congress in 1974. I had worked behind the scenes and as the candidate's wife in John's congressional campaign in 1976, organized a Mondale-Ferraro fundraiser in 1984 and a couple of major pro-choice fundraisers.

I had volunteered a lot of my time, and understood the importance of volunteer work. But this was different. I wanted and needed a paid job. Boxer's two opponents in the primary, Lieutenant Governor Leo McCarthy from the Bay Area and Congressman Mel Levine from

Los Angeles, were better known. The initial polling showed McCarthy favored by fifty percent of voters, Levine at about fifteen percent and Boxer at not even one percent. Her campaign was a long shot but I knew she could win. I knew she would be a great senator, and I wanted to be a part of making that happen.

The Anita Hill hearings had energized women (and good men) who were ready to work for Boxer. They had seen with their own eyes that the Senate was an all-male club. As Barbara herself said, "It seemed that nobody ever noticed before that there were ninety-eight men and only two women in the Senate."

Each of the fifty states is represented by two senators who serve staggered, six-year terms. But in 1992, because Senator Alan Cranston was retiring, there were two seats to fill in California. Barbara Boxer was running for one and Diane Feinstein for the other. This was a first. We had had two men representing California in the Senate since California became a state in 1850! So why not two women? But it was a hard sell to many who also thought that California voters would not vote for two Jewish women. Barbara's response was, "It's just what the Senate needs, a double dose of chicken soup." I always loved Barbara's way with words.

Not to be outdone, Feinstein's campaign was creatively spotlighting the imbalance of female senators to male senators with her slogan "Two percent is not enough. It may be good enough for milk, but not for the U.S. Senate."

Besides Boxer and Feinstein, Patty Murray from the state of Washington and Carol Moseley Braun from Illinois were running for the Senate in 1992. Victory for all four would make the United State Senate six percent women. A possible six out of 100, and the media started calling it "The Year of the Woman." Wow! Six out of a hundred. Can you hear my sarcasm? As of the spring of 2018 there are twenty-three women senators, which is twenty-three percent. We're getting there but still a long way from the fifty percent of the population that is female.

Boxer was a congresswoman from northern California, liberal Marin County, just north of San Francisco. Most of the state's voters lived in the southern part of the state where she was completely unknown. Back then California was not the "blue" state it eventually became. The conventional wisdom at the time was that Boxer was too liberal to win, but I knew differently. I could feel the excitement from the women I was talking to. They were ready to work their hearts out for her. Excited to be a part of this historic campaign, I was now being parachuted out into a bigger world than I was used to. Barbara was too. As she said in her book *The Art of Tough*, "…campaigning for the Senate in a state as big as California, which is larger than many entire countries, has to qualify as one of life's most abnormal experiences."

To do this, Boxer's campaign divided the state into about ten regions. I was hired for the primary campaign to organize the Central Coast counties of Santa Cruz, Monterey and San Benito. This was more than I had expected to take on, never having done political work beyond my own county. Neither had I been the one in charge, the one who stood up and talked in front of an audience. I loved the organizing part of the job. I was in my element. By now, speaking to smaller groups was okay, but I was still uncomfortable when I had to speak in front of a large crowd.

At the clinic, forty years old, I'd been punching a time clock, earning $7.50 an hour. I wanted greater autonomy and more opportunities to use my initiative and creativity. Now, working on Boxer's campaign, I was free to innovate, giving directions with no one watching over my shoulder. This was my bailiwick! I could come up with an idea, do the planning and carry it out. While some people may not handle this kind of freedom well, I discovered that I thrive on it. My experience raising three children, organizing communities and doing political advocacy all contributed to my confidence and competence as a paid campaign worker.

Boxer's campaign had to raise millions of dollars. The candidate "dialing for dollars" is one way. But Barbara came up with a play on words to help raise some of the needed money. Taking off from President George H.W. Bush's successful charity, "A Thousand Points of Light," Barbara invented "A Thousand Points of Loot." The idea was that a thousand house parties would each raise a thousand dollars. You could have a party with ten people at $100 each or a hundred at $10 each.

So I set out to facilitate Boxer house parties in every corner of the Central Coast. The campaign sent me plenty of campaign materials: issue papers, bumper stickers, T-shirts, her famous "Boxer shorts" and Boxer nightshirts that said "Boxer for Senate: You'll sleep better at night." A VCR tape — an uplifting infomercial — of her talking about who she was, what she had done and wanted to do was played at each party. And we raised thousands of dollars.

I wasn't given a budget. Since I had no money to work with creativity and ingenuity counted. I was fortunate when a local attorney with an empty space upstairs from her office volunteered it free of charge. I gathered my core team, and we transformed it into Boxer's Central Coast Primary Campaign Headquarters, an invaluable place to hold meetings and conduct campaign work.

My goal was to get Boxer's name out there —everywhere. Enthusiastic volunteers came pouring out of the woodwork. They set up information tables in shopping malls, in front of the post offices and libraries and any public place that would allow it. While some of them were holding Boxer signs at busy intersections, others walked door-to-door handing out Boxer literature. As in my early days of community organizing, I coordinated a speakers' bureau, sending Boxer supporters to speak to community groups, campaign forums and churches, and marshaled all the troops for a big push to get out the vote on Election Day.

Deciding to take advantage of the influence of local elected officials, with their high profile and their own following, I organized a press conference with current and former women elected officials — city council members, county supervisors, school board members — who supported Boxer. We gathered at the County Building in downtown Santa Cruz, two volunteers behind us holding up a huge banner made by a volunteer that said, " Barbara Boxer for U.S. Senate: 98 to 2 Just Won't Do." Having the endorsement of people already popular in the community was priceless. The press conference got great coverage. At this one event we were able to reach thousands of voters with Boxer's name and her stand on the issues.

Then a couple of the male elected officials said, "What about us?" Boxer supporters themselves, they wanted in on the excitement, so we held another press event with current and former male elected officials.

Barbara ran a creative and relentless campaign for the Democratic Primary. She was everywhere, but flying under the radar. McCarthy and Levine didn't seem to notice that she was gaining ground. Toward the end of the primary she toured the state for twenty-four hours straight, arriving in Santa Cruz at four in the morning. My job was to notify the press and get people to show up at that ungodly hour. Denny's Restaurant at the top of Ocean Street was the only place open that early, and as the main route into Santa Cruz, it worked very well. Surprisingly, an excited group of about twenty supporters actually showed up to talk to Barbara about the issues, and the local paper even turned up to interview her.

Before going to Denny's, Barbara came to see her Central Coast campaign headquarters and freshen up. I still remember how nervous and excited I was as I got up at two in the morning to show her around the office. I made lots of coffee and set a table with croissants, jam, fresh strawberries and orange juice. She was duly impressed and grateful for the professional quality of the campaign we were running.

Despite the huge time commitment and the challenges presented by the campaign, I was having a ton of fun. It was exciting to have so many people who wanted to help. Managing the volunteers was a big part of my job. Of course, there were a few with quirky personalities. I had to figure out what to have one shabby, frenzied, middle-aged woman do so she wouldn't harm the campaign. She didn't listen very well, so it was hard to give her direction, and I never knew what inappropriate thing she might say. She wanted to walk precincts and talk to voters, but I was more than dubious about how she would represent the candidate. I have always believed that there is a place for every volunteer — so, instead of turning her away, I asked her to help put packets of information together. She was happy to be of service, and I was happy she was not talking to voters.

Hundreds of volunteers came out of the woodwork, excited to help elect the first woman senator from California. One young single mother, living on welfare as she put herself through law school, appreciated the opportunity to be involved in the campaign, learn the issues and see how a political field organization was run. She was a perfect example of a woman down on her luck and working hard to better herself. We kept in touch for a while and I was happy to see her reach her goal of becoming an attorney and getting off welfare.

Three University of California Santa Cruz students worked as interns, offering their youthful energies in a myriad of ways, while gaining valuable experience. The office walls were covered with evidence of our efforts. There were enormous volunteer sign-up sheets. There was "The Road to the Senate" poster picturing the Capitol building at the end of a yellow brick road covered with hundreds of yellow brick-shaped pieces of paper bearing the names of volunteers. My mom was on the phones and John and the kids helped out when they could. It was a family affair.

Since Barbara was not supposed to win, money was not coming into her campaign as it was for McCarthy and Levine. Because of this she didn't have the funds to run ads until the last ten days of the campaign. Fighting the odds, Barbara campaigned hard in every part of the state, and won the primary. People gathered at campaign headquarters to celebrate.

Happy and high on the adrenalin of a win, we turned to our new challenge; the general election campaign. Barbara would be running against Republican Bruce Herschensohn, a politically conservative television commentator from Los Angeles.

The county Democratic Party opened a headquarters to house all the Democratic candidates running in the general election, and I moved our operation right in and started to set up shop. It was a warehouse-like building, with a cement floor and high ceilings, within walking distance of downtown Santa Cruz. The goal was to have people constantly coming and going, creating a lot of noise and excitement, signaling that everyone has something to offer.

But with no walls enclosing my designated area of the headquarters, in contrast to the secluded upstairs apartment headquarters we'd used during the primary, I felt distracted and exposed. Fortunately, one of our Boxer volunteers worked in construction and offered to pay for and build temporary walls around our designated area. I accepted gratefully. This made meetings and phone conversations much easier.

Late one afternoon I got a call from Boxer's state field director in Los Angeles. She wanted me to plug into a conference call that night. I was tired, had been working non-stop, and while I was always accommodating, this time I just couldn't do it.

Most every night John was home with the girls, making dinner and helping with homework. They were older now — Kelly was sixteen, Sara thirteen and Lesha eleven, but I had committed to being home that particular evening. I knew the field director was stressed, with huge challenges of her own, but I also knew it was not mandatory that I be available.

"I am so sorry, I can't make it. I've got three kids and I promised them I'd be home tonight."

"Well, you will just have to figure out if you can do this job and have kids too."

I was shocked. Angry tears welled up as I thought about how much I had poured into this campaign — really what my whole family had given to it. I thought about why I was doing this and who it was for. I thought of Barbara Boxer, who supported women being able to work and have a family at the same time and would not appreciate this kind of remark.

I went home, spent the evening with my family and after a good night's sleep was ready to continue my work. The call went on without me, and the next day I was briefed on the high points. There was no ground lost. Lesson learned.

....

Family life was challenging during this time. Campaign work really *is* 24/7 and I was not home very much. It took years to find out what effect my absence had on the girls. It was neither all good nor all bad.

Sara told me recently, "I remember coming home after school and having the house free for my friends and me to hang out unsupervised. Kelly and I hung out a lot and it was fun having an older sister to be friends with. Lesha seemed so much younger even though she and I are only 18 months apart."

Kelly said, "After school was boring. I spent a lot of time watching TV, eating Cheetos and thinking about boys." One of her friends, who had an abusive father, spent a lot of time at our house and ended up being sort of our fourth daughter. Her situation gave Kelly a different perspective on our family: "Even though you and dad weren't home with us after school, this made me feel and appreciate the stable home life we had."

I have always said Kelly was born mature and has been a thoughtful caretaker ever since. She says that taking Christmas gifts to the children at the migrant labor camps when she was only five years old had a huge impact on her and instilled a desire to give back. At seven she decided she didn't want to eat meat anymore, and became a vegetarian. At fifteen, all on her own, she decided to volunteer for Earth Save. It's an organization founded by John Robbins, a Santa Cruz resident and heir to the Baskin Robbins ice cream fortune. He wrote the 1987 bestseller, *Diet for a New America*, about the connections between diet, physical health, animal cruelty, and environmentalism. So for Kelly, the choice was a perfect fit.

But like many a parent, I only learned when my girls became adults that they had done their share of experimenting with marijuana and alcohol. I would like to think I would have noticed and done more to steer them away from drugs, but am thankful that they came through their teen years basically unscathed.

John and I eventually learned that Lesha had been depressed and anxious in her teens. Like me, she was never a very good student. School was hard for her. In fact, she hated it, and didn't care about much else, either. She had no insight into her situation or her feelings and assumed everyone felt as disconnected as she did. This was before there was much understanding in the school systems that different children learn differently. Lesha came through it all right, but I do regret that I didn't give her more of what she needed during those difficult early years of her life.

Sara's friend Denine, and Lesha's friend Julia were also at our house quite often after school and practically became family members. They were part of a group of boys and girls that hung out together and liked each other just as friends — which was much different from when I was their age.

The girls did engage in our world of activism a couple of times — stuffing envelopes, passing out fliers at fundraisers and coming with me to pro-choice marches. But they got quite bored with it all, not appreciating the impact of what they were doing. They were too young to realize you can change things, that citizen activism can affect how decisions are made and how those decisions can affect their own lives.

Sara acknowledges now the intense dedication of her parents to being informed citizens, standing up for women's rights, and working to elect fair and just leaders. She didn't quite "get it" back then, but she did take it in stride. "We were told 'shush' more times than I can count when the news was on. We listened to oh-so-many political discussions over dinner. But I was still so young that I really didn't understand much of it and why, in particular, it was so important that Barbara Boxer be elected."

....

In the general election I was given responsibility for Santa Clara County, home of Silicon Valley, which enabled me to take my community-organizing skills to a much larger population of voters. I had the help of an amazing group of women who called themselves DAWN: Democratic Activists for Women Now. It was formed by women who were determined to help elect Barbara Boxer and turned out to be invaluable to me and the campaign. Many of the women had never been involved in politics before, but here, just as all over the state, women were coming out in droves to do what they could. They were wonderful to work with and made my job much easier.

It was a hard race. For hundreds of miles along the California coast, from the San Francisco Bay Area to Los Angeles, the political scene is mostly liberal. The Central Valley and inland areas, however, are more conservative. Many in the political press labeled Boxer's opponent Herschensohn as "ultraconservative." He thought *Roe v. Wade* should be overturned. He believed the U.S. Department of Energy should be abolished, and said in 1989, "I would like to see oil exploration in the plains, in the coastal waters, drilling everywhere."

Herschensohn was trying to paint Boxer as an out-of-touch, liberal, free-spending Washington insider. At the same time, Boxer was having a hard time making people see what an extremist he was. He came across as reasonable and rational. The *New York Times* quoted Sherry Bebitch Jeffe, a political analyst at the Claremont Graduate School, saying of Herschensohn, "He reminds me of Ronald Reagan. You might hate what he stands for, but he's a decent human being. He's very media friendly, while Boxer comes off as overly shrill."

Mainstream media never uses the word "shrill" to describe a man who is speaking out about his beliefs and principles. If women dare to step out of the role society expects them to play by enthusiastically or emphatically expressing strong opinions, they are tagged with unbecoming and even insulting descriptions. A man behaving the same way would be called a strong leader and characterized as taking charge. Unfortunately, as recent elections have demonstrated, this is still the case.

The polls showed Boxer leading, but the race was tightening, arousing a lot of excitement. Then, four days before the election, Bob

Mulholland, political director of the California Democratic Party, confronted Herschensohn at a campaign appearance in Chico. Brandishing a large poster advertising a strip club, Mulholland shouted, "Should the voters of California elect someone who frequents the strip joints of Hollywood?" This plunged the final days of the campaign into a furious exchange of accusations. Many called Herschensohn a hypocrite for patronizing strip clubs while embracing conservative religious values. Herschensohn accused Boxer of an organized last-minute political smear, even though no evidence ever emerged that she had ordered the disclosure or knew about it in advance. He spent the waning days of the campaign having to answer those allegations — and had to admit he'd visited the clubs.

On Election Day, Boxer won by five percent. Boxer's and Feinstein's victories in the general elections were historic on two counts. First, California had never before had two U.S. Senate seats at stake in the same election. And, for the first time, two women senators represented a single state.

Campaigns are always full of personal stories, and I have mine. Both of them involve John, whose spontaneity, rebel nature and willingness to act outside the box have always been a big attraction for me. These two stories are indicative of the many reasons why I love him.

When Barbara won the general election, a group of us piled into our Dodge Caravan (dubbed the "Choice Mobile" because it was the vehicle of "choice" when my friends and I would go to pro-choice marches) and headed up to San Francisco to celebrate. Boxer's victory party was held at the Fairmont Hotel, a historic city landmark and old-style luxury hotel. Its elegant ballrooms and meeting spaces with panoramic views of the city and the Bay sat high on top of Nob Hill.

It was a little past midnight. Thousands of people who had worked their hearts out were roaming the halls. The excitement was bouncing off the walls. A group of us strolled down wide halls past the large ballroom being prepared for the victory celebration. Reaching one of the twelve-foot-high closed doors leading to a meeting room, we saw a number of people milling around outside the room. Curious, I asked, "What's going on in there?" The room was full of national television cameras and reporters preparing to interview Boxer and Feinstein. We would not be allowed in. "Well," I thought, "This is a good place to hang out for a while. Maybe we'll see some action."

At that very moment a hotel waiter, an innocent-looking lanky young man approached the door carrying a large round tray of assorted drinks and cookies. Ready to enter the room, he was spontaneously stopped by John, who said, "Thanks I'll take that." It all happened in a second. John now had the tray and was in the room setting up drinks on the long buffet table on one side of the room. Boxer looked over at him, smiled and waved in her usual friendly manner. And that is how John, in his new role as waiter, got to watch history being made as the major networks interviewed our new senators Boxer and Feinstein — while I waited impatiently outside. I was jealous, but had to hand it to him for cleverly getting a front-row seat to history.

Six years later, in 1998, Boxer was reelected after a closely watched race in which she won by ten points. I hadn't been active during that campaign because I had a full-time government job (that story to come). But John and I were again at the Fairmont in San Francisco, ready to celebrate. Minutes after the polls closed, CNN and ABC projected Boxer the winner and we all went crazy, laughing, hugging and toasting to Barbara's victory. The ballroom was full of excited well-wishers, as John and I wiggled our way up to the front, reuniting with many people I had known and worked with over the years. After Boxer spoke we were there to greet her as she walked along the front row to shake hands and say thank you. As she passed us, in his typical mischievous style, John dipped under the rope and followed along behind her entourage. This time I wasn't getting left out of John's spontaneous fun and followed right behind him along the roped-off area reserved for the senator and a few staff, waving at people as if we belonged there.

. . . .

With Boxer's win in 1992, it was hard to contain the energy emanating from women in my Central Coast community. Over and over I heard from women saying, "This is only the beginning. Now what can we do?" It *was* only the beginning. The question was how to harness this newfound energy. Women had become painfully aware of how underrepresented they were in the decision-making bodies of our country and they wanted to do something about it.

So I decided to organize a Women in Government Conference. The goal was to educate and encourage more local women to run for elected office, either Democrat or Republican, to serve locally and be in the pipeline for higher office in the future. The Republican Party was a different animal in those days. Republicans were more willing to work with Democrats in office, and had a less extreme ideology. The need was obvious. We needed more women to run for office, and they needed help.

We held the conference in a central location between Santa Cruz and Monterey, reaching out to all segments of the community. About 125 women attended from around the Central Coast. There were workshops where locally elected women spoke in an intimate atmosphere, sharing the ins and outs of running for elective office as well as holding office. Kathleen Brown, then the state treasurer and Democratic candidate for governor in 1994, gave the keynote speech and shared invaluable information about her experiences running for office. She explained how she got started in politics, what was needed personally, professionally and practically. She described what it was like being a candidate and what affect it had on her personal life, both good and bad. She was realistic but positive, sending an encouraging message for women to step up to the plate, because their experience and perspectives were needed. Several attendees came up to me to let me know how much they appreciated the opportunity to ask questions directly of women who had run for office.

EMILY's List (EMILY stands for "Early Money Is Like Yeast"), a political action committee focused on getting pro-choice female Democrats elected to office, had been established seven years earlier, in 1985. The organization's name emphasizes the fact that early fundraising is essential if a political campaign is to attract the money it needs to win. Before the Boxer-Feinstein victories, other than EMILY's List, few organizations existed to support women running for office. In the wake of that sea change, many more were formed. DAWN decided to stay together with the goal of electing women to public office in Silicon Valley. Emerge America, with a presence in twenty-five states, identifies and conducts an intensive seven-month training for women planning to run for office. Go Run, started by The White House Project, trains female candidates in basic communication and fundraising skills and addresses the unique barriers women face in politics.

On the state level there is California List, Women Winning Minnesota, Ruth's List in Florida, Carol's List in Montana, Annie's List in Texas, Sally's List in Oklahoma and Lillian's List in North Carolina and no doubt more that I don't know about. It has been documented that women tend to need more encouragement to run for office and more help when they do decide to take the plunge. Many, like myself, have never wanted to run but have the skills to assist women who do. These organizations were sprouting up all over the country back then and were a tremendous help in increasing the number of women running for office and the number of women winning.

In 2016, EMILY's List launched Focus 2020, a project focused on electing pro-choice Democratic women to governors' seats and state legislative chambers in the 2018 and 2020 elections — before the next redistricting in 2021. And it's succeeding!

Democrats flipped three state legislative chambers in 2016. In Nevada, Democrats picked up ten seats in the state House and one seat in the state Senate to flip both chambers. In New Mexico, Democrats picked up five seats to flip the New Mexico House of Representatives. Also according to EMILY's List, Democrats picked up seats in the Maine Senate, Florida Senate, and the North Carolina House.

But I have never seen anything like 2018! According to the Cook Report, turnout in the 2018 mid-term election was 50.3 percent of eligible voters, the highest in a midterm election since 1914 and the first time a majority of eligible voters cast ballots since women gained the right to vote almost a century ago.

Twenty-five women — a historic number — will serve in the Senate. And six states — Arizona, California, Minnesota, Nevada, New Hampshire and Washington State — are represented by two women senators as of 2019.

Democrats gained forty seats in the House. Candidates supported by EMILY's List alone flipped enough seats (23) to deliver the U.S. House majority to the Democrats. This was the largest gain for Democrats since the Watergate midterm of 1974.

This was the first time Americans elected more than a hundred women to the House of Representatives: Democrats increased their ranks of women from 61 to 89 (46 percent), while the number of Republican women fell from 23 to 13 (43 percent). There will be 36 new women in the House, the highest number in history, eclipsing the previous record of 24 elected in 1992 — the so called Year of the Woman.

Ninety percent of House Republicans are white men, compared to just 38 percent of House Democrats. This is the widest such gap in history.

Before the 2018 election there were 33 Republican governors, sixteen Democratic governors and one Independent (Alaska). After the election Democrats had six more seats. There were six women governors before the 2018 election, which upped it to nine — six Democrats and three Republicans.

After the 2016 election, thousands of women reached out to EMILY's List, about running for office. Since its founding back in 1985, the organization has helped elect 116 women to the House, 23 to the Senate, 12 governors, and over 800 to state and local office.

In 2018, there was a huge drive to elect women. There is no doubt in my mind that this is the effect of Hillary Clinton, blazing the trail and being the first woman to win a major party's nomination for President.

. . . .

After my 1992 work on Boxer's campaign and Bill Clinton's election to the Presidency, I was thrown into one campaign after another, as a national game of musical chairs played out. Our local congressman, Leon Panetta, left to become President Clinton's director of the Office of Management and Budget, leaving his congressional seat open; Sam Farr, our state assembly member, decided to run for Congress in a special election to fill Panetta's seat; and when he became our congressman, my friend and County Supervisor Gary Patton ran for Farr's vacated assembly seat. This all happened in a little over a year.

As I had done with Barbara, I contacted Sam Farr and told him I wanted to work on his campaign. I had known Sam since 1976, when John ran for Congress and Sam was running for Monterey County

Supervisor. He was now a state assembly member. Having witnessed my successes on Barbara's campaign, he hired me on the spot, making me one of two fundraisers in the congressional district. Sam won and was our congressman for the next twenty-four years.

Gary Patton was a longtime friend. Connected by our political work and growing families, John and I had been in birth classes with him and his wife Marilyn when they were expecting their second child and we were expecting our first. Gary, a Santa Cruz County supervisor for twenty years, was a well-known environmentalist and the attorney for the Save Lighthouse Field Association when John and I were a part of Operation Wilder — the group that stopped massive development along the coast just north of Santa Cruz.

Gary was well known in the northern part of the Assembly district (Santa Cruz County), but not so well known in the southern part (Monterey County). He hired me to set up fundraising events, and in the process build his name recognition in the southern part of the district. I started with people I knew from Farr's campaign and began organizing as many gatherings as possible. Sadly, Gary lost the general election to a well-known, well-liked and well-funded moderate Republican named Bruce McPherson.

At this point I was ready for a break from the grind of campaign work — but in January of 1994 I got a call from Kathy Akao. She wanted to know if I would manage her campaign for superior court judge. Kathy was an assistant Santa Cruz County counsel for about eight years, former staff attorney for the Asian Law Alliance in San Jose and a public defender and private practice attorney in Santa Cruz. She was running against an incumbent, which was unheard of at the time. If the candidate loses the race and later appears in the incumbent judge's courtroom, it might be held against them. Future cases could be jeopardized by even subtle prejudices of the judge. I liked Akao's confident attitude and thought she could win. So I agreed to take the job. She was challenging the incumbent Judge George Kovacavich who had been appointed by Governor Pete Wilson. Akao had also applied for the position and was viewed as the top candidate, but was passed over by the Governor. Akao believed that Kovacavich was too much to the right in his views for a county that had become quite liberal.

Kathy had never run for any office before, and gave me complete control of her campaign. The campaign was in a county I knew well. She listened to me, took my lead, and did what I said. She was a pleasure to work with, as were the core supporters who formed her campaign committee. Using her contacts and mine, we set up continual house parties and fundraisers all over the county, covering every city and rural area. She attended meetings and spoke to key individuals, groups, organizations and the press. An attorney friend of hers helped her fine-tune her talking points. The more Kathy spoke, the better she got. It was exciting to see her transformation happening right before my eyes. As her confidence grew, she became a different person.

Kathy's campaign took my skills to the next level. I was not just a part of a campaign team, being field or fundraising staff, as I had been with Barbara's, Sam's and Gary's campaigns; I was the campaign manager. I loved being totally in charge, taking on a novice candidate and watching her grow.

As a Japanese-American, Kathy had a strong following among a small but well-established Japanese-American community, mostly in the southern part of the county. In 1972 her well-known aunt Jeanne Houston, had published an insightful and revealing book, *Farewell to Manzanar*, which was made into a TV movie 4 years later. Jeanne's maiden name is Wakatsuki, and her book tells the true story of her family's experience in the Japanese-American internment camps. President Franklin D. Roosevelt had authorized the infamous camps in 1942 by Executive Order 9066. More than 110,000 Japanese-Americans were interned against their will simply because they were of Japanese ancestry. Kathy's mother was interned at Manzanar in the high desert east of the Sierra Nevada Mountains while her father was serving in Europe with the 442nd Regimental Combat Team. The injustice was striking. Kathy herself had been born in Long Beach in 1948, after World War II.

In 1944, Roosevelt suspended the executive order and closed the internment camps, but the damage was already done. These Japanese-Americans no longer had a home, job or business to go back to. They had to rebuild their lives from the ground up, and the government did nothing to help them. None of these people did anything to deserve being taken forcibly from their homes and put into camps.

Farewell to Manzanar is a moving history and gave me new insight into the historic nature of Kathy's rise to public office. I was honored to play a part in her continuing story.

Kathy won a resounding victory; the local paper announced "Akao Wins Upset." Her victory marked the first time an Asian-American attorney in California had been elected rather than appointed a superior court judge, and the first time a Santa Cruz County sitting judge had been defeated. Later, Kathy would go on to be Santa Cruz County's first woman to serve as presiding judge. In recognition of my work, Kathy gave me a beautiful silver bracelet engraved on the inside with the inscription, "Pat ~ you helped make history. Thanks, Judge Kathy Akao 6-7-94." I will treasure it forever.

I had been busy with one campaign after another, growing every day in my own self-confidence and the freedom I had to be creative. It was exciting and rewarding. I was being shaped and defined by my own interests, choices and actions. For the first time in my life I had my own identity, separate from John.

. . . .

Meanwhile, John was making good money that arrived in the form of a regular paycheck. It felt good to have something we could depend on, but his commute to Redwood City was grueling. He was on the road for more than three hours a day and was coming home looking gray and fatigued. We both knew that couldn't go on much longer. Even though it would mean losing the rare feeling of security that comes with a regular paycheck, I think we were relieved when the company went out of business and John got laid off.

John started work on one of his own projects in Monterey – the development of an outdoor music hall, just south of Santa Cruz. While I was earning $2,000 a month managing Kathy Akao's campaign, he was making no money and using our savings to get his project off the ground. This all felt like déjà vu, a flashback to the mid '80s, when we had been on the downslope of our financial rollercoaster. Then his land-use business was declining and my small income was not covering our expenses. If we'd been paying attention, we would have realized that we couldn't continue that way and survive financially.

We had blinders on again, probably because denial was easier than facing the facts. In hindsight, I think I was using my campaign work and other political activities so I didn't have to pay attention to our dwindling financial situation.

When John's Monterey project didn't pan out, things started going south quickly. Kathy's campaign would soon come to an end and I too would no longer have a job. Paying the rent became difficult and we had to move again, this time to the upper rental unit of Mom's house in the hills above the small town of Soquel, just south of Santa Cruz.

It had now been six years since the trauma and exhaustion of living in the barn. Again, we were moving from a newer home in town to an older country home, although it was a big step up from the barn. Mom was constantly building on her property. She loved the chaos and loved living out in the country. I am more of a city girl, liking things to be clean, more new and orderly. Though it was another big adjustment for me, in my usual way I set out to set up a home for us — again trying to make things as normal as possible.

I kept busy finishing up Kathy Akao's campaign. John was hired as the project manager of a commercial development in Santa Cruz, overseeing the permit process with the city. The girls were now in high school. Kelly could drive and all three were pretty independent, probably enjoying our new country life more than I did.

Addressing the press in front of the County Building with former and current women elected officials in Santa Cruz County. Our goal was to show county wide support for Boxer's 1992 campaign for U.S. Senate.

It was a tough day.

With Barbara Boxer towards the end of the 1992 California Democratic primary at our campaign headquarters during her 4am stop in Santa Cruz before we met up with the press and her supporters at Denny's

My mom and Kelly working at our Boxer campaign headquarters

With Leon Panetta (he was then our Congress member) and Barbara Boxer at a Boxer for U.S. Senate fundraiser in Carmel, CA in 1992 that I organized

*The five Democratic women Senators in 1992 - the "Year of the Woman." –
with the two Republicans that made it 7 out of 100!! 27 years later, as of
2019 there are 25 out of 100 (17 Democrats and 8 Republicans and
of the 25, four are women of color)*

*Newly elected Judge Kathy Akao with her son Kris.
The local paper proclaimed "Akao Wins Upset"*

CHAPTER 10

"YOU ARE PERFECT FOR THE JOB"

Being challenged in life is inevitable, being
defeated is optional.

~ Roger Crawford, Disabled Athlete and Motivational Speaker

It was a beautiful sunny spring morning in 1994. I was sitting at my
desk in the tiny hole-in-the-wall office above a Capitola hardware
store that a friend of mine was letting me use as a makeshift headquarters for Kathy's campaign. I was about to start making campaign
calls when the phone rang. It was my old friend Kirk Mitchel. We had
worked together on Barbara Boxer's campaign. It had been about a
year and a half since we had spoken, so I was surprised and pleased to
hear from him. We chatted a bit, and then —

"Hey, Pat. I have the perfect job for you. Just send your résumé
to this fax number in D.C."

I wasn't looking for a job. I was knee-deep in managing Kathy's
campaign, with the election only a couple of months away. It was a
hard race, and my plate was full: organizing fundraisers, setting up
debates and sending out volunteers to walk precincts.

"Thank you," I told Kirk, "but I already have a job, and it isn't going to end until the election on June 7th."

"That's okay, because this is a government job and they move at the speed of government. You know — really slowly. Unlike the speed of political campaigns."

Later I would come to understand what he meant.

"What's the job?"

"It's about childhood immunization. It will use all your campaign and community organizing skills. You're perfect for it. Just send your résumé."

The project was out of the U.S. Department of Health and Human Services. Kirk was one of two people already hired for it, and he was helping to identify others who would be a good fit. In the end there would be ten of us. Intrigued, and realizing that I would, in fact, need a new job in just a few months, I polished up my résumé and faxed it to the D.C. number. After that, Kathy's campaign kept me too busy to think about it much.

Several weeks later, I got a call from a Donna Garland with DHHS, who asked if I would fly to D.C. for an interview with Rick Leach, the project director. My flight, hotel and meals would be paid for. She described the job only briefly, and, amazingly, I didn't ask for details.

The call set my stomach churning with my old fear of job interviews. This would be only the second interview in my entire life and it was going to be in the nation's capital. Thanks to the conversation with Donna I knew my community organizing and political campaign work were good experience for the job. But I also knew it would be a stretch.

It would be based out of San Francisco and included four states, so the job would take me out of my local community and expand my working environment. I'd be engaged with people from other parts of the country in a new cause that I didn't yet know anything about. I would be stepping up a few rungs of the professional ladder. Even the trip to D.C. was daunting, since I was far from a seasoned traveler, and aside from the pro-choice march I had attended years before, I had never spent time in D.C.

But I decided I would be equal to this challenge and prove it in my interview. So for the next couple of weeks, in order to feel physically strong and powerful, clear my head and work off some of my nervous energy, I spent whatever free time I could find working out at the gym.

Then it was time to say good-bye to John and the kids; high on adrenalin, I boarded my flight to DC.

I always enjoy a good conversation with strangers, and the five-hour flight provided one on either side of me. Both seatmates asked about my trip, giving me the opportunity to talk about the potential job and my background. This turned out to be great practice, and I jotted down notes for the upcoming interview. I was thinking positive thoughts and visualizing everything going well. Physically in shape and mentally sharp, I had the feeling this job was meant to be.

Then — the plane touched down and my nerves started up. I managed to retrieve my bag, get a taxi and check into the hotel. One moment I found myself pumped up with self-confidence, the next, scared to death; not knowing what the hell I was doing there. It had been many years since I lived in Switzerland, and that was when I was a teenager and my mom was managing my life. Now I was the adult, on my own with a job interview in the nation's capital, yet feeling like the proverbial mom who didn't get out much, hesitant to venture into the big city.

Lying in a strange bed far from home with my future teetering on the horizon did not make for a restful night. I couldn't sleep but set the alarm anyway for fear of oversleeping. I finally did nod off, awoke to the buzz of the alarm all ready to go and with a full charge of adrenalin. I had to talk my mirrored image down into a confident calm while getting dressed and fixing my hair. Taking a deep breath, I put a smile on my face and stepped out into the big city.

My destination was at the foot of Capitol Hill — the Hubert H. Humphrey Building, headquarters of the U.S. Department of Health and Human Services (HHS). People in business suits were coming and going, looking important. I took the elevator to Rick Leach's office, where Donna Garland met me with a big smile. Warm and friendly, she put me at ease immediately. I followed her down the hall to a room with a large oval conference table, where we joined Rick and Ron Stoddard, a Public Health Adviser from the U.S. Centers for Disease Control (CDC).

Rick was open and jovial. He made light conversation and made me feel right at home. I can banter with the best of them, and was in my element talking about my start as a community organizer in the early 70s, my social activism and political campaign work. I kept waiting for the interview to start. After about half an hour Rick told Donna to get the paperwork for me to fill out, and I was hired— just like that. The second job interview of my life turned out to be four of us sitting around a conference table having a casual conversation. All interviews should be that easy.

About a year later Donna told me in passing that before my interview she had received a call from the White House recommending me for the job. Of course, that definitely got her attention! I have always loved to reach out and network, so before my flight to D.C. I had called Marsha Scott, whom I'd met while she was campaigning for Bill Clinton and I was working on Boxer's campaign. She was an old high school friend of Clinton's in Arkansas, and after he took office, she went to work as Head of Correspondence and Presidential Messages. So I called her, told her about my upcoming job interview and asked her to call Rick Leach's office and recommend me for the job. She did just that — and it obviously didn't hurt my chances at getting the job.

. . . .

Just a few years previous, in 1989, there had been a nationwide measles epidemic. It brought attention to the fact that only fifty-five percent of children under the age of three were getting all their shots at the right time. So in 1992, newly elected President Bill Clinton created the Childhood Immunization Initiative (CII).

There were numerous causes for the country's poor vaccination rates including: recent changes in the healthcare system, the fact that many people lacked health insurance, an ever-increasing number of required vaccinations for babies and children, and a mobile population. And ironically, because the vaccine had in recent years done such a good job lowering the incidence of measles, many young parents didn't have experience with this deadly disease and didn't know how important it was to immunize their children. I would soon learn how complicated the situation was.

The initiative included several programs. One was Vaccines for Children, which made immunization affordable for families who didn't have health insurance. It operated in tandem with the Children's Health Insurance Program (CHIP), which First Lady Hillary Clinton helped create. It provided health care coverage, including immunizations, for children in families who were not poor enough for Medicaid but could not afford commercial health insurance. Part of my job was to work with the state immunization programs to identify children without coverage and enroll them in CHIP.

Another part of the initiative was outreach and education to increase awareness and, working with local and state health departments, to bring diverse people, agencies and organizations together to address these problems. Ten of us Regional Outreach Consultants or ROCs ("rocks") would work in each of the ten Health and Human Services regional offices around the country.

My office would be in San Francisco. John and I talked about me working from San Francisco, an 80-mile drive from our home, and decided that since this would only be a seventeen-week contract, it wouldn't disrupt our family too much. Besides, we needed the money. My stint with Akao was over and John was between jobs at the time.

. . . .

"How do we put the public back into public health?" This was something I heard Rick ask many times. His vision was ambitious; to mobilize all different sectors of American society to work together on the common goal of protecting children from preventable diseases. This was a model UNICEF and other organizations had used globally for quite some time. So, Rick thought, "How do we rally America to do something that America believes in?"

One piece of the puzzle was to create local and statewide coalitions. Another was to identify existing successful programs and replicate them in other parts of the country. Since Rick understood both government bureaucracy and campaign organizing, he was perfect for this task.

The people Rick was looking for to help him had experience in community organizing, political campaign fieldwork, press operations and labor organizing. Unlike the CDC Public Health Advisors, who move every couple of years to a new state for a new assignment, we were native to our assigned regions of the country, with knowledge of the local culture and politics. And we had the freedom to see and act on what was needed in our specific area of the country.

We were not there to replace bureaucratic structures but to enhance them. We were to use our political campaign and community organizing tools to raise the immunization rates.

. . . .

On June 7, 1994, Kathy won her election. A week later, on June 15th, I was on a flight to Charlotte, North Carolina, to attend the annual CDC National Immunization Conference. This was my first day on the job.

I checked in at the hotel, not knowing what to expect since I hadn't been given much information about the job or the conference. Feeling excited, I was looking forward to this next adventure. At this moment, as at so many other critical junctures in my life, it struck me how much of my enthusiasm for new experiences, even in the face of scanty preparation, stemmed from the adventurous spirit my mom had instilled in me.

The hotel featured the most elaborate gym, pool and spa I had ever seen. I thought, "Wow, this job is going to be great!" As it turned out, over my seven years traveling around the country in this job, few of the hotels were as lavish as this one.

About two thousand people were attending the conference from all over the country—mostly public health professionals from state or county health departments. By contrast, I knew nothing about immunizations beyond the shots my baby girls were given. I had never heard the word epidemiologist, had no disease-related education, and at that point in my life had not attended a conference of any kind. This one, however, would not be my last.

Not all ten of us ROCs had been hired yet, but those who were met with Rick. His instructions were to go out and mingle, attend various workshops and report back what we had learned. The problem was that all I heard in these workshops were acronyms. My repertoire to date was limited to HHS and CDC; but APHA, MMWR, NACCHO and many more were mysteries. I had to laugh to myself as I sat listening to this completely foreign language.

Introducing myself to people from my Region 9, which included California, Arizona, Nevada, Hawaii (yes, I eventually got to work there) and the Pacific Island Territories (unfortunately never got there), I collected business cards from every one of them, making a note on the back of each to help me match faces to names. My natural outreach and networking juices were flowing. I was in my element.

As I met many of the public health staff from my region, I could tell they were curious and a little bewildered about me. What was I doing at their conference? They weren't given any more information about us ROCs than we'd been given about them.

Our program was innovative — not typical for government. The ROCs worked within the Public Health Service, but in a creative, out-of-the-box — that is to say, non-bureaucratic — way. We functioned in stark contrast to the low-key CDC Public Health Advisors, who oversaw grant money. By design and training, they kept in the background in well-defined, supportive roles to various city and state immunization programs. We, on the other hand, had no money to give out and were expected to be somewhat innovative, with a "go forth and do good" mandate. In many ways, communicating with the CDC Public Health Advisors was like trying to mix oil and water.

It wasn't until the last session of the conference, after most people were already on their way home, that the ROCs were given the podium. Robin Scheeper, the ROC from Region 10, spoke to the entire conference, or what was left of it. She talked about the kind of work we would be doing with the state and local health departments on outreach and education programs to raise immunization rates. Unfortunately the room was basically empty, and I thought to myself, "Boy, is this how we rate? Not such a good way to start a new job."

. . . .

From the conference I was whisked directly to San Francisco, where I was shown my new office in the Federal Building at United Nations Plaza. Our first directive was to organize Regional Outreach Conferences in each of the country's ten HHS regions, even though ROCs still hadn't been hired for all of them.

The goal of these three-day conferences was to bring together people who didn't normally talk or work with each other — people from health care, nonprofits, service organizations, government agencies and more. Our task was to give them information on the state of immunization around the country and why the rates were so low, so they were all on the same page. From there, we were to build structures that would enable everyone to work together. Since I had been bringing people together to work on many different issues for the last twenty years, this was right up my alley.

The first two conferences had already taken place. The third was to be held in Los Angeles — in my region, and the planning was well underway.

A few days before the conference, the phone rang. It was Donna.

"So what session do you want to present?"

I thought she was kidding. She wasn't.

My heart started to pound out of my chest. "Could I do this job?" I was happy to be able to get my feet wet slowly but this was too much, too fast. I thought, but didn't say, "Excuse me, but I'm not ready for this yet!"

A few days later I found myself facing 400 people in a massive Los Angeles hotel conference room, about to present an overview of Clinton's initiative. I took a deep breath to calm my nerves and scanned the room. About three rows back, I spied a friendly face. It belonged to Sandy Ross, program manager for the County of San Diego immunization program, whom I had met briefly at the Charlotte conference. Now her big, friendly "You can do it, Pat" smile warmed me like the sun and made me feel as if it were just the two of us having a conversation as the rest of the audience listened in. I wound up doing better than I thought I would.

With practice, I not only overcame my paralyzing fear of public speaking — I actually started to like being on stage. At a ROC meeting years later, we were all given certificates commending us for our particular strengths. Mine read "Ms. Microphone Bakalian." I'd come a long way!

After the LA gathering I became part of a conference production team, a traveling roadshow for the seven remaining regional meetings. We developed the programs, put together the materials and facilitated the workshops. At the end of each day we gathered in one of the small hotel conference rooms (sometimes before and sometimes after a few martinis at the hotel bar), to debrief and go over the next day's plan. Imagine a room of hyped-up, loud and crazy extroverts. It was great fun. I was making new friends and having a ball.

Many of my team members were more experienced and more widely traveled than I. A few had organized national events and press conferences. As we were getting to know each other, they shared with me what it was like for them to travel around the country being the point person for high profile events. It all sounded very exciting. My experience had been closer to home and seemed much less sophisticated. I thought if they knew my limited background they would be unimpressed, so I didn't share all that much. In hindsight, this seems crazy. Why was I holding myself back? It's interesting how we compare ourselves to others and come up short, how we qualify ourselves in situations based on things that don't matter, when we have the ability to do a good job.

Santa Cruz was too far from San Francisco for me to commute every day, so I left for my office on Monday mornings and drove home on Friday evenings. In between I lived at the Mayoko Hotel, in San Francisco's Japan town district. The hotel staff got to know me, and a few times gave me a special room with a sunken Jacuzzi tub and sauna, prompting an excited phone call to John.

"You can't believe the room I'm in! You need to jump in the car right now and join me!"

But he never did.

By now Kelly, who had always been pretty independent, was eighteen and getting ready to go off to college. She was fifteen when she took her first job at a local video rental store right down the street. We told her then we would match anything she saved, and in about a year she had saved $1,200, which she used, with our help, to buy her own car. At sixteen, she and her friend Stacy moved in together, into a nearby apartment. Today it is hard to believe we let her do that, but she always seemed much older than she was, and we were close by to keep an eye on things. When I learned that Kelly and her friend Denine took themselves to Planned Parenthood to get on the pill, I was glad we had always been open with the girls about their changing bodies, sex and relations with boys.

Sara was sixteen and had a steady boyfriend who was having troubles at home. He was a nice guy and we felt bad for him, so when they came to us with the idea that he move into our house, we agreed. It was as if the girls had an adopted brother and for the short time that he was with us there were no problems — except that he was pretty messy in their bathroom.

Lesha was fourteen, starting high school and growing up fast because of two older sisters. School was still hard for her so we were happy to find an alternative school, West Beach High, which was able to give her more one-on-one instruction.

John was the "house husband," with the kids Monday through Friday. He had always supported me in anything I wanted to do, and this was no exception. Having this kind of freedom for the first time in my life was a true gift, something I would have done for him without any hesitation.

....

When the regional conferences were over, I started working with local and state public health departments in my region to form immunization coalitions. We identified and invited the obvious partners to the table, created meeting agendas, educational materials and action plans. All told, between 1993 and 2000 the ROCs helped establish or reorganize about two hundred immunization coalitions around the country.

Since, at the time, there was still no ROC hired for Southern Illinois, I was sent to the Chicago area to facilitate a planning meeting with a local group. It was ten at night by the time I landed in St. Louis (the closest I could get to my destination) — much later than I had anticipated. I didn't have the different time zones down yet, nor had I anticipated how far I would have to drive to Carbondale, the home of the University of Southern Illinois. It was the longest hundred miles I had ever driven. The night was as black as coffee. The two-lane road was unlit. Occasionally a semi would barrel on by, faster than I thought safe, shaking my car in its wake. All I wanted to do was to climb into bed and go to sleep, but the road was interminable. When I finally made it to the hotel, I was completely wound up, unable to stop my mind and fall asleep, knowing the next day was going to come way too soon. Then, before I knew it, I was up and out and facing a room full of 50 people looking to me for direction. They, however, turned out to be wonderful, and the daylong session went well. This was my trial by fire.

We ROCs were on our own, like free-floating balloons. We did face some of the same challenges, but our regions were very different from each other, and we differed from each other, as well. I thought we needed something to acknowledge the unprecedented nature of our work and reinforce our emerging team spirit, so I asked my friend Jan Janes, a graphic designer, to help me design ROC t-shirts. They were blue with a red-and-yellow Superman logo, with "ROC" replacing the "S" in "Superman," and they bore our new motto: "We Go Where No ROCs Have Gone Before." They were a great surprise and a big hit.

....

As our seventeen-week contracts came to an end, Rick worked with CDC staff to incorporate our outreach work into their National Immunization Program, creating the new Community Outreach and Planning Branch. We were all asked if we wanted to continue as permanent federal employees of the CDC. I was enjoying my independent lifestyle, knew there was much more work left to do and didn't want to drop the ball just when things were gaining momentum. So after talking with John and the girls, I submitted my application.

The application process was cumbersome, but this time I had a leg up. I had been doing the work for four months and knew exactly what I needed to write. I was interviewed in my office in San Francisco, on a conference call with four people in an office somewhere in Atlanta. The experience was nothing like my friendly, laid-back interview with Rick Leach. I was told that my style, competence and sensitivity to the "other side" — meaning the private sector — was evident.

I passed the test and became a "Fed."

Shortly after I was hired, my new boss, Shawnett Crawford, said to me, "Now we own you." Physically bristling at that comment, though not replying back to her. I had never considered myself owned by anyone—not then or ever. This was a heads up that I was no longer in Kansas anymore; meaning that now I was a government employee. They now had much more control over me and what I did, than during my seventeen-week contract work for Rick Leach.

Since I was now a federal employee, the CDC would no longer pay hotel and meal costs. I needed to find a permanent place to live in San Francisco. Luckily, Kirk introduced me to his friend Catherine Blum, who had just bought a three-story townhouse at the top of Potrero Hill and had an extra bedroom to rent out. She and I hit it off instantly and I moved in the next week. Catherine was about six years younger than I, and had a whole different lifestyle. She had never been married and didn't have kids. So I started to live what felt like two lives. There was my workweek with a single woman in the big city, and my weekend as a wife and mother in the rural hills of Santa Cruz County.

Occasionally I would join Catherine and her friends for dinner, laughs and good conversation, but most of the time I just came home, made a quick dinner, had a glass of wine, and crawled into bed with a good book about the time she was going out. I had quiet mornings drinking coffee and reading the paper, and headed into the office before she even got up. It was a perfect arrangement and the rent was reasonable.

I loved the hard work, and I loved the independence. I was relieved not to have to take care of John and the kids, not to have to make meal after meal for the family, day after day. At forty-five, for the first time in my life I was experiencing both physical and emotional independence. I was earning more money than ever before — a fabulous boost to my self-confidence and sense of security. People all over the country recognized my skills and viewed me as an expert. I was finding out what I was capable of. I loved what I was doing — and was getting paid for it. This was my time.

In terms of the family, my job was a financial windfall, especially considering the financial rollercoaster we'd been on over the years. But it posed some real challenges to our marriage. Weekends were the only times John and I were together. We did all the routine stuff — grocery shopping, cooking, cleaning and caring for the kids, but we weren't connecting emotionally. I feel very lucky that we had a strong foundation having spent so much time getting to know each other at the beginning of our relationship, or the times that we spent apart would have been more detrimental to our marriage. But it didn't help that we both came from families that taught us not to speak about what we were feeling and that we were passing this trait on to our kids. I know they missed me being home during the week but they didn't say anything. In hindsight, I wish I had paid more attention while home on the weekends and asked more questions about what I was missing in their lives.

. . . .

At the CDC I was free to set my own priorities and make my own travel arrangements. It was like being an independent consultant, but at the same time I was a government employee – a very unusual situation. I had heard that back at the height of the AIDS epidemic the CDC had a program employing staff who functioned more independently and with less governmental constraints than usual, but it wasn't the norm — and neither was our situation.

The ROC's were an anomaly to the way the CDC usually conducted business. The challenges were many as was the fun and the rewards. Some at headquarters in Atlanta got it and some didn't. A few who understood the benefit of our work were great supporters. For us, who had no previous experience working for the Federal government, this was very much appreciated and was a breath of fresh air.

As the CDC consultant, along with the California Department of Public Health and a group of about 250 local and statewide leaders, we established the California Immunization Coalition. Our purpose was to create a vehicle to work together to access each other's expertise and networks. This group is still going strong in 2019, but this type of collaboration was rare at that time.

My job also included helping local counties create their own strong viable immunization coalitions. But California is an enormous state, I was only one person, and I couldn't possibly provide the local communities all the help they needed: materials, consultations, workshops. So, working with the CDPH staff, the statewide coalition director Margaret Baker, her assistant Kit Cole and my longtime friend and former ROC Kirk Mitchell, we created the California Intern Project. This was an innovative model program in which we hired grad students in public health as interns and trained them to establish local immunization coalitions.

Meanwhile, a problem was brewing with the statewide coalition. Decisions made by consensus among coalition leaders were being reversed after the fact by CDPH. As the official proponent for coalition-building, I knew this high-handedness would, at best, create dissent, and at worst cause organizations to leave the coalition. I raised the issue with a number of people, but no one listened, so I decided to put my concerns in writing.

Characteristically informal, the ROCs had neither letterhead of their own nor access to CDC's that I could use for my letter. So I decided to create my own CDC-ROC letterhead. Perhaps I would have checked out this rogue move with someone in the bureaucracy if I hadn't been at home on painkillers, recovering from a back injury caused by lugging suitcases all over the country. But in my fuzzy state I didn't, I just faxed my letter out to coalition leaders and CDPH officials.

Was that a huge mistake! While the powers-that-be had taken no heed of my persistent complaint, it took them only a few hours to become outraged by my unorthodox letterhead without addressing what my letter actually said.

The phone rang the next morning at ten o'clock. It was Shawnett, my CDC boss in Atlanta. She had been contacted by my CDPH contact, who had gone ballistic on her about my crime, and now Shawnett was doing the same to me. I listened, stunned into silence, turning cold, barely breathing, gripping the phone till my knuckles turned white. How could this be happening? I had always tried to be liked by everyone, and up until this fiasco I was.

Shawnett described my actions in the most unflattering terms. She asked me for an explanation, and I somehow managed to give her one. She said she knew I had meant well and had not sent the letter with malicious intent, so she wouldn't fire me. But she did forbid me to do any work in California for an extended period of time — it ended up being for two years.

That evening, worn down from back pain and raw with emotion, I cried as I told John what had happened. He was wonderful as always.

"This is good," he assured me. "You'll be getting the same money for less work."

It didn't make me feel better, but he was right. I had been spread way too thin, trying to work effectively in four states plus Guam. Now, with the biggest of those states off my plate, I could do a better job in Arizona, Nevada and Hawaii. I continued to operate out of my office in San Francisco even though I wasn't even allowed to talk to the San Francisco Health Department just three blocks away.

I was terribly shaken, devastated at being exiled from my home state, where I had developed so many good working relationships and done outstanding work. In fact, the CDC had been planning to give me an award for the California Intern Project. Now that would not happen. I was being severely punished — not for doing the wrong thing, but for doing the right thing in the wrong way. My motive had been to help. I'd believed that once the right people read my letter, they would make the needed changes.

The decision to create my own letterhead seems naive to me now. But, to my credit, I took responsibility for this error in judgment, and as soon as I could pull myself together wrote the CDPH a letter of apology. A few years later, Donna Garland, who had been CDC's deputy branch chief at the time of the incident, told me she felt some of what had happened was her fault. She said she had not sufficiently guided the ROCs through the trails of government protocol. This admission didn't change anything, except that it did take out some of the sting — albeit belatedly. I never did find out whether the problems I raised in that letter were corrected.

This was a big bump in the road but I still felt I was making a difference. I eventually bounced back from my blunder and started to enjoy my job again. In Nevada I worked with the Department of Health and Human Services to form a partnership with the federal Women, Infants and Children's (WIC) program, a natural repository for immunization records. In Arizona, I worked closely with the Arizona Partnership for Infant Immunization, a statewide coalition, and the Maricopa County Health Department to organize private physician seminars to raise the doctors' awareness of children in their practice who might not be getting immunized on time. These seminars also helped develop cooperation between the public health system and doctors in private practice, where most kids got their shots. The seminars were successful, so a group of us put together a guidebook, *Creating Effective Private Physician Seminars: A Planning Document*, for use by other communities.

Traveling on a government expense account was an unremittingly austere endeavor —but there were a couple of memorable exceptions. Once, on checking into my usual hotel in Phoenix, I was told there had been a mix-up and they didn't have a room for me. So, they sent me to a hotel in Scottsdale – still at government rate. It turned out to be a luxurious resort with a full spa, beautiful pools and a suite with all the amenities. I called John to convince him to join me, but he was unable to drop what he was doing to get on a plane. A year later, though, he was able to join me on a working trip to Hawaii. After conducting a daylong immunization seminar, I was delighted to have him there with me.

Despite the many good things the ROCs were accomplishing, we faced unique challenges. We offered our coalition-building, outreach and educational services to the state public health departments, and some city and county health departments, as a free resource. But in many cases those entities did not understand the purpose or value of working with us. This was new territory for the public health community. They were used to working with people from the CDC who came with — and oversaw the use of — grant monies. But we had no money, so many of them didn't know what to do with us. This presented an extra burden to us ROCs. We had to sell ourselves, and let the public health personnel know why working with us helped the people they served in the community. Part of my approach to this problem was to try to learn everything I could about what the public health departments did and how they functioned, so I could coordinate with them more effectively.

Meanwhile, people at CDC headquarters in Atlanta didn't always understand the challenges the ROCs dealt with in the field, so we did not receive as much support from them as we would have liked. In fact, an oil-and-water relationship too often prevailed between us and our co-workers in other branches of the CDC National

Immunization Program. Once, in the Atlanta office for meetings, I was walking down the hallway and heard someone say "ROC Alert! ROC Alert!" The snarky tone of voice exposed the attitude that as a ROC I was not "one of them."

Initially, many in Atlanta saw us as people with a mission to distribute trinkets to the public—balloons and refrigerator magnets with immunization messages. Peg Harrington, a friend and fellow ROC, told me that on one of her first encounters with a CDC staffer, he said, "Oh, so you are one of the magnet-and-balloon ladies." And some thought we were political appointees crashing their party. Perhaps they thought of us as government fluff. The autonomy we enjoyed compared to their world might have also been irksome. And I'm sure it leaked out that we were getting paid on the same level as many who had worked their way up the ladder over years of government service. That could understandably cause resentment. Whatever the reasons, there was a wall between us that hindered good working relationships.

While it was a challenge to work under these circumstances, there were some CDC staff members who were supportive and wonderful to work with. When I left my job, I appreciated the understanding expressed by a former colleague who wrote a letter of recommendation for me.

He understood that even though management at the CDC had hired us to expand its role to non-traditional partners, the rank-and-file employees who we dealt with were not fully on board. He understood and appreciated how difficult our jobs were; having been tasked with engaging people and organizations from "outside the box" of public health with those who were bound by the traditional walls of bureaucracy.

He wrote, "Unfamiliarity with public/private partnership building by some in Atlanta resulted in loss of influence and respect for the role they (the ROC's) had been asked to do often, causing headquarters staff to side with state/local public health, leaving Pat and the other ROC's at risk."

. . . .

President Clinton's Childhood Immunization Initiative was successful. The proof was that in seven years childhood immunization rates rose to an all-time high. Meeting that goal meant that priorities and funding would naturally be channeled to other pressing issues. The National Immunization Program was to be re-organized. While building partnerships and coalitions had been an essential part of the initiative, the work of the ROCs would no longer be necessary.

I was offered the opportunity to stay with the CDC, but that would mean moving to Atlanta, to a completely different kind of job. It didn't take John and me long to say no to that. Leaving California, our grown-up daughters and my mom was not an option for us. Some people said I was crazy to give up "a cushy government job," but I knew I wouldn't have been happy. The rigid, slow-moving culture of a traditional government position would have felt like prison to me.

So with way too many boxes in my car, I left my San Francisco office and apartment, and headed back to Santa Cruz, to John and the kids and my next great adventure.

*In my San Francisco office in the Federal Building at 50 UN Plaza.
I had the walls plastered with maps of my region*

*The ROC's with our boss Rick Leach (back row 5ᵗʰ from the left), his assistant
Donna Garland (front row 6ᵗʰ from the left) and Ron Stoddard
(holding the baby) from the CDC in our ROC t-shirts*

A Calvin and Hobbes cartoon with a personal message a friend sent me after I was kicked out of the state of California

Having a great time in the staff room of the 2nd National Conference on Immunization Coalitions in San Diego. Amazingly we were all wearing black and blue. I call this picture "the Blues Sisters."

Something new in official portraits

This photograph released by the Department of Health and Human Services on Thursday shows the official department portrait of Secretary Donna Shalala. Along with other members of President Clinton's Cabinet, Shalala is striking a blow against dull tradition, the glowering "Our Founder" portrait of the department boss. Shalala dropped the formal stuff in favor of this shot with some kids.

I always loved this very different "official" photo of Donna Shalala,
The Secretary of Health and Human Services. I had it on my office wall to
remind me why I was doing this work

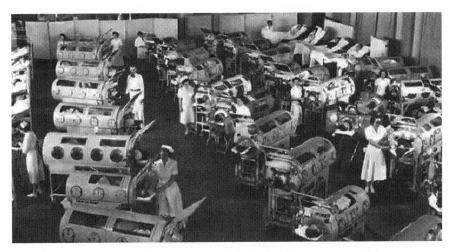

Polio victims in Iron Lungs in the 50's. John spent a week in
an Iron Lung when he was 5 years old.

CHAPTER 11

INTIMACY

Those failures that I ran from taught me nothing.
Those that I confronted, cozied up to, and understood
were the ones that permitted me quantum leaps forward.
In another way of looking at it, they became the
compost from which new growth emerged.

~ Jane Fonda, from her book *Prime Time*

After seven years of living mostly in the big city, I was back home in Santa Cruz. Things had changed. The kids had all moved out and were finding their own path through life. I was unemployed. After catching my breath, I interviewed for some jobs I thought would be perfect—but wasn't hired.

But I was undaunted, and my independent entrepreneurial spirit was starting to kick me in the ass. My position at the CDC had been reorganized out of existence, but I saw a way I could capitalize on the expertise I'd gained there. Now two hundred immunization coalitions existed around the country, many still in need of help. I would create Bakalian Consulting Group.

Faithful to my collaboration mantra, I would help the weaker coalitions learn from the strong ones. I would call my first endeavor "The Immunization Coalition Sustainability Project," because the coalitions, no longer in start-up phase, needed to turn their attention to sustaining their efforts. Figuring out which coalitions needed help would take research and documentation, but I was superbly equipped to assess what programs these coalitions were undertaking, how they were structured, which ones were functioning well and which ones were not.

But who would fund this effort?

Having worked at the CDC I knew that pharmaceutical companies were where the money was, and I had established working relationships with a number of pharmaceutical reps. Thinking they would be a good funding source, I reached out to Frank John at Aventis Pasteur, who had seen me in action over the years, and who, I thought, respected my professionalism.

I called him one morning at his office in Colorado Springs, and based my pitch on the fact that we had spent seven years building and strengthening immunization coalitions around the country, and now needed a study to find out what they were doing and how well they were doing it.

"You and I put a lot into this project over the years, Frank, and we both know how important it is to the health of children all over the country. It's critical now to assess where it is, and if those coalitions need help. I'm ready to do this. Do you think Aventis Pasteur would be interested in funding it?"

"A terrific idea, Pat! We need to do it, and I will help you get the money."

I thought I'd pass out. Frank understood the idea instantly.

After several weeks of meetings, phone calls and emails, Aventis Pasteur gave me the green light for a two-year research grant of

$169,000. I was elated, but didn't truly understand what a major coup this was right out of the gate for my fledgling business.

This was a big deal — and a big project for one person. I needed to find a partner. During this time I was working on a small contract with the Los Angeles health department, doing an organizational assessment of their immunization coalition. It was there that I got acquainted with Lucinda Connelly, a Ph.D. student in public administration who was writing a grant proposal for the coalition. We hit it off right away, had an easy and comfortable relationship.

"So, Lucinda," I said one day, "how would you like to partner with me on a research project?"

In about five minutes flat she understood why this study was important and decided to come on board.

The first step was to survey the 200 coalitions around the country to discover which ones were thriving and which were floundering. We identified eighteen of the most successful — and from them chose eight of varying sizes from different parts of the country – some rural, some urban. We developed a standardized questionnaire that we'd use to conduct in-depth one-on-one interviews. We split up the list. I went to Savannah, Georgia; Columbus, Ohio; Kansas City, Missouri; and San Diego, California. Lucinda visited the other four.

We didn't have one bad experience. We produced a report of our findings with recommendations and a catalog of fifty-eight of the most successful programs, and sent it out to more than three hundred individuals and organizations around the country.

Our report showed that education and outreach was happening everywhere! In schools, beauty parlors, grocery-store parking lots. And when some coalitions branched out to include adult immunizations, it even happened in casinos. Coalitions helped states strengthen school immunization requirements. They facilitated Medicaid-funded vaccine registries.

The news media was addressing concerns about the safety of vaccines. An episode of the TV show *E.R.* featured an episode about infectious diseases and childhood immunizations. That inspired one coalition director to ask her local NBC affiliate to do a follow-up show with a local doctor and public health nurse talking about the importance of vaccines and what was happening in their state. The station did it.

But the study also revealed a developing problem. State and local coalitions were not getting the tools they needed from the CDC's annual Immunization Conference. A group of us from public health departments, CDC and coalitions around the country, understood this and a few years earlier had decided to organize an annual conference focused on giving these coalitions the specific assistance they needed. I was a part of this group.

The first National Conference on Immunization Coalitions took place in San Diego in 1999. Thanks to a lot of hard work and commitment from many people, it is still going strong, now called the National Conference on Immunization Coalitions and Partnerships. The fourteenth conference was held in Hawaii in 2019. Attendees come eager to learn about coalition building and management, fundraising, project evaluation, leadership development, establishing partnerships, policy advocacy, and communication. The conference also gives them a place to network and share their successes and their challenges.

Lucinda and I presented our research findings at the Sixth National Conference in Norfolk, Virginia in September 2004. Close to four hundred people were there, representing some one hundred state, regional and county immunization coalitions. We were well received. People approached us afterwards with questions, and told us over and over again, "Thank you so much for your work." They wanted more information and could see how our study could help them do their jobs better.

After years of skepticism from some of the CDC establishment, we especially appreciated the recognition of Dr. Walt Orenstein, the former director of the CDC immunization program. He wrote, "Coalitions are critical to assuring efforts to prevent diseases are successful. The Immunization Coalition Sustainability Project report is impressive and provides valuable and comprehensive information on what should go into an effective coalition." His letter validated not only my past work, but also the significance of this research project and the work Lucinda and I did to bring it to life.

The study, of course, was also the launching pad for the next stage of my work. I now knew which coalitions needed my services, what their major challenges were and how I could help them. I sent letters and emails to coalition staff around the country, national organizations, state and county Public Health Departments, the CDC, and private companies.

A number of states responded positively to my outreach. New Mexico was starting an immunization coalition from scratch. They hired me to help reach out to necessary partners, to develop a coalition structure, a strategic plan and organize their first general meeting. I knew that a well-known keynote speaker would attract more people and media attention so I contacted Amy Pisani with Every Child By Two, the national organization started by former First Lady Rosalynn Carter and former Arkansas First Lady Betty Bumpers.

"Amy, do you suppose Rosalynn Carter would speak to the group?"

"What a great idea! I will ask her."

I have always believed that if you don't ask, it is a "no", so you might as well ask, because it could be a "yes." To everyone's delight both Rosalynn Carter and Betty Bumpers said "yes," and were delighted to lend their voice and visibility to our efforts.

Each client had slightly different needs, so I tailored my assistance to fit the unique situation of each one. I had previously worked with the Northern Nevada Immunization Coalition to help them establish their structure. Now I helped them with their planning process and advised them on how to work most effectively with their state health department. In West Virginia I did an assessment, provided materials, facilitated planning meetings and helped organize their first annual immunization summit. In Oregon, I again did an assessment of their fledgling adult immunization coalition, working with its leaders in order to attract new partners and expand their work throughout the state.

My expertise - coalition building - had been fine-tuned over the years and was welcomed and appreciated at last. I didn't have to sell myself, as I did while working for the CDC, to reluctant state health departments. These clients knew they needed my expertise and saw me as the perfect resource. They were a joy to work with.

Life was good. I was working out of my home office, enjoying my travels, meeting and working with interesting committed people.

But immersed in the work at hand, I was neglecting to bring in more contracts, and over time requests for my services stopped coming in. Meanwhile, funding was becoming a major issue across the country. Most immunization coalitions got the majority of their funding from state or county public health departments, which had started to funnel limited resources elsewhere. Their rationale was similar to the CDC's when it eliminated the Regional Outreach Consultant positions. Since the goal of increasing numbers of immunized kids had been met, there was no more need to fund outreach. I couldn't overcome that trend, and in hindsight, I should have put more time into diversifying — offering my services to other issue coalitions, collaborations or non-profits. But I didn't, and my clients were drying up.

. . . .

John's land-use work may have been inconsistent over the years, but it was not without great successes. People were willing to pay him large sums of money for his expertise. He was able to get permits for every one of his projects over his thirty-year career, which cumulatively resulted in adding hundreds of acres to the California State Parks.

He was a critical player in getting Elkhorn Slough, between Santa Cruz and Monterey, designated as a marine sanctuary, now known as The Elkhorn Slough National Estuarine Research Reserve.

He was instrumental in getting a bill passed for the expansion of Natural Bridges State Park, a swath of beach and woods adjacent to Santa Cruz. The alternative was a sixty-unit condo.

On the land next to Pismo State Park, along the Central Coast of California, owners had tried to put a big mobile home park on the sand dunes. With John's guidance, that land was purchased and an additional five hundred acres was added to Pismo State Beach.

Pogonip, a beautiful open space above the city of Santa Cruz, was purchased as a city park with John's help.

And John was the project director for the University of California, Santa Cruz Marine Research Center, the birthplace of the Coastal Science Campus of UCSC.

But now John's land-use business was beginning to encounter more hassles and headaches than profit. It became extremely difficult to get anything approved in Santa Cruz County, even development that was good for the community. He never worked on anything that wasn't reasonable and environmentally sound, but there were more and more hoops to jump through, always with some faction of the community in opposition. It was frustrating for him, and I felt his frustration. So in 2003, when John joined forces with Dave Reinhart, the son of one of his old college friends, I was thrilled. His entrepreneurial spirit would now be unleashed, enabling him to propose and develop projects of his own.

Dave was working with the California Trade Association, a government agency that helped California businesses sell their products in foreign countries. Through that work John met Gao Yang, or Sonny, as we came to know him. Sonny was the assistant to the director of the California Trade Association in Shanghai, and with his help John was introduced to the possibility of land-use and other business ventures in China. They became close friends and partners, creating Golden Allied Enterprises and eventually opening up an office together in Shanghai at the prestigious United Plaza building. Their projects were varied —from a golf course to a vineyard to development of an electric bus.

John was eager to learn about Chinese culture and ways of doing business. Sonny introduced him to Mr. You Yi-Chen, who became another business partner. Mr. You was known as the father of the Chinese auto industry because in the mid 1980's he had set up the first joint venture between an automobile company (Volkswagen) and the Shanghai government, becoming its executive director. He introduced John to many influential people in Chinese industry.

To make this all work, John took an apartment in Shanghai, living there for a month or six weeks at a time, coming home for about three weeks between trips. These frequent and extended business trips to China, however, took a toll on our relationship. While I was working for the CDC, the longest I was ever away from home was two weeks—and that was only once or twice in the seven years. Normally I was home every weekend. He always whole-heartedly supported me in whatever I pursued, and I was in full support of his China ventures.

John's absences, however, were much longer and proved to be a bigger challenge than I expected. Nevertheless, I figured John must have had a hard time coping with my absences when I stayed in San Francisco to work during the week. But he never brought it up at the time, so neither did I.

Now our long separations became difficult for me. I lacked clients and was home full-time, trying to figure out my next step without the benefit of John's input or any distractions from the kids. Our roles were completely reversed, and I was lonely.

I was "between jobs", but it felt more like an identity crisis. I would wander through the house with a cup of coffee in hand, often staying in my pajamas until noon. All alone without my own work, I felt unanchored. I did a lot of thinking, searching for where to put my energies.

Normally, I would have bounced ideas off John and shared my feelings about the void in my life. But talking on the phone with him in China was difficult and annoying. Our voices were delayed by a few seconds, making it hard to respond to one another and stay on the same subject. The difference in time zones made it even harder. Shanghai is fifteen hours later than California, so the best time for us to connect was during his morning, which was five or six the previous evening for me. He would be getting ready for work, thinking about the day ahead, while I was ending my day thinking about how alone I felt. The phone calls weren't helping.

I looked forward to how we'd reconnect and spend time together during his visits home —but that wasn't what happened. His non-stop flight from China to San Francisco took about twelve hours. Needless to say he was exhausted when he arrived. I expected us to return to our old familiar routine once he recovered from jet lag — but that didn't happen either.

I know now that he was thinking — but not sharing with me: "What information do I need to put together and get to Sonny? What didn't I complete before I left? What do I need to do when I get back to Shanghai?" Then, in a few short weeks he was gone again. I wanted to be as supportive of him as he had been of me, but I was struggling.

The strain of being involved in projects in such a far-flung country was enormous. John became single-minded, investing everything in his work — financially, physically and emotionally. There was nothing left for me. Meanwhile, he didn't let on how worried he was about the financial aspect of his projects. To deal with his stress, he would have a few drinks after dinner and promptly fall asleep on the couch. When he checked out like that in the evenings, I felt abandoned and annoyed.

I knew he was not intentionally trying to hurt me, but I still felt hurt and very alone. I was looking for the intimate connection we had always had, but now had lost. I was frustrated and tired of feeling like I was living alone.

Just as our financial straits had become a catalyst to move to the barn almost twenty years earlier, this breakdown in our relationship motivated me to action. One evening, anguished over our situation, I gave him an ultimatum.

"John, you are shutting me out. You're drinking too much, and it has to stop. We need to get counseling or I'm gone."

He might not have been able to understand what I was going through, but neither did he want me to leave, so he acquiesced.

"Okay. I will see a therapist with you."

This was not easy for him. In fact it was a miracle. He has always been a very private person and didn't think much of therapists. Having experienced the Armenian Holocaust, his family was close knit and tended to shut out the world beyond. He grew up with the mantra "need to know" and always told me, "You don't tell anyone anything unless they need to know — and no one needs to know anything." So John was initially perfect for me: someone who learned not to share his feelings, married to someone who learned not to share her feelings.

As in all marriages, we had our good and bad times. When things got bad, I would try and try to get him to let me in.

"What are you feeling?" I would ask him. He would answer, "I don't know — what does that question even mean?" — having no clue as to what I was talking about. Then I would ask, "Are you feeling sad? Are you feeling angry? Are you feeling upset?" I would go through all the feelings I could think of. What I got back was a blank stare. It never worked.

....

For the past twenty years I had been seeing Virginia, a wonderful acupuncturist who was also someone I could talk to about what was happening in my life. I asked her if she knew someone who could help us.

"Yes." She said she was happy that I had asked, "I know the perfect person for you. His name is Gary. He does couples' therapy. Here is his phone number."

I called him right away and was grateful that we were able to schedule appointments with him between John's trips to China. When we met for the first time, he came across as a kind and compassionate person. John and I felt at ease in his tiny, very cozy office, sitting on a couch across from Gary in his overstuffed chair. John surprised me by being much more open and vocal than I had expected. I credit Gary for this.

Over thirty-five years of marriage we had become quite distant. Now, things started coming out in our sessions with Gary that enlightened me about what John was experiencing and how he was feeling.

I told Gary, "Most evenings, when John is home, he drinks and then falls asleep on the couch. This makes me feel like I have been abandoned."

Then John explained, "Every evening I start feeling anxious and what helps me cope with it is alcohol."

"Coping" — that's one way to put it. But what he was actually doing was using alcohol to escape the stress.

Meanwhile, I was in shock, to learn about his anxiety. I'd experienced anxiety a few times in my life, so I understood how it feels. It is not fun.

Confused, I asked, "Why haven't you shared this with me before? What else are you not sharing?"

This new information was a crack in the wall between us - an important opening we desperately needed. I wanted to understand my husband better and I also knew John didn't understand how our lack of emotional communication affected me.

"Gary, I explained, "there are times when John is not being himself, but does not tell me what is going on with him. Just a small example — recently when we were getting ready to go out to dinner, he started acting uptight. He didn't say 'I'm tired' or 'I'm pissed and I don't want to go out.' So I was left wondering what was going on with him, and if it was my fault — blaming myself, so typical of women— and if he thought he had to even go if he didn't want to? Why wasn't he telling me what was going on with him? His behavior was making me not want to be with him."

Gary explained that many men believe that it is the male partner's job to take care of and please his woman, to avoid disappointing her. If they say they're going to do something, they're honor-bound to follow through. Otherwise they assume the woman, in her disappointment, will exact a price for weeks to come.

"Oh my god!" I responded. "He will pay the price for weeks to come? Instead of just talking about what each person wants? Where does that come from?"

"That's all a part of the patriarchal overlay that men have absorbed for years. It's bad for everyone — men and women. I do hope this is an 'older generational thing' and that male-female relationships are evolving."

To hear such insights, particularly from a man, was helping both John and me. I remember Gary saying, "Don't ask him if he feels this way or that. Just watch him. When I hear someone start haranguing me with 'what are you feeling'? I shut down." He said, "Let him know you're sensing something is bothering him, and that you would rather know what it is than to continue with what the two of you had planned. If the plan needs to be followed through, acknowledge his change in demeanor and let him know you're more than willing to listen if he wants to talk about it. Then give him the space and time to decide."

I could do that, and hoped it would make John feel free to tell me how he felt.

Gary told us that many of the couples he saw were like two ships passing in the night. Both people desperately wanted to meet in the middle and connect and were making every effort, but couldn't see that their communications weren't working. So Gary would kneel next to the husband or wife and say, "This is what I heard you say," and then say to the spouse "Is that what you said?" This was a way of showing each spouse what they intended to convey was not being heard.

I was grateful to hear Gary say, "I don't think this was happening with you two. What I can see is that John is terrified about what is going on with his business and, by his nature, he is putting on a good face, because of his deep sense of obligation for your well-being."

I had communicated to John what was going on for me with our lack of intimacy. And now, in therapy John was revealing how stressed he was about his work in China.

Gary helped us by articulating what I was projecting and what John was feeling. He showed me that from John's perspective, it appeared I had lost faith in him. Worse, he thought I was doing that as a result of my own fears and doubt. I had always been a partner who bolstered John when he felt uncertain, as he did for me, but now I was feeling doubt too, which made him feel even more scared. He thought of himself as the guy who brings home the bacon. As an entrepreneur, sometimes it worked and sometimes it didn't, but in the end he always came through. To be robbed of that identity would make John feel as if his soul was being taken away.

I said, "Our income has been like a rollercoaster ride, fluctuating over the years, but when it was down John always got it up." Oops.

We all stopped for a minute to have a good laugh.

I went on to explain that what I meant was that I had always believed I could depend on him. This time it felt different — not because I doubted John, but because the world economy was very precarious. Would he be able to pull off his business ventures? I didn't know if things were going to work out as they had in the past. I was fearful and I hadn't been sharing my feelings with him either. It turned out that we were both hiding our fears and worries from each other.

An entrepreneur with solid projects, John was working hard to get funding in China. The money would appear to be forthcoming, and then something would happen to make it evaporate. The fact that he never accepted failure made me believe in him. I was hoping that whatever he did would work out. I was trying to be supportive, but I was terrified.

"I don't think you have given up on your relationship or have gigantic problems, but what I do see is a lot of fear," Gary said.

In another session we talked about the assumptions that we had brought to the relationship from our birth families, and how they affected our relationship. Of course, for me the whole father-daughter relationship was negatively charged. For girls, our relationship with our fathers, or lack of one, affects how we relate to men; a nurturing father-daughter relationship can help give a girl the self-confidence to go out into the world, while a difficult one can compromise that confidence.

This subject came up when I confessed that while still working for the CDC I started to be concerned about my time apart from John and about our relationship. To sort it out I went to a therapist in San Francisco. We talked about how the dysfunctional relationship with my dad was affecting John and me. I had always been afraid to talk to my dad — afraid of the reaction I would get when I told him what I thought — because so often what I got back from him were hurtful put-downs. I never knew what to expect or how to react so I chose not to speak up at all.

Sharing this with Gary and John, I realized I had transferred this behavior to John, who, unlike my dad, was always understanding and said I could tell him anything. It was now clear why I was holding back my feelings from John and not speaking up. I had been conditioned from childhood. This was something I had to work on. I now had to change this old pattern of communication.

Meanwhile, I learned a whole different set of tactics from my mom; to make everything an "adventure" and flow with things when I'm put in an uncomfortable situation. As a result, the habit that kicks in when I'm under stress is to keep things rolling happily along. In the process I suppress any negative emotions. This served as a survival system when I was younger, but now it was getting in the way of a candid, open relationship with my husband. This realization was one of those huge "aha moments" that gave John and me a big start toward improving our relationship.

In contrast, John was raised with women who adored him, which may have made him feel even more responsible to give me what I wanted.

"Many men's need to please the women they are with," said Gary, "stems from their getting the message when they were young that if they didn't please their mothers they might be abandoned and not get the love they needed. This can lead to the need to please their adult partners for the same reason — to avoid being abandoned— an unconscious attitude that's interwoven with the patriarchal role of male as caretaker."

I think these insights let John off the hook a little. Although his childhood was nurturing and his self-esteem was bolstered, the "No Talk Rule" was in full force. It was ingrained in him to keep a tight lid on his internal world. Now he needed to be more open about what he wanted and not just focus so much on what I wanted.

Therapy with Gary also helped me see the differences between the ways in which John and I do intimacy — which led me to wonder what exactly is intimacy?

I've always understood intimacy as being about vulnerability and trust; about being open with each other and willing to share deep feelings without fear. I was yearning for that kind of intimacy. But what is intimacy for a man? John was trying. He would do things I wanted to do even if he didn't want to do them. Was that being intimate to him?

I asked Gary, "What does intimacy look like for a man? You told us that you're in these men's groups and you feel that men want more intimacy. What does that look like?"

"Intimacy is a word that's thrown around a lot. To me, intimacy is if I am lying side by side with my wife and we're having a conversation that feels completely authentic. There are no overlays. There's no saying something to try to get something out of the other. There's no trying to create an impression. We are in the moment, we are present together and we are sharing whether it be physically, verbally or somewhere in between, or even silently together."

Hearing intimacy explained from another man's perspective was helpful to both of us.

"That is exactly what women want!" I replied. "But women are more verbal about our feelings. I want John to be more verbal – to tell me what he is feeling."

Gary told us that when he and his wife get together with other couples, the women tend to chat with each other and feel connected that way.

"The men and I probably share about five percent of the words that the women share, and still feel just as connected with each other as my wife does with her women friends." Then he went on to tell us how intimacy looked in his men's groups.

"In one of my groups, with incredibly evolved men, there is a great deal of intimacy. We spend the first five or ten minutes telling dirty jokes, which brings us into the room. Now we feel really connected because we have laughed together. That feels really intimate to me. I don't experience that kind of intimacy with women generally. Very rarely do I share a dirty joke with a woman and feel like that is intimate."

"So", I asked, "is it possible that two people can be in the same room, with one person feeling intimacy, and the other not? Can it then shift, where the other person is experiencing intimacy and the other is not? Do you think it is possible for men and women to be emotionally intimate in the male way and the female way?"

Gary's response was what I expected. He said, "I think it is possible, but very difficult. Men and women are just different and I am glad about that."

I said I was glad about that too. Then a light bulb went on in my head: What I needed to do was to figure out what intimacy means to John. I needed to recognize there is an emotional world in men that is every bit as deep as women's, just expressed differently. If I could recognize when John was feeling intimate, even when I wasn't, I could at least appreciate the moment, and him, in a whole new way. I felt a wonderful sense of hope for us, and our future together.

We couldn't afford to see Gary more than about eight times, but we were already making important changes. I felt I was actually living with somebody again. I felt we were connecting. We were talking more — both of us. When we left Gary's office we would talk about what we had learned and how we felt about it. Just the fact that John went with me, and not begrudgingly, was amazing.

I knew there was no way I wanted out of this relationship. John was — and is — my life partner. He and I are good for each other. He's the kindest man I know. He has a depth of kindness and compassion at his core that has been hard for him to reveal at times.

I couldn't bear to be in a relationship with less individual freedom than John and I give each other, but, on the other hand, I had learned that too much independence could separate us. Our sessions with Gary and our willingness to change helped us find our way to the best of both worlds. We learned that we had to reprogram ourselves out of our destructive childhoods, and we were both willing to work on doing it.

I love the saying of John C. Maxwell, the leadership expert, "Change is inevitable, growth is optional." I believe that growth, in the case of John and me, was a matter of opening up to things we were discovering about ourselves, and each other. I was learning that my desire to have intimacy with John on *my* terms was unrealistic and wasn't going to work, because he had his own way of being intimate. So we both tried and somehow muddled through. Change was happening in our lives and we were both growing. He stopped drinking so much and we were both opening up more about our feelings.

John continued his business trips to China, but he shared much more with me, and I did the same with him. I felt closer to him and was better equipped to be present for him. He had a lot to deal with, but at least he knew I was a hundred percent in his corner whatever the outcome. Buoyed by our renewed connection, I began feeling free to refocus on finding what was in store for me next.

Lucinda and I signing the Immunization Coalition Sustainability Project contract with Aventis Pasteur, Inc. (later to become Sanofi Pasteur) in our kitchen

Before the kick-off event for the New Mexico Immunization Coalition, former First Lady Rosalynn Carter and Betty Bumpers (former First Lady of Arkansas), co-founders of the national Every Child By Two advocacy organization (Now it is called Vaccinate Your Family), along with New Mexico's First Lady Barbara Richardson meeting with WIC staff and families at La Familia Medical Center in Santa Fe to discuss the importance of immunizations

CHAPTER 12

HILLARY AND THE LITTLE GREEN PIN

Always aim high, work hard, and care deeply about what you believe in. When you stumble, keep faith. When you're knocked down, get right back up. And NEVER listen to anyone who says you can't or shouldn't go on.

~ Hillary Rodham Clinton

I joined John for my first trip to China in the spring of 2005 and soon came to love the culture and excitement of Shanghai, a city of sixteen million people. Through John I met many warm and friendly people.

John and I spent one of our first evenings there with John's business partner, Sonny, and his parents. They hosted a dinner for us at a popular restaurant where the Clintons had eaten in the 1990's during Bill's presidency. Meng Yankun, Sonny's mother, was then the chair of the Shanghai Women's Federation (SWF), one of three women's organizations in China under the leadership of the Chinese Communist Party. Founded in August 1950, SWF was established to represent and protect women's rights and interests and to promote equality between men and women.

Meng and I shared a mutual interest in equal rights for women, so I was excited to meet her. A smart, friendly, gracious woman, Meng was curious about the changing lives of women in America.

With Sonny there to translate, Meng had many questions for me. "Is your current government receptive and supportive of women's changing roles? What kind of organizations are working for women's equality, and what kind of challenges do they face?

These were big questions. I did my best to give her an overall picture but also wanted to know about the status of women in China.

As in virtually all countries of the world, Chinese women are, to one degree or another, second-class citizens. What we know about the status of women in a certain country is based on what we have heard or read, rarely on what we have seen in person. I was excited to learn a little about my Chinese sisters from Meng, who believed strongly in equal rights for women and who, through her work with the SWF, was doing what she could to bring needed changes to China.

As a result of government approval following the Communist Revolution, women's rights groups became increasingly active in China. One of the most striking manifestations of the social change and awakening that accompanied the Revolution has been the emergence of a vigorous and active Women's Movement.

Meng said certain reforms had significantly changed the lives of women: "The People's Republic of China announced publicly the commitment toward gender equality." But in China, as in any country, society can be slow to change. Efforts of the new Communist government to create gender equality were met with resistance in the historically male-dominated Chinese society. So while the legal and social status of women has greatly improved in the last few years, it is still inferior to men's.

Progress, Meng told me, has been incremental. For example: the marriage contract was traditionally between families, not between two individuals. Reform started, she said, with the Marriage Law of 1950, which banned the most extreme forms of female subordination and oppression. It was followed by the Marriage Law of 1980, which banned arranged and forced marriages, and shifted focus away from male dominance and toward the interests of children and women. It gave both men and women the right to divorce; and encouraged sexual equality by making daughters just as valuable as sons, particularly in regard to eligibility for old age insurance. Then, the amended Marriage Law of 2001 said that all property acquired during a marriage was seen as jointly held, and the concealment of joint property was punishable. In current-day China, women enjoy legal equal rights to property.

I learned that in 2004, the All-China Women's Federation compiled survey results to show that thirty percent of families in China experienced domestic violence. The 2001 Marriage Law amendment had offered mediation services and compensation to those who were subjected to domestic violence. But it wasn't until 2005 that domestic violence was finally criminalized by the Law of Protection of Rights and Interests of Women.

As recent as 2019, a government directive banned employers in China from posting "men preferred" or "men only" job advertisements. It included prohibiting companies from asking women applicants about their childbearing and marriage plans, or requiring them to take pregnancy tests.

I enjoyed our conversations, sharing what we each knew about the state of women in our respective countries. What I did learn was that there was so much more to learn.

Meng and I kept in touch and the following year, in the fall of 2006, she invited me to attend the Shanghai Women's Federation International Forum for Women's Economic Development and Participation. Since 1998, every two years the Shanghai Women's Federation hosts an International Forum. Women come from all over the world to learn from each other and share their work related to the economic, social and cultural development of women.

This was an immense honor. I was grateful, and thrilled to participate in a gathering that supported women on an international level.

"Can you invite a few American women to speak at the Forum?" Meng asked me one evening when we were again having dinner with her and her husband.

This came completely out of the blue. After a day or two of panic, I figured out whom I could ask to join me in China.

A few years earlier I attended a meeting at the University of California Santa Cruz Women's Center. The director wanted input to start a training program for female students who wanted to get involved in politics and even run for office. I met Marcy at that gathering. She had been a project manager for Aetna and then Bank of America, traveling all over the United States and the world to manage the design and construction of their new offices. She was now retired, and like me, in search of her next adventure. We quickly became friends, and discovered that we were both passionate about women's rights and searching for the best place to put our time and energies. We went to D.C. a couple of times for EMILY's List conferences and met with women from the National Organization of Women (NOW) and the National Council of Women's Organizations.

I had a hunch that she'd have a whole Rolodex of names to consider for the forum, so I gave her a call. Could she go, and could she help me find a few other women to attend and give interesting presentations? The answer was an excited "Yes".

She reached out to Kerry Haley and Lorraine Hariton, whom she knew from the Forum for Women Entrepreneurs and Executives in Silicon Valley. Kerry was the vice president and general manager of the Wireless Division at Citizens Communications, and Lorraine was the CEO and president of Apptera, Inc., and CEO of Beatnik, Inc. They would share their experiences and challenges as professional women in the United States.

Meng, wanting to get as much public attention as she could for the forum, arranged for free publicity on a popular TV show and asked Lorraine and me to be part of it. Was I game?

Wow! There was no way I could say no.

I was going to be on Chinese TV! Nervous, excited, thrilled and apprehensive — all at the same time — I had no idea what to expect when we got to the television studio. Lorraine was told that she would share the stage with four other women, each from a different country, while I would be seated in the front row of the studio audience. My job, and that of a few others next to me, was to comment on the discussion onstage when the television cameras panned over to us. My headset translated everything to English so I could understand all the speakers.

Professional hairdressers and makeup artists got us ready for primetime. I have never worn much makeup; and having my face covered in perfumed cosmetics only added to my discomfort. I didn't have any experience in this arena, and was trying not to look like the amateur I was.

We all took our places and the show started. Lorraine and the other women on stage were interviewed about their professional experiences — by a confrontational male host who was more than a little chauvinistic.

"What is it like for *women* in the corporate world?" Cloying.

"How is a woman's behavior and experience in the corporate work environment different from a man's?" Provocative.

"What are the challenges that women face?" Condescending.

I wondered, was this an act to make the discussion more interesting, or was he showing his true colors?

When it was my turn to respond, I found it hard to relax enough to make an intelligent contribution to the discussion. Today, about the only thing I remember about my performance is that I felt awkward, but with no negative feedback I should assume I did just fine. I wish I could do it again. I would be much more relaxed and have more fun with it.

The next day, while Lorraine and Kerry were busy with their workshop presentations, I was interviewed by a lovely man from a Shanghai radio station. The questions this time were more relevant to me personally, so they were easier to answer.

"How have things changed for women in the United States? What were the challenges of owning my own business?" he asked, following up on a casual conversation we had before the show. He spoke perfect English, and far from being condescending, he seemed truly interested in what I was saying. And I wasn't covered in a thick layer of makeup! I was relaxed and enjoying myself, and left the show feeling that it went very well. Being a part of The Shanghai Women's Forum was a gift I will cherish forever.

....

Back home, I was distracted from my search for meaningful work by the presidential campaign that was starting to rev up. This would be no ordinary election and I couldn't wait to get on board.

On January 20, 2007, Hillary Clinton announced her run for the presidency. I had first become aware of her in 1992 during her husband's presidential campaign, when I was working for Barbara Boxer. I knew she was the first First Lady to have an office in the West Wing of the White House. First Ladies normally concentrated their time and energy on less weighty or controversial issues than Hillary Clinton's focus. She chaired the Task Force on Health Care Reform —

convening hearings, testifying before Congress and helping to draft legislation. She led the fight to pass the Children's Health Insurance Program (CHIP) that helped parents whose children lacked health insurance. This issue was especially close to my heart: More kids with health insurance meant more kids were likely to be up-to-date with their immunizations, which would further my work for the CDC as a part of President Clinton's Childhood Immunization Initiative.

She came to the White House with an established career of her own and was not about to fade into the background, especially when it came to issues she cared about. This was all very different from the way previous First Ladies had functioned in the past. While I found all this admirable, there were many who saw it as unbecoming a First Lady or, for that matter, a woman. But Hillary did not hesitate to challenge old-fashioned expectations of how women are supposed to behave, and what they are supposed to do.

Here was a woman who didn't just make speeches. She acted on her beliefs. She started her career working for the Children's Defense Fund because she understood that healthy children are the future of our country. I read her book *Living History* in 2003 and came away with even more admiration for her accomplishments as well as the barriers she had overcome as a woman in politics, especially in the days when there weren't as many women in leadership positions as there are now.

I admired her as a woman who was creating a new role model of how a smart, talented, capable woman looked and acted. And, I felt a connection with her because she and Bill seemed to have an egalitarian relationship just like John and I do.

Hillary, as candidate for the presidency, was already familiar with the kinds of intricate political issues and decisions that presidents face. She could summon her experience as an attorney, First Lady of Arkansas, First Lady of the United States and United States senator to navigate the complexities of the office with wisdom and strength.

I loved hearing Hillary say that she was given much in her life, and it was her duty to "do all the good you can, for all the people you can, in as many ways as you can, for as long as you can." This has been my lifelong belief and way of being in the world as well.

The list of Hillary's accomplishments is long and impressive. Now that she was running to break the highest and hardest glass ceiling, I was not going to miss being a part of it. I was all in and ready to do anything I could. My passions were not only reignited with the prospect of working to elect the first woman president of the United States, but for a woman who had done so much good over her lifetime and whose morals and values I shared.

In October of 2007, I went to a Hillary organizing meeting in the back of a pizza parlor. It was in the same Capitola shopping center where I'd run the campaign office for Kathy Akao some thirteen years earlier. I'd come full circle, except this campaign was for president, and this time I was a volunteer and not paid staff. Now, I sat with fourteen men and women around a large table, listening to a young campaign worker talk about Hillary and the campaign's plans. We were each given the names and emails of everyone who attended, but no specific direction about how to proceed. So, after giving some thought to what I'd be getting myself into, and with no job prospects in sight, I sent out an email to the group.

"Are any of you interested in meeting again to talk about forming a local "Hillary for President" campaign?"

One person responded; her name was Tricia Spiegel.

We first met over tea at her house in Aptos, just south of Santa Cruz. Clicking instantly, we became a dynamic duo. For the next year we put our lives on hold, volunteering our energy and expertise, working almost full time to create a local Hillary for President Campaign.

Our first task was to enlist the help of a few influential Democratic activists in the area.

Among the first people I called were Karen and Darrell Darling, a couple who ran a local bed-and-breakfast. They were Santa Cruz Democratic Party leaders and well-known Hillary supporters. I told them what Tricia and I were planning, and asked them to be a part of our leadership team.

The Darlings had become acquainted with the Clintons through personal tragedy. Their son, who worked in the Clinton administration, was killed in the same plane crash that killed Secretary of Commerce Ron Brown. Hillary had spoken very graciously at their son's funeral in Santa Cruz. They did not hesitate to say, "Yes, of course! Anything we can do to help."

Since our goal was to coordinate grassroots support in the three-county Central Coast area, we reached out to a prominent Monterey County businessman and California Democratic Party leader, Shawn Bagley, as well.

We set up shop in the small apartment below Tricia and Rich's home. It didn't take long for it to start buzzing seven days a week with volunteers who: called voters, made signs, got dispatched to go door-to-door or sit at campaign tables at the downtown mall.

We developed our own database of supporters, which grew to about eight hundred fifty people, two hundred of them active volunteers. We sent them a weekly email newsletter with: articles about the campaign and policy issues, invitations to debate-watch parties and fundraisers, requests for help with phone-banking, how to contribute online and other activities. We created a full-fledged local Hillary Clinton campaign.

On top of regular campaign activities, Shawn Bagley organized a "First in the nation Primary" event in Salinas before the real primaries and caucuses had gotten underway. The intention was to get press coverage and attract volunteers. We enlisted the support of local California Assemblywoman Anna Caballero and United Farm Workers co-founder Dolores Huerta to speak in support of Hillary. Other well-known people were there to speak in support of Senator Obama and Senator Edwards, the other Presidential candidates. It was a perfect way to convene activists from around the Central Coast and was great fun. About two hundred people turned out, mingled, bought t-shirts and buttons, voted for their favorite candidate and signed up to volunteer.

The following month, we excitedly welcomed Hillary to town to speak at a rally at Hartnell Junior College in Salinas, where she accepted the endorsement of the United Farm Workers. This was last-minute and unexpected, so with the help of a few Hillary staff, we scrambled to get the venue ready. Backstage that day, along with Tricia, her husband Rich, Shawn, Karen and Darrell, I introduced myself to Hillary Clinton.

Knowing I had only about thirty seconds, I blurted out, "Thank you for running, Hillary! I am working very hard and know you are going to be a great president." We hugged and I had my picture taken with her. I found her approachable—a warm, caring and genuine woman I could work my heart out for. There was no doubt in my mind about what I would be doing for the coming year.

. . . .

One day the phone rang — it was Lorraine Hariton — my friend from the Shanghai Forum.

"How'd you like to go with us to work in Iowa for Hillary?"

"Yes! Of course!" I answered without hesitation.

The Iowa caucus on January 3, 2008, was to be the first test in a very long and hard-fought Democratic primary battle between Senators Clinton, Barack Obama and John Edwards. Lorraine was reaching out to her network to raise money for Hillary and recruit volunteers to campaign in Cedar Rapids.

I wanted to go, but I had one big problem: how to pay for my trip. John was fighting tooth and nail to get funding for his projects in China, I had no job prospects, and we were barely keeping our heads above water. But I was determined not to miss this opportunity.

John solved the airfare problem — he gave me airline miles he'd racked up from his many trips to Shanghai. Yippee! No expense there! But I would need money for food and three nights in a hotel. More passionate than proud, I humbly reached out to my friends and fellow campaign workers. "Can you help pay my expenses to work in Iowa for Hillary? Any small amount would be so appreciated."

They wanted me to go as much as I wanted to go and contributed whatever they could. I felt blessed and grateful.

Lorraine rounded up thirty-five of us from various parts of the country including: a woman from Palo Alto and her grown daughter from Florida, a woman who came with her twelve-year old daughter, and two husband-and-wife teams. One woman flew in from India, where she had been working, and brought us all t-shirts that said "Team Lorraine" — which is what we called ourselves. It was a wonderful group of warm, passionate, vital and interesting people whom I loved getting to know.

We got to work: phoning people to invite them to rallies where they could see Hillary in person, as well as identifying Hillary voters, making sure voters knew where their caucus site was and finding out if they needed a ride. One day Jericka Parker, a young woman from Cedar Rapids, and I were followed by a local news crew as we campaigned door-to-door.

"Hi babe! Guess what!" Excited, I called John. "I'm gonna be on the news! Tell the kids and the volunteers — I'll send you the link."

"Fabulous!" He was proud of me, and happy to see a little of what I was doing.

Meeting residents one-on-one was interesting and rewarding. People were friendly and amazed I had come all the way from California. Many opened up to me about the issues they cared about and how they were having a hard time getting by. I could definitely commiserate.

My biggest challenge was dealing with the cold weather in Iowa. Unused to snow, I had not been so miserable since our winter in Canada a lifetime ago. If I was going to keep going; there was no doubt that I needed to break down and buy some warm boots.

All of us volunteers worked hard all day, but it wasn't all work. I felt great camaraderie and had some fun times after-hours hanging out at "The Democrat," a local pub near campaign headquarters. The place was buzzing with activity as we enjoyed a drink and a bite to eat while sharing our experiences of the day and the latest political news.

I was able to see Hillary speak twice while I was in Iowa. The first time was in Cedar Rapids, the second in Vinton, thirty-five miles north. Four of us piled into my rental car, and even though Vinton is a fairly small town, we managed to get lost on some of the neighborhood streets (this was before GPS and smart phones). Once, when we stopped to ask a young man for directions, he peered intently into the car and exclaimed, "Wow, are you Hillary Clinton?" Flattered, I giggled and assured him that I was not, but that I certainly did support her! Afterward, we all had a good laugh imagining Hillary getting lost driving a bunch of her friends around the back streets of Vinton, Iowa, no Secret Service in sight.

Iowa is one of thirteen states that hold caucuses instead of primary elections, as in California. Witnessing the caucus process was a real eye-opener for me — baffling, in fact.

In 2008, the states that held primaries averaged four times as many voters than the states that held caucuses. No surprise, given the obstacles I saw firsthand that face voters in caucus states. Caucuses, unlike primaries, require voters to show up at a specific place on a specific date and time—regardless of work schedules, health issues, available transportation, weather or childcare needs. Stranger still, the voters in caucus states are required not to cast a private ballot, but to stand up in front of their neighbors, friends, and spouses and declare who they are voting for.

Some primaries, like California's, allow voting by mail. People can vote in the privacy of their own homes, have weeks to cast their ballots, and can drop them off or mail them in. This enables all registered voters to take part in the democratic process, no matter their age, health, mobility, work or family responsibilities.

In Iowa, by contrast, there were hundreds of caucus sites around the state, about the same number as there would be polling places in a primary. On caucus night, our group worked a two-county area, each of us assigned to a caucus site. Our job was to help each of Hillary's local caucus captains get people to the caucus, explain what to expect if they were new to the process and make sure they didn't defect to another candidate. Some sites were small and some quite large. Some were held in high school gyms while others were smaller, like the one I was assigned to, which was held in a local bar and grill out in the country.

Traveling about fifty miles north of Cedar Rapids in my rental car, driving the back roads, dark and flat as far as the eye could see, in the middle of nowhere, I thought, "Okay, this is going to be an experience!" I met Rosemary, Hillary's caucus captain, in a bar and grill. I was there to help her, so as she talked to her neighbors, I did the same.

It was January, seven in the evening, already dark out, and bitter cold. While walking door-to-door for days before, I met many older women who just couldn't caucus; it was too much for them to deal with at their age and frail health. I talked with younger people who wanted to vote but had to work that night. Nurses, waitresses and many others working late shifts couldn't afford to take the time off. Others had young children who needed to be in bed before the voting even started.

Hillary won my caucus site but lost the state, coming in third to Barak Obama and Senator John Edwards. Disappointed but undaunted, with a much better view of how our election process works, I headed back home.

. . . .

I landed in Houston about a month and a half later, along with my friends Roxie Gribble and Danyel Hosier. Even crazier than the Iowa caucuses, in Texas voters actually had to cast their ballots twice! They called it the Texas Two-Step, because they have both a primary *and* a caucus. This strange and unique way of choosing delegates started in 1976, when state party leaders added a primary to the existing caucus.

Early in the morning of March 4, Election Day, after three days of calling voters and walking door-to-door in Houston neighborhoods, the three of us headed over to the Hillary headquarters to get our assignments. The place was buzzing with energy and excitement. We had been told how this was going to work, but I didn't really believe it until I saw it with my own eyes.

After Texans cast their secret ballots in the primary election, they have to go back to their polling site that same evening and cast another vote — a public vote in the caucus. If they don't go back and caucus, their primary vote is reduced to 3/4 of a vote compared to the whole vote counted for someone who had voted in both the primary and caucus. Thankfully, for the 2016 election the Texas Two-Step was changed to a primary election only.

Our voting site was in a large auditorium at a local high school. Judith Lichtman, an attorney and senior advisor for Hillary's campaign, met us there. Her job was to make sure everything was done legally. The turnout outstripped everyone's expectations, which posed problems as the day wore on. Roxie, Danyel, Judith and I talked to Hillary supporters all day, reminding them to come back at 6:30 that night to caucus. Many seemed to know the drill, with most of them accepting this unique requirement. Everything was going along smoothly until seven in the evening, when the primary voting was supposed to end and caucus voting was supposed to start.

Anyone who was in line to vote in the primary before seven would be allowed to stay and vote. So the polls closed at seven, but voting continued for hours. By that time it was dark and getting cold. Because of a shortage of voting machines and a greater than average turnout, there was a line stretching out the door and as far as you could see down the street. There were parents with young children who were hungry and bored, elderly and some disabled people who were cold with no place to sit down. Our job was to keep Hillary voters there, but standing out in the cold for three hours waiting to vote, especially since they had already voted in the primary earlier that day, was not an option for many, and they left. It was ten o'clock when the last person in line cast their ballot in the primary. Now, the caucus could start.

Once the caucus began, voters had to sign in before taking a seat. There weren't enough sign-in forms, so those in charge were actually creating them by hand. It was noisy, chaotic and disorganized, and it didn't end until midnight. We heard some sites didn't finish up until two in the morning.

What I saw up close and personal in Texas and Iowa was *not* democracy in action, and was not something I had ever experienced before. It was not one person, one vote. The Texas Two Step and Iowa caucuses disenfranchised people by making it difficult to vote and, in the case of Texas, required them to vote twice in the same day. When the votes were counted, Hillary narrowly won the Texas primary, but lost the Texas caucus.

Unwinding after the day's chaotic intensity, our team crowded into a local bar, where we were excited to receive the news of Hillary's dual victories in Ohio and Rhode Island. They turned up the volume on the TVs and we joined the cheering crowd when Hillary said, "For everyone here in Ohio and across America who's ever been counted out but refused to be knocked out, and for everyone who has stumbled but stood right back up, and for everyone who works hard and never gives up, this one is for you."

....

The Pennsylvania primary was coming up next, and Roxie and I decided to go. Again I used John's miles, and my wonderful friends chipped in to help me pay for food and the hotel. We were going to work in Carlisle, a town of about 18,000 people just outside of Harrisburg.

On one of our first nights there, we were invited to a local Democratic Club dinner and debate between a representative from Hillary's campaign and one from Obama's campaign. (Senator John Edwards had dropped out by then.) The long, narrow room had three rows of tables filled with chattering, excited people. Both Roxie and I were super excited to see that Rob Reiner, the actor and director best known for his role as the son-in-law of Archie and Edith Bunker on the *All in the Family* TV show. He was there to speak on behalf of Hillary. After he spoke, people huddled around him. Roxie and I squeezed our way to the front of the group itching to say a few words and get our picture taken with him. He was extremely warm, friendly and obliging as we posed for a picture.

The crowd couldn't have been more friendly and welcoming to us out-of-towners. An older, long-time local Democrat heard we were staying in a dingy cheap hotel in Harrisburg and had another idea in mind. "Jim, I want to introduce you to these two lovely young ladies. They have traveled here all the way from California to help get out the vote for Hillary. They are staying in a not so nice hotel in Harrisburg. Can you help them out?"

That was all that needed to happen.

"I have just remodeled a B&B in town and am a staunch Hillary supporter. You are welcome to stay at my place, no charge."

This was an offer we couldn't refuse.

When we arrived at the Orris House Inn that night, we both thought we had died and gone to heaven. It was a grand Victorian, beautifully refurbished in perfect period style, with the most comfortable beds and top-of-the line bedding. We were treated like royalty. Jim even brought croissants, fresh fruit, fresh squeezed orange juice and coffee to our rooms each morning. Most of the time we got drenched walking door-to-door in the rain, so coming back to this lavish home-away-from-home was pure joy. Now, that was the way to campaign and just goes to show you, if you put yourself out there, you never know what is going to happen.

. . . .

Roxie and I returned home from an exhilarating time in Pennsylvania, where Hillary won by nine percent. Despite this clear victory, there were increasing calls in the media for her to drop out of the race. They assumed she had no chance of winning the nomination in the long run, even though the delegate count was close. We thought their assumptions were premature. This call to drop out was not coming from Democratic Party leaders or Obama's camp. It was coming from the mainstream media.

A *New York Times* editorial quoted Howard Kurtz's online blog "beseeching her to get the hell out of the race."

On the *Times* opinion page, Maureen Dowd sarcastically made her point with a Dr. Seuss rhyme: "The time is now. Just go. ... I don't care how."

Across town at the New York *Daily News*, a bitter Mike Lupica was steamed over the fact that Clinton "won't quit" the race.

And weeks earlier, *New York* magazine had fretted about which senior Democrats would be able to "step in" and "usher Clinton from the race" or if Clinton, obsessed with her own "long-range self-aggrandizement," would finally figure it out herself.

At this point in the primary race, the delegate count was very close — too close to call — so why the push for Hillary to quit from so-called journalists who were supposed to report the news, not create it based on their personal biases? I thought these comments from the mainstream media were disturbing and sexist. No man would have been treated like this. Women all over the country who had been paying attention were pissed. What the fuck!!

Until Hillary's presidential run I had never seen journalists take it upon themselves to tell a candidate when they should drop out. That decision was normally based on how much money a campaign had, how many primaries or caucuses they were winning and what their advisors recommended. The press was totally ignoring the fourteen million voters Clinton had at that time (she ended up with almost eighteen million) and that she was our *representative* in this race. No other previous candidates were told to quit. No other candidates had been routinely depicted in the media as being self-absorbed. It drove me crazy, as it did millions of her supporters.

Throughout the campaign I was keenly aware of the endless examples of sexism being spewed out by the media. I had thought that at this point, as a country and a society, we were further along in our evolutionary path, but what I saw was the continued and accepted role of sexism in the media. There was an endless barrage of insulting comments that couldn't help but affect voters. The "N" word is off limits, but the "B" word is not; in fact it was said and written over and over again about Hillary, as in a widely distributed poster that read "Life's a bitch, don't vote for one!"

This is some of what was actually said on TV. Tucker Carlson at MSNBC said, "When she comes on TV, I involuntary cross my legs." Neil Cavuto on Fox said, "Men won't vote for Hillary Clinton because she reminds them of their nagging wives." Marc Rudov, author and radio host on Fox News said "When Obama speaks, men hear 'take off for the future' and when Hillary Clinton speaks men hear 'take out the garbage.'" On The O'Reilly Factor, Bill O'Reilly asked Rudov, "What is the downside of having a woman become the president of the United States?" with Rudov responding, "You mean besides the PMS and the mood swings, right?" Jack Cafferty on CNN's Cafferity File, said, "She morphed into a scolding mother talking down to her child." Mike Barnicle on MSNBC's Morning Joe said, "When she reacts to Obama she looks like everyone's first wife standing outside probate court." Randi Rhodes called her "a fucking whore." Maureen Dowd of the New York Times claimed Hillary "has turned into Sybil." MSNBC reporter David Schuster asked whether her daughter Chelsea was being "pimped out." Chris Matthews declared, "The reason she's a U.S. Senator, the reason she's a candidate for president, the reason she may be a front-runner is her husband messed around. We keep forgetting it. She didn't win it on her merit." And not to be outdone, comedian and magician Penn Jillette joked on MSNBC that Obama's success was due to Black History Month and Hillary's success was due to "White Bitch Month."

The Hillary-bashing went on week after week, month after month, with not a word from anyone from the Democratic National Committee. It seemed endless to millions of her supporters. But all of this sexism and misogyny had an unintended effect. Women were waking up to the sexist double standard that was being inflicted on Hillary. Women of my generation had felt and experienced sexism all our lives to some degree or another. We had learned to deal with it and to repress it—but now we recognized the anger that had been festering just under the surface. When we witnessed what the press inflicted on Hillary — an extremely smart, capable woman very much prepared to be president of the United States – our old wounds were broken open and bleeding. It was an unforgettable awakening.

Some tended to see sexism as other women's problem: If it wasn't happening to them personally, it wasn't happening at all. In an April 13, 2008, article in the *New York Magazine* entitled "Feminist Awakening: Hillary Clinton and the Fourth Wave." Amanda Fortini wrote:

> *But as our first serious female presidential candidate came under attack, there was a collective revelation: Even if we couldn't see the proverbial glass ceiling from where we sat, it still existed — and it was not retractable.*

I'd had my own experience with media sexism toward a female candidate. After my time in Shanghai and before Hillary's run for the presidency, I managed the campaign of Santa Cruz Mayor Emily Reilly, who was running for the California State Assembly. One day I got a call from a female news reporter who wanted to do a story on Emily's clothes.

She said "I have noticed that since Emily has thrown her hat in the ring, her wardrobe has improved."

The news story she was planning to write was not going be about Emily's stand on the important issues facing the people of the Central Coast; it was going to be on Mayor Reilly's fashion sense. This story would never have been proposed for a male candidate. I was amazed and annoyed all at the same time and told the reporter, "I can't schedule an interview with Emily for you if the topic is going to be about her improved wardrobe; not her stand on the issues important to the people of the Central Coast." I was truly taken aback, and managed to be clear with her without revealing my outrage.

．．．．．．．．．．．

After the Pennsylvania primary, I decided to run for delegate to the Democratic National Convention. I had never done this before, and didn't know much about being a delegate, but I had put my heart and soul into Hillary's campaign and saw no reason not to take this next step. California had held its primary, and Hillary won the state as well as my congressional district, which was allotted five pledged delegates according to the Democratic Party rules – three for Hillary and two for Obama. Excited to have this new experience, I joined Shawn Bagley and Karen Darling to run as a slate. Two of our Central Coast for Hillary volunteers, Shawn Kumagai (who I am very happy to say is now a newly elected city council member in Dublin, CA) and Jill Burtenbach, made an electronic flier for us, and emailed it to our volunteers and supporters.

On the same day, in each of California's fifty-three congressional districts, people would gather to vote for whom they wanted to go to the Democratic convention as a delegate for either Hillary or Obama. It was up to us candidates to get friends and family to vote for us. Now it was my turn, after working on so many other people's campaigns. I called everyone I knew and asked them to go to Monterey and vote for me.

On a beautiful sunny Sunday afternoon, I found myself among people from all over the district who had gathered in front of an auditorium where the delegate election was being held. After pleasantly socializing outside, we all got in line to sign in and vote. It was all very civilized and orderly compared to what I had seen in Texas. I was feeling comfortable, greeting people who were there to support me. About fifteen people were running for three delegate slots. We each gave a short speech, and as the votes were tallied I found out I had won one of the three seats.

Pledged delegates are selected based on the party primaries and caucuses in each state, where voters choose among local people vying to represent their candidate. The Democratic Party also has super-delegates. These people are distinguished party leaders and elected officials, including governors and members of the Senate and House of Representatives. They are seated automatically and are free to support anyone they want.

The 2008 Democratic primary elections were very close, with a lot of twists and turns in Florida and Michigan that I don't have the space to get into. According the Real Clear Politics website, even though Hillary won the popular vote by 176,465 votes, Obama ended up with more total pledged delegates (1,766.5 to her 1,639.5 — a mere difference of 127 delegates).

I was incensed at how this kind of thing can happen. For example the whole state of Wyoming had a grand total of 8,760 people vote for president at their 2008 caucuses and were given twelve pledged delegates to the Democratic National Convention. In comparison, in my California Congressional district, about 95,000 people voted in our state primary election and were given five delegates to the convention. Each of the Wyoming and California Central Coast delegates counted as one vote for our Democratic presidential nominee, but represented a vastly different number of people. As a delegate, I represented 95,000 people. A delegate from Wyoming represented just 8,760 people.

Because Obama ended up with more pledged delegates, a greater number of superdelegates (463 to Clinton's 257) decided to support Obama; the final tally was Obama 2,229.5 to Hillary 1,896.5 — a difference of 333 delegates.

Many of us giving our blood, sweat and tears, traveling to a number of states, seeing firsthand the undemocratic caucus system used to elect our party's nominee, felt very strongly that changes needed to be made in order for future elections to accurately reflect the choice of the people.

. . . .

With Obama having enough delegates, on June 7, 2008, Hillary officially, and very graciously, suspended her campaign. Senator Obama's campaign took over both the Democratic National Committee (DNC) and the administration of the convention. Not long after that, rumors started spreading that Hillary's name would not be placed in nomination, even symbolically, as other second-place candidates in past elections had traditionally been. It wouldn't have changed the outcome of the convention, but it would have recognized her historical campaign and the hard work of the thousands of people who volunteered their time and gave their money to support Hillary's presidential candidacy.

In 2008, Hillary had only 333 fewer total delegates (including both pledged and superdelegates) than Obama. In 1980 Ted Kennedy had 750 fewer delegates than Jimmy Carter; in 1988 Jesse Jackson had nearly 1,400 fewer delegates than Michael Dukakis; and in 1992 Jerry Brown had 600 fewer delegates than Bill Clinton. Every one of those second-place candidates — all men — had his name placed in nomination.

After a long and hard-fought primary between Clinton and Obama, there was a lot of talk about having a "unified" convention. But many of us felt strongly that the only way to achieve unity was to have Hillary's name placed in nomination in this historic election. Anything other than that would be a threat to a "unified" convention, leaving Hillary delegates feeling invisible and disrespected, diminishing the historic nature of her campaign. Only if the Clinton delegates were allowed to vote for their candidate, we believed, would they accept the results as legitimate and go on to vote and work for the Democratic nominee.

As Hillary's delegates, we were not receiving any direction from her campaign. Meanwhile, the state Democratic parties were major obstacles, refusing to provide us with any delegate contact information. So a handful of people started calling as many delegates as they could find, one by one, to assess how much support there was for putting Hillary's name in nomination and asking for names and contact information of other Hillary delegates to increase our numbers. We were enlisting those who were committed to honoring their pledge to vote for Hillary to join a Google Group set up by Sacha Millstone, Monisha Merchant and Mary Boergers — Hillary delegates and Democratic Party activists.

For the Hillary delegates to unite in this effort, we had to be able to communicate with each other. The Google Group was an essential vehicle for doing that, but only about fifty delegates nationwide knew about it. How were we going to obtain the names and phone numbers of more than 1,600 pledged Clinton delegates across the country to invite them to join?

Undeterred, four dedicated volunteers accomplished the bulk of the work of contacting Hillary's delegates — Michele Thomas, John West, Suzanne Grier and John Siegel. They were not delegates themselves but had been invited to join the group

John Siegel was the one who called me. "Our group is working to have Hillary's name put in nomination, but the party is trying to block us. Would you join the effort? Help contact other delegates in California?"

Without hesitation, I said that I would. I immediately asked four others, Roxie Gribble, Geri Kaspar, Prameela Bartholomeuse and Dale Schroedel to help me call the 204 pledged delegates for Hillary in California. At the same time, web sites like Together4Us and I Own My Vote were publicly calling for Hillary's name to be placed in nomination, and a roll-call vote to be taken.

Then, early one morning, Linda Shaw, a Hillary volunteer from Benbrook, Texas, who had spent endless hours phone-banking in state after state, found what we needed in the DNC rules. A candidate's name could be placed in nomination, even over the objections of other candidates or the DNC, if the candidate submitted a written request supported by a notarized petition signed by at least three hundred delegates, with no more than fifty from each state.

Thus "The 300 Group" was born: a grassroots effort to put Hillary Clinton's name in nomination. Separate from the Democratic Party and even from Hillary's campaign, we started quietly asking each Hillary delegate we could find to print, sign, notarize and mail back to us our petition to satisfy DNC rule requirements, believing that the petition drive could do no harm and might be of help. We were working toward a real nominating convention with two names on the ballot, followed by a roll-call vote — exactly as had been done in the past.

We weren't naïve in our enthusiasm. We were well aware that every aspect of Hillary's role at the convention would likely be determined by negotiations between Obama's campaign and hers, rather than by any DNC rules or our petition. So as our Google Group grew, we discussed whether and how we might influence the negotiations between the two camps. Various ideas were floated, one of which created division among the delegates. Some felt we should just continue quietly gathering petition signatures, while others believed we should go public with our petition in order to strengthen Hillary's hand. Still others wanted to publicly threaten a protest at the convention if Hillary's name was not placed in nomination. This third idea provoked outrage and anger from delegates who feared we would embarrass our candidate by even hinting that disruption was being considered.

After much discussion, we decided to lie low and continue to reach out to delegates who would sign on to our "300 petition." But as we reached more and more delegates, we started getting resistance. State party leaders were telling Hillary's pledged delegates not to sign, saying that it would be divisive and would hurt Obama and the party. To counter their influence, and because it was almost impossible to reach delegates without having their contact information, we decided to go public.

The petition was still circulating, as we revealed it to the press, broadcast it in the blogosphere and talked about it on the airwaves. We explained that the only way to bring the more militant Clinton delegates behind Obama would be to let the Clinton delegation fully participate in the election process. Far from being divisive, as the Obama campaign apparently feared, an open election would be the key to unification. That was our message. And yet, even though our message was getting out there, we were still having difficulty finding California delegates and convincing them to sign. Then something very interesting happened.

Senator Clinton was at my friend Lorraine Hariton's home in Los Altos Hills for a "unity" fundraiser. Supporters of Hillary and Obama were gathering to mend fences. I was there, and after Hillary spoke, I spontaneously reached for the circulating microphone to ask her a question.

I was strong and clear when I told her "I believe it would help unify the party if your name was placed in nomination. There is a petition being circulated to do that. What are your thoughts?"

Hillary's answer was what we needed. She said she thought her delegates should be able to vote for her, and if they couldn't, it could be a threat to party unity.

This was just what we'd been hoping and working for. Simone DuBois videotaped our exchange and put it up on YouTube. It was picked up by the national media outlets (and later mentioned in the book *Game Change* by John Heilemann and Mark Halperin). As a result of what Hillary said, a lot more Hillary delegates in California were receptive when we called to ask them to sign the petition. Otherwise, I don't think we would have amassed the signatures we needed in time. I thought the Universe was truly working.

On August 14, just eleven days before the start of the convention, as people all over the country continued to sign and mail in their petitions, we were told by Hillary's campaign that she and Obama had agreed; her name would be placed in nomination for the sake of unity. Since we weren't in communication with the Clinton campaign, we didn't know if our petition drive had anything to do with this, but we felt victorious anyway.

Unfortunately, those good feelings were short-lived. Having been adversely influenced by their state parties, which were controlled by Obama's campaign, the number of pledged delegates committed to vote for Hillary was shrinking. Many had decided party unity meant not voting for Clinton, as they were pledged to do.

How were we going to make sure those elected to vote for Hillary actually did so? We needed a letter addressed to Hillary delegates that would explain why they should vote for her. But how were we going to get this letter to them — delegates from all over the country? We didn't have email or snail mail addresses. Time was short. The only option was to give each Hillary delegate our letter at the convention. We had state captains whose job it was to get this letter to their people, but in a state the size of California this was almost impossible. Once at the convention, delegates were dispersed everywhere, attending a multitude of events.

Then, Hillary solved the problem. All of her delegates and their guests were invited to a gathering where she told us, "I am releasing you to vote whatever way you chose."

At that point, many delegates found our arguments to vote for Hillary quaintly irrelevant. I talked to a lot of California delegates who took Clinton's "delegate release" to mean she wanted us to vote for Obama. But I still felt I needed to honor the people who had sent me to the convention to vote for Hillary.

Before going to Denver, I had called Gloria Allred, the civil rights lawyer noted for taking high-profile, and often controversial, cases particularly involving the protection of women's rights. I knew she was a California delegate. I asked her if she would research the California Democratic Party rules, and specifically whether we, as California delegates, were bound by the rules of the California Democratic Party to vote for the candidate we were elected to represent? She said she would.

Good thing that she did! One morning at breakfast, as we were trying to figure out how to proceed, she told us that state party rules required that on the first ballot, California delegates are required to vote for the candidate they were elected to represent.

Exactly! This is what we wanted to hear. But how could we communicate this to all the California delegates?

Gloria asked Art Torres, the chair of the California Democratic Party, if she could address the delegates at the morning's breakfast meeting. He refused. So, in true Gloria fashion, she took a table napkin and tied it across her face as a gag. This, of course, instantly attracted the press, to whom she announced that she had been silenced — gagged — by the California Democratic Party. She told reporters that the state party chair would not let her inform the delegates of this rule, which she proceeded to describe in full, in the process publicizing it to an even wider audience. Unfortunately, by this time most California delegates, having finished breakfast, were on their way out the door.

....

This was the first Democratic convention I ever attended. Downtown Denver was overrun with delegates, volunteers and press. Our hotel lobby was buzzing with chatter, people connecting with old friends and making new friends with fellow campaigners. The 300 Group rented a condo just off the main street, as a place to gather; and where delegates could turn in their signed petitions. People came with signs they made for Hillary rallies; they organized parties and planned meetings.

The 300 Group had succeeded in collecting about 600 signed petitions, twice as many as we needed. To commemorate Hillary's historic campaign, a little green "300" pin was given to each person who signed the petition, with a number engraved on the back signifying the order in which their petition was received. I proudly wore my #16 pin and it is still one of my cherished possessions.

The press was keenly aware of our actions. I was stopped and asked questions a number of times. The little green pin was the most coveted convention souvenir in Denver. Amazingly, I was offered $500 for mine, but there was no way I would part with it, then or ever.

In Denver, the personally signed petitions were delivered to Senator Clinton in a beautiful leather binder. A 300 pin was framed in a shadow box and presented to her with a two-page letter, entitled *Little Green Pin*, telling her our story. In the end, she decided not to file the petitions to put her name in nomination. She didn't need to. Obama's campaign agreed to have her name symbolically placed in nomination.

In hotels all over Denver all the delegates cast their vote. Of the 1,639.5 delegates pledged to Hillary, 1,010.5 voted for her. I felt happy and proud to have been one of them.

Later, as the roll call of the states was read from the convention floor, many states passed, so that when they got to New York, Hillary was able to graciously call for a unanimous vote for Senator Obama to be the Democratic presidential nominee.

It took a while for the adrenalin to subside, but eventually I headed home to Santa Cruz. It was back to the reality of my day-to-day life — and some very challenging situations.

View from John's apartment in Shanghai – the old and the new colliding

The beautiful Yun Brocade given to me by Meng Yankun (Sonny's mother and chair of the Shanghai Women's Federation)

With attendees of the Shanghai Women's Federation 2006 International Forum on Women's Development and Economic Participation. From left to right: Ms. Chonchanok Viravan (Thailand) Chairwoman of the International Federation of Business and Professional Women, Ms. Irene Natividad (USA) Founder and President of Global Summit of Women, myself, Lorraine Hariton (USA) with the Women Entrepreneurs and Executives of Silicon Valley, Ms. Yankun Meng (China) Chair of the Shanghai Women's Federation, Ms. Mandisa Khumalo (South Africa) Wife of Consul General of South Africa in Shanghai and Ms. Yanling Li (China) Director of the P. R. Department, Shanghai Women's Federation

With my door-to-door partner Jericka Parker and the neighborhood we canvassed in Cedar Rapids. It was super cold for this soft California girl!

Making phone calls for Hillary in Cedar Rapids

Meeting Hillary back stage in Cedar Rapids, Iowa with other Hillary volunteers

Campaigning in Houston, Texas for Hillary. Roxie Gribble (on the right), Danyel Hosier (on the left) and I with Gavin Newsome (then Mayor of San Francisco, now California's Governor)

Roxie and I with Rob Reiner after he spoke at a Democratic dinner in Carlisle on behalf of Hillary and the amazing B&B we stayed at – for free!

Walking door to door in the rain with Roxie and her friend,
Andrea Post in Carlisle, Pennsylvania

With Hillary backstage in Harrisburg, Pennsylvania after she
spoke the night before the primary there

At the Democratic Convention in Denver 2008. John West engraving each of the "300 group" pins with the number based on the date their petition was received. Mine was #16.

The little green pin

Michele Thomas and I talking with attorney and CA delegate Gloria Allred

Gloria Allred gaged in order to get press attention. She asked and was denied the ability to speak to the entire California delegation.

271

*Being interviewed and asked about my 300 pin in the hotel lobby
by the Times of London and Politico*

With Gloria Allred at the Democratic Convention in Denver 2008

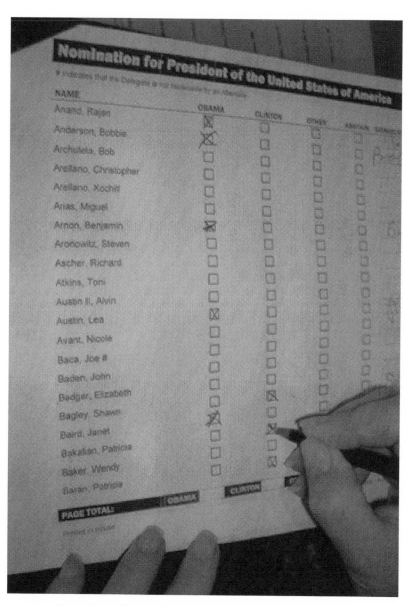

Voting for Hillary Clinton for President at the Democratic National Convention August 2008

CHAPTER 13

HEARTBREAK AND THE
CRASH OF '08

Not everything that is faced can be changed...
but nothing can be changed unless it is faced.

~ James Baldwin

Flashback: It's 1996, I am at a national CDC meeting in Atlanta. My brother Steve calls: "Dad has had a brain hemorrhage. He's not expected to live much longer." I'm on the first plane to Eugene, Oregon.

Six months earlier, Dad had reached out to me after we saw each other at Steve's wedding. We hadn't seen or talked to each other for fifteen years — since the "Black Easter" episode in 1981 — the time he accused me of manipulating and tricking him into coming to Easter dinner when Mom would be there as well. I wondered why he wanted to get together, but didn't ask. He had flown down to California from Oregon, and we met at a hotel near the San Francisco airport. I felt some anxiety, but also a growing confidence that I was a different person now, and this was an opportunity to prove it to myself. Dad

275

had always brought a hidden agenda or unexpected put-downs to our encounters. Now, after so many years, and given the trouble he was taking to fly down to see me, it was hard for me to imagine that he had something bad up his sleeve.

We spent four hours together, eating lunch and talking. "Dad, the girls have grown up to be beautiful, smart, capable young women. Here are a few pictures I brought to show you."

He averted his eyes and started talking about something else. He did not want to see them. I suspected it was because he was protecting himself from being hurt, but I wasn't sure, since we didn't talk directly about what he was feeling when I tried to show him the pictures.

Dad and I shared a liberal political philosophy and the understanding that we live on a fragile planet that is our responsibility to protect for future generations. We both loved to travel – experiencing different peoples and cultures. I told him that I thought we had a lot in common, and that if he got to know me, he would like me. I don't remember a response. To most of my comments and questions there simply was no response. He didn't have anything "bad" up his sleeve as he so often did in the past, but he was no more approachable than he had ever been; he just wasn't giving me grief. I was not, to my great relief, nervous or uncomfortable. I felt sympathy for him, for the way he had chosen to live his life and for the family he was missing out on.

And that was it. We didn't plan to speak or write again, and we never did. It didn't occur to me to ask why he wanted to see me on that occasion, after all those years; I didn't know if his purpose in coming had been satisfied, and I didn't care. Driving back to Santa Cruz, I had the feeling that something was finally finished between us. Alone in the car, I screamed to let out all the tension over the unspoken questions and answers left between us. Talking out loud, I told myself, "You did a great job. You weren't nervous and you stood up for yourself. You have changed." I didn't want any of it left inside of me. Happy about the person I had become, I was going home to John and the girls with a smile on my face, relieved of the lifelong burden of having him negatively affect me. I was proud of myself.

Now, half a year later, I was on my way to see my dad on his deathbed. Despite our virtually non-existent relationship, he was still my father, and I needed and wanted to be by his side as he passed. As it turned out, Steve called to tell me he died while I was changing planes in Salt Lake City. By the time I got to Dad's house, my two brothers were there — Steve with his wife Sheila, and Peter with his wife Stacy and their nine-month-old baby girl, Carli. Carli brought some joy to the somber, uncomfortable mood. Having a baby around always adds light and laughter. I was grateful for that.

Since I had never visited my dad's house in Eugene while he was alive, I felt like an intruder being there without him. I looked around in hopes of learning something about him. His house was much the same as the apartments he had lived in years prior, sparsely furnished with only the necessities. I didn't see family pictures or other objects that would make a house feel warm and cozy. The only thing that would tell a visitor that I existed was a small glass paperweight with my picture inside sitting on a bookshelf near his desk. I had made it when I was about eight years old and in the Brownie Scouts. That was the only thing of his I took with me when I left.

My two brothers and I were uneasy and stiff with each other as we talked about the things we had to take care of: notifying people, arranging for the memorial service, figuring out what to do with Dad's ashes. Peter was the oldest son, but he also had a rocky relationship with Dad. Steve, the only one who was at all close to Dad, took charge.

About forty people gathered at Musgrove Family Mortuary in Eugene, with quite a few there from the community. Dad always did well with strangers — or at least with people who required less intimacy. Many people approached me and said things like, "Your dad was such a kind and generous man." They said he had done a great deal for the community. And went on to say "I had no idea he had any children."

My cousin Judy heard the same kinds of things, and told me, "I was stunned, because he always appeared to me to be such a recluse. I remember once when he visited our home in Madison and he brought his photos to show us from his last trip. I think he had gone to China or someplace in Southeast Asia. There were absolutely no scenery shots. They were all photos of children. It was the strangest thing. And he told me about some of these kids. I just sat there thinking, "What about your own grandchildren?" I just didn't get it.

The service was short and rather cold compared to others I had attended. A few years later my cousin Judy told me "I remember you holding my hand with such force that it felt like all the sadness that you weren't able to express over the years was flowing through your tight grip on my hand." Judy and I rarely saw each other, but for some reason when we did, we always easily reconnected.

When Judy's mom, Dad's sister Ruth, got up to speak, it struck me how impersonally she spoke about her brother, her only sibling. It was apparent that they had not been close. She sounded like someone who had never met Dad and was delivering a canned funeral speech. There was no warmth in her words, and that actually made more sense to me than the strangers who were gushing about what a great guy he was.

Steve knew that Dad wanted to be cremated and have his ashes poured into the creek not far from his house in Eugene. So we set out to honor his wishes. Walking up a hillside outside of Eugene to a small creek surrounded by big old trees and moss-covered rocks, Peter, Steve and I slowly performed the ritual Dad had wanted. Afterward, I wandered alone up the hill, trying to hold back my tears until I was a safe distance away. I didn't want to cry in front of my brothers; I didn't want to share my sadness with them. That is the way we grew up. But I couldn't stop my tears, all the years of sadness flowing out of me — not sadness over losing my father, but the sadness of never having had one. All of my hopes that someday he might change were gone.

A few days later I found myself, with my two brothers, sitting across a large oval, polished wooden table from Dad's attorney, banker and accountant for the reading of his will. So many emotions had flowed through me in the last two days. I felt numb, disconnected, as if I were in a movie, as I stared at the three serious, older men on the other side of the table.

The attorney spoke. "Your father has set up two trusts to take care of your sister Susan and has left his piano to his niece Judy. He has left everything else — his house, car, belongings and financial investments to his youngest son Steven. Do you have any questions?"

Peter, Steve and I sat there silently listening. We asked no questions. I had expected this but was still stunned. We got up to leave and thanked the three men. They must have wondered what kind of zombies we were not to have reacted to the shock of that news. We didn't look at each other or say a word about it. We just got in our car and drove away.

I was bewildered. Would my father's bizarre treatment of me ever end? My dismay wasn't about the fact that he had written me out of his will; it was about what he'd thought of me, whether he even saw me as his daughter. I never knew who I was to him. At times he seemed to want to bond with me, but then something always stopped him from giving me his love. This final act of rejection was so complete; I felt a visceral cutting away of the man who had given me life.

There was no doubt in my mind, that if I were Steve I would have said, "This is it. This is where it all ends. This is where the sickness of our father stops. Whatever he left behind is going to be split among all his children, because that is the right thing to do." But that was me. It was not Steve.

Even as my feelings faded over time, I never approached either of my brothers to ask how they felt or what they thought about our father's will. I especially wonder what Peter went through, being the oldest son and just as discarded from dad's life as I had been. I didn't know much about their relationship, because we never talked about it. I wonder if Peter had letters from Dad like the ones I had. I wonder if Peter had his own version of my "Black Easter."

About a year after Dad died, John and I were sitting in the office of a friend, an attorney, talking about how Dad had disinherited Peter and me. We showed him some relevant documents and asked for his thoughts. He told us there was a strong case to be made that my dad had no legal right to leave us out of his will.

Much of my dad's wealth came from my grandfather Otto, whose will mandated that his estate be handed down to his living heirs. To cut Peter and me out, Dad had set up the two trusts for Susie with the stipulation that when she died the trust funds would go to the State of California — which obviously was not a living heir of my grandfather.

With this knowledge and some trepidation, I called my brothers with this information and asked each of them, "Would you agree to challenge our father's will?"

To my surprise, there was no argument or even a discussion; they both agreed. So we joined forces, hired an attorney and despite Dad's wishes, after much time and effort, I received my inheritance.

. . . .

Santa Cruz is a very expensive place to live, which makes it hard to save enough money for a down payment on a house. We had rented for years but with my inheritance we were now able to buy our first home, a beautiful custom-designed house overlooking the city of Santa Cruz.

I loved its openness and magnificent views. Almost every room had a view, but it was the master bedroom that sold us. On the second floor, it had wall-to-wall windows and a glass door leading out to a small balcony with a panoramic vista of both Monterey Bay and the Santa Cruz Mountains. A large kitchen was the center of the house physically and socially, with a dramatic ten-by-twelve-foot skylight shedding a glow over the gathering place for our family and friends.

The formal dining room was elevated a few steps and opened onto the living room, which had a beautiful marble-faced fireplace and a wall of windows expanding our vista all the way to the Bay. From the family room, two sliding glass doors led to the main deck, which we used for family meals and business meetings. John and I each had an office. Being able to use our home for both family and business gatherings made it the perfect house for us.

Mom was as thrilled for us as we were. She was stunned by her ex-husband's will and felt terrible that his behavior had extended beyond her into the lives of her children. I guess she'd hoped that by divorcing him she could protect us from the pain she experienced with him.

Successfully contesting his will and being able to purchase our own home felt like healing for her as well as for me and John. This was 1997, Kelly was in her last year at San Francisco State. Sara was just starting the University of California Santa Cruz and living on campus, and Lesha was at home, finishing high school. John was fully engaged in the projects of his land-use business, and I still worked in San Francisco during the week at my CDC job. John and I were both feeling a sense of accomplishment and satisfaction in our respective careers.

Moving out of Mom's rustic old country house into our new, modern, expansive house in town was thrilling. I felt a sense of security that had been missing from living all of our lives as renters or as guests of family members giving us a helping hand. This was our place and no one could tell us what color to paint the walls or where to hide the Christmas presents. I felt on solid footing. No one could evict us, or so I thought.

....

Over the twelve years that we owned our home we saw its value more than double. We had no idea what was causing such a crazy increase, but as the years passed, it helped us pull some money out when our finances were strained. Then the crash of '08 caught up to us.

Life got steadily more challenging. At first John and I were both working and bringing in steady incomes; our financial roller-coaster ride was on the upswing. Then, three years into owning our home, John closed his land-use business and started working in China, which ended up being a financial drain.

The China projects all looked good on paper—but no matter what country, money is key to launching a business venture. John's potential investors were backing out of their agreements. Some funds materialized and investments were made, but more money was needed.

All of this was happening at the same time as the Wall Street and housing crash that eventually imploded in September of 2008. Unfortunately, the crash abruptly choked off funding sources and caused John's businesses to slow down and eventually to close after years of hard work and unfulfilled plans. John was deeply disappointed.

He had fallen in love with the Chinese people and their country, and had been warmly welcomed into their homes and offices. His Chinese associates recognized and appreciated his knack for bringing people together to solve problems and get things done. Even though his efforts were not rewarded monetarily in the end, working in China taught him a lot and gave him lifelong friends. He has often said, "China was the best business experience I have ever had. I got more back than I put in."

Meanwhile, I had been reorganized out of my job at the CDC, and three years later my consulting business dried up when clients no longer had the money to hire me. Both of our businesses were in trouble, and jobs in our fields were nonexistent. To add to the outflow of funds during this time, we happily put Kelly and Sara through college, helped pay for their beautiful weddings within three years of each other, and helped Lesha financially when she was between jobs. Now our financial roller coaster was starting to nosedive.

Our personal decline reflected what was happening all over the country. In the years between 2006 and 2008 the economy was tanking. Jobs were disappearing in historic numbers. Ironically, it was also the peak of the real estate bubble, so the value of our house was climbing uphill rapidly. It was the one source of cash we could turn to until we were generating income again. Anyone with a mortgaged house was lucky enough to take advantage of the inflated real estate market, which eventually proved to be a thin bandage on a bleeding artery.

In September of 2008, a huge shockwave hit the world with the collapse of Lehman Brothers. It was the first domino to fall in an extended financial crisis the world had not seen since the Great Depression, and we were in the direct path of those falling dominoes. With the economy in a full-scale decline, the real estate bubble burst and the value of our home began a steady decline. Borrowing against the equity led to a mortgage that outweighed the value of our house. Our loss of income made it impossible to keep up the payments.

To get by, John and I took any jobs we could find just to keep food on the table and the lights on. I worked at Costco as a food demonstrator. Going into it without dread or resentment, I said "I love talking with people, this will be a fun experience."

Most of the people who worked with me were women like me who desperately counted on their jobs to get by. We were paid just above minimum wage. Our supervisor was a jerk who astounded me every time he repeatedly declared, "I hate all women." For some reason, he enjoyed sharing horror stories of his ex-wife with me, who, I could only assume, triggered his hatred of "her kind." Why did he think I was interested? It got so bad that, as he continued his ranting day after day, I found it impossible to continue working there.

I was grateful when a friend hired me for a two-month contract with the Department of Government and Community Relations at the University of California Santa Cruz. It was only for two months, but at least it was more up my alley. My job was to reach out to faculty, staff, students, alumni community leaders, business and legislative leaders, inviting them to a Forum on the Budget and Public Higher Education.

Through a friend, John and I also got jobs making survey calls for a few months for a local labor union in San Jose, a forty-minute drive over the Santa Cruz Mountains. We both continued looking for full-time work but jobs were nowhere to be found for people in their 60s, no matter how hard we looked. Later I would read, that during this time – and maybe even now, the odds of someone in their 60's finding a full time job was about 18%. I could testify to those terrible odds.

Sadly, despite all our efforts, the time came when we couldn't hold on any longer. Reluctantly, we filed for bankruptcy and started the process to short-sell our beautiful home.

Looking back, I realize we were luckier than most. At our ages, we were past the expense of raising young children and had already paid for college and weddings. John was receiving Social Security and I was about two years away from getting mine. We cut way back on expenses, spending our small monthly income only on the basics: food, utilities, gas and car insurance. Luckily we didn't have a car payment or much need for new clothes. We didn't go to movies or out to eat. Thank God we were healthy, because we both went without health insurance until we turned 65 and became eligible for Medicare.

In the midst of this very stressful time I often went to see my mom. Since I was the organized one between the two of us, Mom would enlist my help in getting her many projects and papers in order. She was brilliant and creative and always had several irons in the fire, but as a product of the Great Depression she was accustomed to keeping everything — as she said, "just in case I need it someday."

As she got older and began feeling overwhelmed by her possessions, she needed me more and more to help her clean out and organize all 80 years' worth of her life.

"Mom, how many empty jars or scraps of wrapping paper do you really need?" I asked, as we laughed together.

We went through stacks and stacks of papers. I threw away as much as she would let me, in some cases tossing things when she wasn't looking, knowing she'd never miss them. At times ambivalent about needing my assistance, Mom wanted to feel she was capable and could manage things herself. Many times as I was in the middle of helping her she would change her mind and say, "I want to do that myself."

Driving to Mom's on a beautiful sunny Santa Cruz summer afternoon in July of 2009, the redwood boughs looked especially deep green against a cloudless blue sky. We had plans for some serious purging, aiming to tackle her office desk and shelves, which were piled high with books and papers, much of which she didn't need or want. But on that day Mom and I sat barefoot, curled up on her massive, very cushy orange sofa. Instead of organizing and throwing things out, we talked for hours.

I told her about the financial problems John and I were dealing with and how the "Crash of '08" was hitting us hard. "Mom," I said, "I'm not the person I was just six months ago. John and I are going through rough times financially, but we are closer in spite of it all. He is finally really listening to me. We're a team. I've taken charge of our finances, as meager as they are, which I'm better at handling than I was before — or than John ever has been."

To my amazement, in the midst of all the extreme stress and uncertainty, I was feeling strong both within myself and in my marriage. I was changing, and Mom shared in the pleasure of the changes she saw in me.

When I told her I wanted to write a book about my political activism, her eyes lit up and she clapped with excitement. She was happy for me, and also shared a little about the book she planned to write about her own life.

Five days later I headed back to Mom's once again for a bout of cleaning, determined to be productive this time. I was running late, so I called ahead. No answer, so I left a message: "Mom, I'll be there soon, just have to make one stop."

Finally arriving at her house, I knocked. She didn't come to the door. I knocked again but no answer. I figured she'd left her hearing aids out and couldn't hear me knocking. This had happened many times before, so I thought nothing of it. Letting myself in, I called out over and over again "Mom, where are you?" as I wandered through her house.

Then my heart stopped. There she was lying on the floor next to her bed, fully dressed in her gardening clothes. Her mouth was open with her swollen tongue hanging out. She was still breathing. In shock, I irrationally told myself she was just in a deep sleep and felt instantly relieved.

Nudging her, I said, "Mom, wake up," over and over and louder and louder, as fear started to overtake my whole body. I suddenly realized I was the only one there, and I needed to do something. In my panic, I didn't even think to call 911; instead I called John. "Oh god! Babe, I found Mom on the floor unconscious. I can't wake her up. I'm scared. What do I do?"

I was not thinking clearly. While John was on his way over, I called the EMTs, who talked me through what to do before they got there. John arrived with our youngest daughter, Lesha, who temporarily had moved back home. We watched as Mom — still unconscious — was being put into the ambulance. Tears flowing down my face, I got into the car with John, and we followed in silence.

Mom was in her mid-80s. Over the past two years, she had been in and out of the hospital three or four of times, but always recovered from the minor strokes that put her there. I fully expected her to do the same this time. When we arrived at the hospital, we learned that the emergency crew had brought her back from the brink of death during her ambulance ride. They didn't know that it was Mom's wish not to have extraordinary measures taken to save her life. Mom had given me a copy of her DNR (Do Not Resuscitate), but in the chaos of the moment it never crossed my mind.

Now, in the emergency room, she was being kept alive by machines. The three of us sat there for what seemed like forever, waiting for test results. Finally, the doctor came out. "I'm very sorry to tell you that your mother has had a massive brain aneurysm. She will not recover."

I insisted on seeing the brain scan. I wanted to see for myself. I needed proof. I was in a state of shock and disbelief. Just a few days ago she was fine, and now she was gone. The doctor said her brain had died instantly, but her pacemaker was keeping her alive.

It all seemed like a bad dream as John and I called our other daughters, Sara and Kelly, and my brothers. Kelly and her husband, Damian, lived in San Diego; my brother Steve and his new wife Tish in New Hampshire. They would get on the next plane. Peter lived a few hours' drive away in Napa and would come as soon as he could. Sara and her husband, Craig, lived closer, in San Jose, and could come immediately, so we waited until they arrived.

Standing around Mom, holding each other up as tears flowed with our words of loving farewell to our family matriarch, we gave the doctor the okay to turn off her pacemaker. I wish we hadn't been forced into that responsibility; I would have preferred that she be allowed to go naturally, as her body was trying to do. I'm grateful for modern medicine and the additional years of Mom's life it gave us with her — but in the end, medical intervention intruded on the peaceful flow of living and dying.

The following days, as the family gathered, were a blur. I had known intellectually that Mom would be gone someday, but emotionally I was not ready. She had said over and over again that she was going to be around for another ten years, and, damn it, I believed her. I fell into an incredibly deep sadness.

I don't believe she had a conscious knowledge of her impending death, because she wouldn't have hesitated to share that information with me, but looking back I could see that she had been getting ready to go. She always followed her intuitive urgings with complete trust; chalking it up to the Universe working. She'd been on a trip to India on a spiritual quest just nine months earlier. And many of her close friends told me they had wonderful intimate conversations with her just days before.

She may have been ready subconsciously, but I wasn't ready on any level. I still miss her every day.

The view of the Monterey Bay from our beautiful house on the hill custom designed by a local architect

My mom at her 80th birthday party with me and my daughters.
From left to right: Sara, Lesha and Kelly on the deck of our house

CHAPTER 14

NEW BEGINNINGS

Every decision you make is not a decision about what to do,
it is a decision about who you are.
~ Neale Donald Walsch, Author

Mom's home and her property were like a diary of her life after her divorce from Dad. As the saying goes, "If walls could talk …." Hers could write at least a few books. They would be page-turners with one unusual character after another entering the plot. Her evolving life was like a living plant that grew in the wild and evolved from something simple and mundane to a complex organism.

In 1968, Mom was new to Santa Cruz and looking for a home of her own — her first after her divorce. The first property she looked at evoked love at first sight, and she never looked further. It sits in the hills a mile above the small town of Soquel (pronounced so-Kel), just south of Santa Cruz, on a winding narrow road fringed by forests of redwood trees, prolific ferns, mushrooms, moss and wild flowers.

I learned from Mom's tapes what it was like for her when she found her new home.

I was standing down near the creek on the property, and said, 'Do you mean people own this?!' It was just like a beautiful Ansel Adams picture. So it bought me. I did not buy it. I sold my house in Palo Alto for $55,000 and bought my house in Soquel for $31,000. At that time I was so much involved in my hippy life that I don't know what I thought. I just know that this house chose me. And I had such strong feelings about it that I just went ahead and blindly bought it. And ever since it has been my learning place.

The house was on Glen Haven Road, on a two-and-a-half-acre wooded lot with a creek running through it. It had a large living room with a fireplace, a big country kitchen with a wood-burning stove, three bedrooms and two bathrooms. It was old and rundown with no central heating. There was a huge three-sided shack on the property that was filled to the ceiling with junk the previous owner had left, and a small run-down cabin that had served as a storage unit over the years. Under Mom's ownership, Glen Haven grew over time to become a three-family structure with rental income supporting her for many years. The home's evolution began shortly after she acquired it.

She described in her tapes how, one beautiful spring day, driving back from Santa Cruz on the winding two lane road up to her house she stopped to pick up a couple of hitchhikers. They were two young men, UC-Santa Cruz students, who were working at the campus's Alan Chadwick Garden, an internationally known site for training, teaching and research in organic horticulture and agriculture.

She engaged them in conversation about their work. She was fascinated by their knowledge and gardening endeavors, and asked if they would like to see her garden. There was a lot she needed to do to it and was eager to hear what they thought.

I can imagine her proudly walking her property like a peacock, plumage fanned out for all to see, giving them the grand tour of her home and garden. She could tell they were in awe, and that the wheels were turning in their heads. Inviting them in for iced tea, she proposed, without much thought, that if they wanted to clean out the old cabin down the hill they could live in it in exchange for developing her garden. They accepted, and before she knew it, her property had become an extension of the Chadwick Gardens.

Mom loved to garden and the idea of having help from a couple of innovative, non-commercial gardeners was very exciting. The cabin became a habitable cottage, and an area of her property became a prolific vegetable and flower garden.

After a few weeks of getting the run-down cabin ready for occupancy and the gardening underway, one of the young men came to Mom with a proposal. He had a friend coming up from Southern California for summer school and she was looking for a quiet place to stay. Would Mom consider renting a room in her house? This was a match made in the magic of Glen Haven. Mom thought at the time:

> It never occurred to me what I was going to do with the house, so I said "sure." So she came and was my first renter and my garden was established by these wonderful students.

This was the first of many renters who would come and go over the almost forty years Mom lived on Glen Haven Road. She went on to say:

> After a while I got tired of living in the house with someone I didn't know too well; I wanted my privacy, so I came down here in the basement.

The house had a laundry area and workshop in the basement, which she creatively transformed into a tiny Hobbit-like kitchen area, a bathroom with a claw-foot bathtub, and a nook for reading, sleeping and watching TV. She was not one to hire designers, architects, construction crews or the like. She was the designer, and she engaged people who loved to jump into her projects with her.

> *I hired a man to cover the roots of the redwood trees and build a bathroom and my bedroom. One of the kids at the Free School built the rest out of recycled material. I did get a friend who was a contractor who did the framing.*

The Free School that Mom mentioned was an amazing alternative school (before there were alternative schools) that she was instrumental in establishing; and where she was one of its teachers. She held "class" at her house for the middle-school-age children whose parents wanted something outside the public school system. This was the early '70s, when the "establishment" was being challenged on every level and Mom was no longer afraid to question authority.

She lived in her basement studio for about five years before she met a Scottish carpenter, with whom she embarked on her next building adventure. He told her he had always wanted to build a house. She thought, "I always wanted to build a house too" — and so her next project was launched — a larger home for herself, about seventy-five feet down the sloped property from the original house.

Hearing my mom's recorded recollections about this part of her life, I thought, "Oh, this is so Mom! And typical of what I love about her."

> *"Let's do it." It was one of those things you just jump in and you never really think through, and I realized I must*

have been a builder in a past life, because for one thing it comes very easy to me to know how to do things. At that time I had moved from my renovated space under the main house into the cabin vacated by my gardeners. The cabin had cold running water and didn't have a bathroom. I had a camper with a bathroom in it I parked right outside the door, and showered at the spa I belonged to. The cabin had a wood-burning stove and felt so cozy.

I could completely concentrate on this building job. It was wonderful. I designed it. It was a part of me that just blossomed. One of my favorite stories was all of a sudden this big, big dog appears, and I thought it must be a neighbor's dog. He would come every day and lay down watching us build this house. One day he brought a friend (another dog) along. The friend got bored and wandered off, but he stayed. I think he was a reincarnated builder who just loved building too.

At that time there was an acre next door I could have bought for $7,000, but I didn't because I had too much land to take care of. The lot was sold to a contractor who was building a house, and here I was building a house illegally over here. We knew we were illegal. That was when I planted the cedar trees to try and hide what we were doing.

Then when we had the foundation laid, the man who was doing the framing for the foundation told me he was going to be finished by a certain time so I could order the cement truck to come. When the cement truck came he wasn't finished, so rather than have to pay for the cement truck to go away and come back again, which would have cost a lot more (I was on a tight budget), the cement guy very obligingly started at one end while the frame guy was working as fast *as he could at the other end. Unfortunately, when the cement guy got to the lower part, the framing wasn't quite done so well, so we had a very wide foundation there—which ended up saving the house from damage in the 1989 earthquake!*

I learned how to build a house from this Scottish carpenter. Every morning we had this codebook from the county and if we had any questions we would call the county and get the answers. We just learned how to build a house and it was so much fun. Everything that went into the house, except the framework, was recycled — including the windows up along the top. They are kitchen cabinet windows, which open up to let air in. It was so much fun, but by the time it was ready to move into I didn't want to leave the cabin, because with the cabin I had this wonderful sense of the difference between housing and shelter. The cabin was shelter. It was so elementary — just having that kind of simplicity — not to have the kind of house where you have all kinds of space so you can invite people in. It was an experience of what shelter means to people on the desert or wherever. But of course I did move into the new house.

She lived in this new structure for about ten years, renting the main house to supplement her income to a variety of people, including John and me and the kids for a couple of years. Then one morning she woke up to a knock on her door. It was an inspector from the County Building Department. He was polite but insistent when he said, "This building is illegal and has to come down or be reduced in size. You have three months to make it right." Busted! She hadn't gone through the lengthy and expensive process of applying for permits. Knowing that she was taking a chance, she had hoped to slide under the radar.

My mom and my husband had a wonderfully atypical in-law relationship and together they schemed about how to deal with her criminal status. John, who at the time was immersed in his land-use consulting business, came up with an idea.

"Why not build an addition connecting the two houses and make it one big single-family home? That would make it legal."

And of course, that's what she did, excited to have another building project to work on. When it was finished she lived in the middle unit we called "the connecting room" and rented out the top and bottom living spaces even though it wasn't legal to have rentals.

The addition was a beautiful, self-contained unit with big windows looking out onto her lush, green landscape. The living room had a high-pitched ceiling with glass-paned cabinet doors for windows like the ones she had put in the lower house. The grounds weren't professionally groomed; she used the natural elements and flow of the land creatively. Everywhere you walked were fruit trees she'd planted, a circle of tall bamboo to sit inside and meditate, or a koi pond to relax beside.

While this worked wonderfully for her, it proved to be a major challenge when it came time for us to liquidate her estate. From top to bottom the house just kept going on and on, with hallways and doors and stairs leading from one area to another. Over time she blocked off the access ways between the connecting room and her tenants' spaces to accommodate their privacy. Now Mom was gone, and those walls and doors would have to be de-constructed so we could sell her house as a legal single-family dwelling.

After mom's funeral service and before my brothers returned to their out-of-town and out-of-state homes, we walked together through the whole property. My brothers were familiar with Mom's quirky house but I wanted them to see firsthand the extent of what John and I were going to have to deal with. I hoped to elicit some recognition, understanding and support from them. Even though I was the executor of her estate and the only sibling living in the area, I somehow imagined that my brothers and I were in this together as a family and that they would be there to help me — even from a distance. That was a mistake and not at all what happened.

I had alerted mom's tenants that we would be selling her property as soon as possible so they would have to move. The walk-through after mom's funeral was my first glimpse at the renters' units. In the upper unit, boxes were stacked waist-high lining the hallway, making it necessary to turn sideways to get down to the bedrooms. Shelves were stuffed with junk and boxes, hiding the fireplace from view. The dining room was crammed with desks and filing cabinets, stacked with more junk and more boxes. This would all be gone when they moved out, but my biggest concern was that both units overpowered us with the smell of cat urine. It made me want to cry.

As we headed to the lower unit, I found myself repeatedly asking, "How do people live like this?" They paid their rent on time, so Mom had left them alone, not paying any attention to the condition of their place. As far as I could tell, they had never cleaned anything. The toilet was stained beyond redemption, and the stench was nauseating. The kitchen sink was stained and encrusted with dried food.

The help and support I was hoping for from my brothers was not forthcoming. I gave Steve the benefit of the doubt because he lived across the country, but Peter only lived a few hours away. He did come for a couple of days to help us go through the mounds of Mom's stuff — a drop in the bucket of all that had to be done.

To rub salt in the wound, I learned that my brothers went on a vacation together following Mom's funeral. I remember thinking that I would have loved a call from them just to see how I was doing. But there was no feeling of family. We were separate people who knew each other simply by chance of birth. I felt a complete lack of support, even from afar, for what John and I were going through. But, so typical of me, in the midst of my extreme sadness at the loss of our mother and my brother's lack of help or any understanding for what we had to deal with, I didn't speak up. I didn't tell them how overwhelmed John and I felt by the need to take care of our mother's affairs on top of everything else we were going through with our bankruptcy and short sale of our own home. This was yet another manifestation of the great silence that was so deeply ingrained in all the members of my birth family.

So it was left to John and me to transform this unusual triplex into a legally qualified single-family home. With little cash in my mom's accounts to cover repairs and enhancements to make the house attractive to buyers, the rental income was sorely needed. But our Catch-22 was that the renters had to go before we could fix it up and show it. Thankfully, they took all their belongings with them when they moved out, but there was so much more of Mom's years and years of accumulation to deal with.

There's no cliché more obnoxious or more undeniable than "Life goes on." For me as the executor of Mom's estate, that cliché was kicking my ass when all I wanted was to hide under the covers. Every day I got up and made my long list of to-dos for the job of allocating and relocating what my mom had left behind.

"How about we set a match to it all and walk away." I half kiddingly said to John.

In the weeks and months to follow, John and I vowed not to leave a similar mess behind for our own kids to deal with.

We spent nine months giving away food, clothes and furniture, and dealing with water leaks, propane tanks, toilets and two under-maintained septic tanks. There were 4,500 square feet of interior walls to paint, a huge shed still filled with junk that had to be removed, and fifteen filing cabinets crammed with papers to review, sort, toss or keep. We filled the biggest dumpster I'd ever seen — three times!

Our wonderful friends not only provided emotional support, but also hauled away several carloads of items to be donated. Mom's cybernetic colleagues, Becky Hibit and Phillip Guddemi, spent over a week graciously sorting through over three thousand books and hundreds of audio and video tapes, packing up at least fifty boxes and arranging for her collection to be donated to the Independent Media Center at the University of Champagne in Illinois.

She had some essential cybernetics books that were real collectors' items, because of her long history and friendship with great thinkers in the discipline like — Gregory Bateson and Heinz Von Foerster, as well as her many academic friends in Santa Cruz. I had no idea where to start and was grateful for this help and proud that the school named the donation the "Barbara Vogl Cybernetics Collection and Archive" in her honor.

My cousin Nancy was there to help me go through Mom's kitchen and pantry. "Nancy," I'd say, "look at this. I found some more popcorn way back here in her pantry." We laughed hysterically every time we found more of the popcorn Mom had stashed in every possible corner of her very small kitchen. "I think she forgot she had it and just kept buying more — probably because it was on sale." A member of the "waste-not-want-not" generation, Mom also liked to freeze food. Some we found in her freezer had been there so long it was no longer recognizable.

Sara and Lesha spent many days going through the books and papers hidden in a myriad of nooks and crannies. They tackled her bathroom, with drawers full of seriously expired medicines and a fascinating collection of trinkets and doodads. We were all so tired and our emotions so frayed that it was very easy to break out in moments of laughter, mostly at Mom's expense. Sorry, Mom. The lighter moments kept us going through it all.

The people who had been a part of Glen Haven over the years were never just run-of-the-mill types. One morning, while John and I were busy working around her property, a letter came from the County of Santa Cruz Code Compliance Investigator saying that a complaint had been made about someone living in the "space capsule" next to the fence close to the neighbor's property.

Yes, there was a space capsule of sorts once occupied by a couple of mad-scientist friends of Mom's. They had built a lab and needed somewhere to put it with their Dr. Frankenstein-like equipment. I had no idea what kind of experiments they did in there, but Mom let them put the lab on her property and we dubbed it the "space capsule." Her friends never lived in it, but worked in it during the day. After a few years they moved their equipment out, and Mom then used it for storage for the next fifteen years. It was ridiculous that someone would complain about people living in it, especially so long after the "mad" scientists were gone.

But the code officer refused to believe that the structure was a storage shed. "You need to either tear it down or pay a $1,500 permit fee." Those were our options.

This unreasonable run-in with the powers-that-be was just the beginning of a series of unexpected, baffling barriers to getting the house ready to sell. It got crazy enough to be funny, but it would be a hell of a long time before we could laugh about it. So to keep from getting fined we tore the lab down. It was about fifteen feet square with a few steps up to the door, a small window on each side, a wooden floor covered with a thin utilitarian carpet, and a rounded roof. It took three people four days to dismantle the structure, which was so sturdily built it could have withstood re-entry from space. Most of the remains were discarded in the dumpster we rented, but some weren't and that led to the next episode of panic.

One morning the phone jarred me awake. "Your mother's house is on fire." That is what I heard from our panicked realtor. My stomach tightened in shock and disbelief.

John and I bolted out of bed, throwing on whatever clothes we could find as fast as we could and raced to the house, all the way imagining flames shooting up into the surrounding trees. Lights of fire trucks greeted us, but to our immense relief we found that the people who dismantled the space capsule were simply burning the remaining wood scraps in a small controlled fire. Our realtor, who enjoyed listening to the fire department radio scanner, had misunderstood a report naming the Glen Haven address and immediately spread the word, which became a "house on fire" by the time it was relayed to us.

At the same time all of these things were happening, we had naively entered into a regrettable relationship with mom's handy person. Mom had hired Joanne to keep up the garden and do odd jobs around the house. Heaven knows Mom needed the help. She was in her mid-70s at the time, still involved in a dozen different projects and political groups, and became easily short of breath from emphysema caused by years of smoking. With her huge house and two and a half acres, a willing pair of helping hands was a godsend.

Joanne had been living in her van with her partner, Susan, somewhere in the vicinity. Joanne had kicked a meth habit and was evading arrest for skipping out on a community service sentence. Glen Haven was just that for her — a haven where she could work outdoors, make some money and feel appreciated and respected. She worked for Mom for about ten years, during which time they became good friends. John and I needed help getting the property ready to sell, and Joanne was conveniently available. We let her park her van in Mom's driveway, and paid her for the work she did.

Just before Thanksgiving, as the cold winter rainy season was setting in, I asked them, "Would you two like to temporarily move into mom's middle unit? I know that you have some health problems, and staying out in your van is probably making them worse."

We would have them watching out for the property and they could come in from the cold. It seemed like a win-win arrangement. They agreed and spent the winter months warm and cozy inside.

Then as the weather cleared in early spring, the indoor refurbishing reached a point where we needed Joanne and Susan to move out in order to finish it. We asked them to move back out to their van in the driveway, and told them we would need the van moved off the property shortly, when we started showing the house.

This was 2010, just after the crash of '08. After an agonizingly slow effort at marketing the house, it felt like a miracle when we closed escrow with a buyer. But we hadn't been able to get Joanne and Susan to vacate the premises yet, and though the new owners were wonderful people, they understandably did not want to have these two women living in their driveway. That's when things started getting dicey.

"We can't move because our van isn't running. We're waiting for parts."

This was a big red flag. I was getting nervous that we were going to have a problem. Their van didn't go anywhere, but in a gesture of compliance, they made the decision to move into a hotel. Along with the new owners, John and I met with them at their hotel, asking them to get the van off the property within the week.

"We will leave if you pay for our hotel bill," Joanne replied, "and to have our van towed to where we want it."

I was astonished, and so angry I couldn't see straight. All I could say was "Joanne, how could you do this after all my mom did for you?" She said nothing. I was afraid to say any more for fear of what might come out of my mouth. This, of course, was extortion, but to expedite their exit we reluctantly agreed. James, the new owner, was an attorney so he, on the spot, wrote up an agreement that we all signed. My insides were on fire with indignation. Joanne's timing was impeccable. We were emotionally and financially against the wall. I felt abused and helpless. Then things got worse.

The day before the van was to be removed, we got a call from the California Rural Assistance League. Joanne had sought legal counsel and was backing out of the agreement she had signed at the hotel.

She told us, "This is not valid because it had been signed under duress." Which it had not.

She and Susan had filed papers demanding to stay, not in their van on the property — but in the house — for an additional thirty days. The Sheriff was going to force the new owners to let them move back into the home they had just purchased. Somehow Joanne was able to make it appear as though she and Susan were legal renters and couldn't be evicted with less than a thirty-day notice. The California Rural Assistance League was demanding that we pay Joanne and Susan $1,500 in exchange for dropping the action. Extortion again!

John and I felt responsible for this mess, and horrible about the fallout for the new owners, so of course we shared the cost. I was beyond furious — but as is so often the case, fighting the legal battle would have cost us more than capitulating to Joanne and Susan's demands. The new owners, James and Maranda, were amazing through all of it. They are special people. The story of how they came to buy Glen Haven is a window into their character and explains how they could patiently wade through the ordeal Joanne and Susan perpetrated on us.

....

The real estate market was at an all-time low. "Sluggish" would have been an optimistic description. Like everyone else trying to sell a house during that time, we slowly and reluctantly began lowering our asking price. Mom's reverse mortgage required that her property be sold within a year of her death to prevent foreclosure and we were running out of time. My portion of the proceeds, earmarked for John and me to restart our lives, was a seriously shrinking lifeline.

Every day we would give each other our silent high sign of crossed fingers, hoping for some action, but we were not getting any bites. Then one morning, as I got my coffee and went to my computer, there it was — an email from James. He and Maranda, responding to our real-estate listing, were almost begging us to let them buy Mom's house. James sent a long letter with pictures of his family: Maranda, their four-year-old daughter, and his mother-in-law.

They were living in San Francisco and didn't want to raise their daughter in the city. Maranda's mother lived in cold upstate New York, and they wanted to bring her out to the warm West Coast. The layout of Mom's place would enable them to have her close while enjoying their own separate living areas. They were passionate about organic gardening, art, meditating, and cooking, as well as working from home in a peaceful setting. They thought Mom's place was ideal on all counts.

Looking in different parts of the county, they found themselves on Glen Haven Road and saw the for-sale sign in front of Mom's place. James's letter said that when they first walked around the property they felt "an energy":

*We found your place so irresistible we never want to leave!
Each visit to the Glen Haven home (which we have nick-
named the Heaven house) confirmed that we would be in a
perpetual state of bliss living there. There is a powerful energy force that encapsulates every element of this place. The
flow of the home and how each floor accesses to a beautiful
garden and also has big windows to view the garden even
when the weather is bad. Each space inside and outside has
its own inviting personality, which shows the zest for life
that Barbara put into the property. The home definitely is
not pretty from the street but once inside has an energy that
says something about its owner's vitality... 'My existence on
earth will be an inspiration to those who can look beyond
the facade we all have and learn to fully value the heart of
a person.' Barbara has created a wonderful haven (heaven)
which we are asking you to let us obtain.*

All I could say was, "Oh my god! They are perfect. I can't believe
this!" I started sobbing. A real mess, I ran downstairs to tell John —
with both tears and a huge smile on my face. I just kept saying over
and over, "This is a miracle, this is a miracle."

I know Mom sent this family to her property. Over the years,
she had said many times that she felt she had been guided to buy Glen
Haven and now she was helping the next owners of the property find
it. And she was helping us. The Universe was working.

Initially incredulous, John and I nevertheless couldn't contain a
hopeful excitement. Even though we had an offer in hand, we feared
the worst. Mom had not kept up with the maintenance of her property, and we knew the inspection would uncover problems that weren't
readily apparent. We hoped they wouldn't be deal-breakers.

A few days later we met James, Maranda and their daughter Kayleigh. It was a beautiful, sunny seventy-five-degree day. We had lunch on the patio above Mom's koi pond. Kayleigh was enthralled with the fish.

Maranda explained to us, as James nodded his head in agreement, "Kayleigh is our only child and we want her to grow up around the influence of strong, independent, creative women. We feel that energy here on your mom's property. It's the energy she instilled in Glen Haven. Can you tell us a little about your mom and her life?"

Getting such warm and friendly feelings from both of them, John and I were more than happy to share a few stories about Mom and the strong, creative and caring person she was. This was more than a real estate deal. It was a personal connection with Mom as the link between us.

After they received the inspection reports they emailed us. "We have some reservations about the costs of necessary repairs and want you to know we are continuing to look at other properties."

Yikes!! This news made John and I very concerned.

We had no other interested parties. Panic set in. When they asked for a price reduction we could see the meager equity left for us shrinking still further. But we knew that the reduction would be fair to them, and agreed to absorb a good portion of the repair costs.

During these negotiations we spent every day wading through room after room of Mom's house. Then John and I would return home — not to relax, but to continue cleaning out our own house — all forty years of our stuff — getting ready for our own move, to a yet-to-be-established location on a yet-to-be-established date.

The hurricane of losing our home, packing it up at the same time we were cleaning out Mom's property and trying to sell it, was emotionally and physically exhausting. We were just hanging on from day to day. A friend down the street told us we would always have a place to stay at his house. This stood out in stark contrast to my brothers, who never asked how we were doing or offered any help. Despite the fact that I was keeping meticulous track of expenses and sent them an accounting every month, they had endless questions about the money I had to spend to get mom's house ready to sell. I resented their questions, which seemed to insinuate some sort of malfeasance on my part. Both of them went back to their lives as if nothing had happened with no apparent consciousness of what we were going through.

I had always thought John and I had a close relationship with Peter. He had gone to Canada with us; he lived with us at two different times — before we were married and then after, when he was working at our restaurant. So I never, ever expected what happened about three months after Mom died.

Peter emailed me to say that he wanted to talk. The questions I had been getting from him had an undercurrent of something strained that he wasn't saying. I was happy that he was going to get it out on the table so we could clear the air. We scheduled a phone call, but when the time came, all he said was he had written us an email that he wanted us to read before we talked.

He said calmly, "After you read it, call me and we can talk." "Great," I said, "I am so glad you are telling us about your concerns." We hung up and read the email.

The email literally turned my stomach. Peter was accusing John and me of influencing and manipulating Mom in her later years to our advantage — when, in fact, Mom was totally responsible for her own life. I was shocked! John and I were the only family nearby to help her when she needed it, and now we were being wrongly accused. Not to quit there, Peter also was accusing John of bilking family members years ago in some of his business ventures. He referred to this as the "elephant in the room," as though everyone was aware of John's unconscionable activities yet lacked the guts to confront him. Taking the high ground, Peter was bravely doing the job for everyone concerned — and a few who weren't. He copied the email to all of the people he thought had been cheated by us, and to others who had nothing to do with anything he was talking about, including our cousins and their husbands, *and* to our three daughters and two sons-in-law.

Stunned doesn't begin to cover the way I felt. I had been at Peter's house just a few weeks before he sent his email. He had not mentioned a thing; everything seemed just fine between us. Now he was adopting the role of the good guy sacrificing, himself to make everything right for others. He had no clue what John's business dealings entailed. He was combining John's business dealings with the way I was handling our mother's estate before and after she died, when the two things had nothing to do with each other. And he was wrong on both counts.

We didn't accept any of Peter's analysis. However, *what* he was saying was secondary to *how* he had chosen to broadcast it. He spread his hostile misguided grievances to our daughters and extended family without bothering to talk to us first.

"John, he is saying things that aren't true. The kids have nothing to do with this. Why is he involving them? What is he trying to do?" I rambled on, trying to get some clarity,

In his email Peter also expressed concern for our "financial predicament" while at the same time doing nothing to help, emotionally undermining our ability to cope with it.

As always, John and I were there for each other, and somehow weathered this storm together. My brothers and I are a product of the parents we had, the times we grew up in and what we came into this world with. Interpreting Peter's behavior through the lens of our dysfunctional birth family history helped me to work through my hurt, and eventually move on. He has not to this day reached out and apologized, but I have no bad feelings for him. I have just chosen not to have him in my life.

....

John and I had lived in our beautiful home for twelve years. Our three daughters were already grown and on their own, we had talked off and on about downsizing: selling our 2,800-square-foot home and finding something smaller and less expensive, maybe even moving out of the area even though I felt a need to be close by in case Mom needed me. But emotionally, thinking about downsizing was worlds away from losing our home against our will.

When our finances started down that rollercoaster slide, we could only hope the uphill climb would begin soon. But we would have to lose it all before we could start back up again. It took eighteen months of waiting for the hammer to fall; never knowing when we would lose the roof over our heads. In the end, instead of foreclosure, we were able to short-sell our home and live in it until the ownership transferred. We just had no idea how long that would take. When it finally did sell, we were fortunate to be able to rent the house back from the new owner for a nominal amount for three months, giving us more time to figure out what to do next. Where would we go now, and how would we pay our monthly expenses? Our options were few.

True to form, I decided to change my perspective and let some sun shine through. My childhood upbringing had taught me to tamp down emotional responses to difficulties. My daughters had designated me the "Queen of Denial." Some might judge that as fairly dysfunctional behavior, but who can argue with a party to lighten up the mood? My inner social secretary went into high gear.

Having lived in all parts of Santa Cruz County for over forty years, we knew so many people we wanted to say goodbye to. Our house was still the perfect party place, so why not host one last fling? I named it the "New Beginning" party. And that's how I began to think and feel about what was actually going on for John and me. It was a turning point for us, a time to move into a new way of living. I had enthusiastically organized many events over the years, so putting together the party was my fun in the midst of the hard physical and emotional work we were doing every day.

A party with traditional Armenian dishes and lots of wine and good friends was going to kick off our new life with a bang — even if we didn't know what that new life looked like. To add to the festivities we had a silent auction to sell the few pieces of furniture and odds and ends we had not unloaded in our three garage sales, or discarded on our many trips to the dump. It turned out to be a reciprocating farewell gift. The extra money was a great help, and many of our friends who purchased items later told us, "When we look at what we bought at your going away party, we think of you and the great times we had together." How nice is that?!

From time to time when the girls were growing up, we had temporarily "adopted" some of their friends who had troubles in their own families, providing them with a home away from home. During holidays our adopted daughters joined us to make traditional Armenian dishes like dolma (grape leaves stuffed with meat and rice), cheese boreg (a rich dough filled with a cheese, egg and parsley mixture), and cheoreg (a slightly sweet braided bread served with cream cheese).

Just before our "New Beginning" party I ran into Denine at our local Trader Joe's, who had temporarily been a "fourth daughter."

"Wow, Denine it is so great to see you. You look so happy. Is this your little girl?" I was truly excited to run into her and pleased she was doing so well.

When I told her about our upcoming party, she excitedly said "Can I come and help cook? I would love to spend time with you and see Sara and Lesha again!" (Kelly was living in San Diego and couldn't get away.)

"Of course" I said feeling so happy that she still wanted to join in on our culinary adventures. "We would love to have you cook with us."

A couple of weeks later we were to get the gift of a lifetime. While rolling grape leaves together and talking about old times, Denine, suddenly blurted out, "My mom is so grateful to you, for all that you did for me when I was growing up. She lives in Australia now and just inherited my grandpa's cabin in South Lake Tahoe. She said you can stay there free for as long as you need."

A bolt of electricity ran through me, and goose bumps rose on my arms. John and I had come up with a few ideas about where we might relocate. This was an offer we had not expected. It was the miracle we needed. I was sure that somehow Mom had a hand in it.

Denine's grandpa's place is a small three-bedroom, one-bathroom cabin with a cozy kitchen and living room with a stone fireplace. It's a wood-framed building that sits among tall pine trees in a neighborhood about a mile away from the South Lake Tahoe beach. Arriving with just the basics, we were more emotionally and physically exhausted than we realized. This would be a chance to recover from the hell we'd been through and to figure out our next step.

Utterly grateful, we were now getting by very simply. John's monthly Social Security check and the small amount I had received from the sale of Mom's house were being stretched as far and long as possible. We read, took walks along the lake, watched some interesting DVDs we checked out from the small local library, and slept a lot.

John would look at me and ask, "What percent?" I'd give him a number between one and a hundred, then ask him the same question. It was our check-in lingo to see how close we felt to a full recovery from the disruptions and losses of the past three years. We stopped asking long before either of us reached a hundred percent. We knew that recovery would be a slow and gradual process.

Our peaceful setting in South Lake Tahoe was the perfect balm for our wounds. It gave us both the time and space to begin to recover, but more importantly to see more clearly what we had just been through and what kind of life we wanted to have going forward.

*My mom standing down on Prescott Road near the creek below her house.
She couldn't believe people could "own" such beauty*

*My mom, in 1970 when she first bought her house on Glen Haven
Drive in Soquel, with a UCSC student who lived in the cabin
in exchange for developing her garden*

*Mom at the start of building her own house below
the main house which she got red tagged for*

Building the "connecting room"

Beautiful patio at mom's house where John and I had lunch with the new owners

Mom's "Winchester Mystery" house

*And the endless piles of stuff on mom's property that John and I
had to deal with after she died*

Our much needed retreat in South Lake Tahoe - May to November 2010

The day after we arrived. Snow in May?

While writing this book John and I became grandparents. Johnny, Zoe, Ayla and Mac are a true joy and are the reason, now more than ever, that I do what I do.

CHAPTER 15

NOT NORMAL TIMES

A lot of people are waiting for Martin Luther King
or Mahatma Gandhi to come back - but they are gone.
We are it. It is up to us. It is up to you.

~ Marian Wright Edelman

There is so much going on that is distressing but because
of what I am doing I feel more hopeful and optimistic.
Just doing one thing can change things for a lot of people
so I feel much better about the state of the world now
that I am engaged and trying to do something about it.

~ Liz Torkington, Fundraising Manager for the non-profit One Light Global

After six months in our cozy cabin in South Lake Tahoe, before the winter snow started to fall, John and I moved to Sacramento, California's capital, at the northern end of the state's agricultural Central Valley. Living there was less expensive than on the coast in Santa Cruz or in the San Francisco Bay Area, but was still close enough — about two hours away — from two of our daughters.

For the next six years, we hunkered down there in a compact nine-hundred-square-foot apartment. We could vacuum the whole place in eight minutes! It had taken us a series of purges to get rid of unnecessary belongings and now we were down to what we actually used. We love the lightness that comes with owning fewer possessions; feeling relieved of the relentless demand to endlessly consume.

The transition to a simpler way of life was thrust upon us, but was also something that we embraced without regret. Our income was now limited to two very small Social Security checks, which covered our minimal living expenses with little left over for anything else. But since the "crash" and the loss of our home in Santa Cruz, we had become richer than ever — rich in love of our family and the birth of four beautiful, healthy grandchildren.

For me, the big lesson of the crash of 2008 was that money really doesn't make you happier. I understand more deeply now that a truly rich person is someone who has the support and love of family and friends, knows their own value, is grateful for what they do have, and spreads kindness and understanding. Our losses were dramatic relative to what we had, but unlike so many others, we had our health and a comfortable home, a dependable car and food on the table. We consider these things basic to our lifestyle, but no longer take them for granted.

. . . .

While living in South Lake Tahoe, I had connected with Mom's friend Savanah who had taped her talking about her life for the book she was planning to write. Savanah sent me the twenty-four tapes that I listened to and transcribed, slowly getting to the point of wanting to write my own story.

As I continued to work on my memoir, the 2016 election was quickly approaching. Hillary announced her run for the presidency and my energy shifted to helping her become the next president of the United States. During the primary election, I traveled to nearby Reno, Nevada, with two friends to walk door-to-door with them, talking with people and handing out campaign literature. On the day of Nevada's caucus, the three of us trained caucus leaders worked to make sure everyone was heard and got to vote.

Hillary won the Nevada caucus 52.6 to 47.3. We joined all the other exhausted Hillary volunteers to celebrate, watching the results come in on the many large screen TV's at a local sports bar before heading home.

Throughout the campaign I posted endless articles and videos on Facebook and Twitter. I had built up the number of my "friends" to the maximum of five thousand and "followers" to nine thousand. I was continually keeping my contacts informed about what Hillary was doing and saying, as well as of her background, accomplishments and qualifications to be our next president. It was a big job, but I was rewarded every week as greater and greater numbers of people read and shared my posts. But I needed to do more.

Toward the end of the primary, I found out about some of the Bernie Sanders supporters who were harassing Hillary Clinton superdelegates. A website had been created to make it easy for them to find these people's email, Facebook and Twitter pages, and in some cases home phone numbers. This access enabled them to be vicious and fairly anonymous at the same time. I am not sure how they thought their vicious attacks would turn pledged Hillary superdelegates into Sanders supporters. That was just not going to happen and in fact was backfiring and making the Hillary supporters even stronger. But I was incensed that, because of the ease of social media, people were being attacked. I felt Hillary's superdelegates needed and deserved to receive letters of support. Always a networker, I knew I could reach out to my friends on Facebook for help. But what I needed was the list of the superdelegates' snail-mail addresses, which I was able to obtain through a series of calls and emails to a few key people.

My friends Tricia and her husband Rich, from Hillary's 2008 campaign, joined in the effort and configured the list in bite-size chunks of about fifteen people each. John West and Kim Fredrick, from the 2008 campaign, had established a private Hillary "super volunteer" Facebook page. I used it and my own Facebook friends to recruit letter writers. The result was that more than two hundred people from all over the country wrote some five thousand letters of encouragement to Hillary's superdelegates. Many of them received letters of sincere appreciation in return.

> *It was such a pleasant surprise to open your letter. I had fully expected one asking me to switch to Bernie. Let me assure you that I am a pledged and faithful delegate to Hillary. There is no one better qualified to lead this country. Thank you for taking the time to share your thoughts with me.*

And:

> *Thank you both for the thoughtful letters I received in the mail today. It was a pleasant surprise to receive letters supporting my position with Hillary. As you might guess, I have had a number of communications — social media, emails and letters — from people who do not agree with my support of the Secretary. ...please know that your letters were most appreciated.*

And another:

Thank you for your note of support. It was most welcome after the many negative phone calls. Hillary will make a great president with her integrity, experience and judgment.

And from this letter writer:

I received a telephone call from Congressman Steny Hoyer today. He thanked me for my thank-you note and said he was instructing his scheduler to come find me at the DNC Convention!

I even received messages from the people writing letters saying: *Thank you for the honor of writing letters to the super delegates.* As well as:

I'm disturbed by the pressure being exerted by the Sanders campaign against the super-delegates to capitulate on their commitment to Hillary. I feel I can be of use in composing letters to them to help dissuade them from changing their minds.

It's great to be working with this team again. As long as there's a breath in me, I'll always be willing to do anything — physically, emotionally, financially and mentally — to achieve what's best for our Nation. The superdelegates who I know are getting pissed off at the Sanders harassment. It has gone way beyond lobbying to threats, personal invective, and attempts at public embarrassment.

And after I had sent all of our letter writers an update on our progress, one woman sent this to me, which warmed my heart and made me feel like what I had organized was so worthwhile.

> *Thank you, Pat, for asking me to participate and to contribute in some small way beyond sending donations.*
>
> *Thanks from both Gale and me for the wrap-up on your very impressive project. I had no idea so many letters were being generated. And I appreciated seeing the recipients' responses — you can tell that many of them really felt assaulted by the other side. It feels terrific to have been a part of this!*
>
> *I am keeping the notes I have received, and will treasure them always, as a reminder of our efforts to ensure Hillary's nomination and election. I am so happy to have participated in this project — I am not very good at phonebanking; in fact, I generally dislike talking on the phone. But I really enjoyed writing these notes, and seeing the positive impact our group's efforts have made.*

Writing letters of support to Hillary's superdelegates was just one of so many ways to help — an example of citizen action that is always needed, especially now that our country has, I believe, fraudulently elected Donald Trump.

Throughout 2016, I worked as hard as I could. After a hard-fought battle, Hillary won the Democratic nomination, receiving 3.5 million more votes than Bernie Sanders. The Democratic Convention was the end of July, and John and I opted to watch it all from the comfort of our own living room.

In 2008 I had run successfully to become a Hillary delegate and attended the Democratic National Convention in Denver. Now, living in Sacramento I didn't have the base of support I had built up on the Central Coast of California. I didn't even try to run. There were fifty-three people running for just three slots and I knew there was no way I would get one of them.

Then one morning I picked up the phone.

"Hey Pat, John West here. I have something exciting to share. I have two guest passes to the Democratic Convention in Philadelphia. Do you want one?"

"Oh, my god! Yes, of course I would love one. How did you get it? Thank you so much!"

I was overjoyed and couldn't imagine that I would actually be going to the convention. It was just two weeks away and I was beyond excited.

The whole previous year, my friend John West and I immersed ourselves in campaign ideas, strategies, and information. Now, I could hardly contain myself. Hillary was going to accept the Democratic Party's nomination and I was going to be there in person to witness and celebrate this historic event. This was what I had worked so hard for since 2008.

I jumped into gear to make all the arrangements, grateful once more to good friends who chipped in to help me pay for my airfare and food, and to my new friend, Jennifer McCann, who graciously let me share her hotel room at no cost.

Early one morning in late July, as the sun was just peeking over the horizon, John drove me to the Sacramento airport. A little groggy and with a nervous stomach, I knew I was headed for an experience of a lifetime.

After a full day of travel I checked into the hotel, and rushed to get a taxi to the convention center, not wanting to miss a minute of it. Anxious to get in the middle of the action and to feel the excitement of the crowds, I thought the taxi ride would never end. The driver didn't know where he was going, which just keyed me up even more. When we finally pulled up not far from the entrance to the convention center, I took a deep breath and sighed with relief.

With my expectations already being realized, I soaked up the energies of the crowd while listening to the amazing and powerful Michelle Obama address the convention. I was grateful I hadn't missed her. Many Bernie Sanders supporters were trying to cause disruptions on the floor of the convention center, so when Sanders himself spoke and called for unity, I was happy and thankful.

Tuesday was a real emotional night for me. President Bill Clinton did an incredible job of eloquently weaving together the story of the life he and Hillary had shared with the story of Hillary as the change-maker she had been all of her life. I was familiar with much of her amazing history, and found myself thinking about the millions of people watching on TV who were hearing for the first time who Hillary REALLY is. This was the result, I thought, of the main stream media having done such a poor job of talking about Hillary's life, what she had accomplished and what her policy proposals were. Instead they focused on the false issue of "her emails."

We made HERstory that night when Hillary Rodham Clinton became the first woman to officially become the presidential nominee of a major political party. Tears started to flow down my face as I thought about my three grown daughters and my mother who had passed away seven years earlier. But what really got me was when I thought about my four young grandchildren and the new and more inclusive country they were growing up in.

Before the roll call of the states, a huge screen above the podium came down slowly, displaying small pictures of the forty-four former presidents, all of them male. Then an overlying image of glass shattered to reveal a live video of Hillary, surrounded by a group of young children, addressing the convention. That whole vast room erupted with screaming, cheering and clapping. Many of us were weeping tears of joy. Being there and feeling the energy was something I will never forget. I was flying so high that night that it was nearly impossible to calm my brain enough to get to sleep.

Wednesday night, President Obama was thrilling — he lit up the convention center. Thursday night was over the top. I was impressed by the people who produced the convention. They did an extraordinary job enlisting many speakers who shared touching stories of how Hillary played a role in their life. They ranged from the Mothers of the Movement (whose sons and daughters were killed needlessly at the hands of the police) to Sarah McBride (a proud transgender American), to Demi Lavato (living with mental illness), to Cheryl Lanker (a victim of Trump University). But the highlights for me were Khizr Khan and the Rev. William Barber. Mr. Khan and his wife, Ghazala, are Muslims, Pakistani immigrants and Gold Star parents whose son proudly served our country and died in action. I was riveted by Rev. Barber — a powerful speaker, and thrilled when he said, "When religion is used to camouflage meanness we know we have a heart problem in America."

I could relate to many of the speakers. It was truly moving to have my values validated and reaffirmed by regular people and prominent figures alike. That whole week the crowd was wild with appreciation and support. This was only my second convention, so it is hard to judge, but in my mind this one will be hard to beat in terms of pure joy and the messages that were conveyed.

Simultaneously energized and exhausted — no one got much sleep all week — I headed home with my huge Hillary signs in tow. Seeing my signs one flight attendant, smiled, gave me a high-five and kindly put them in a safe place. She would not accept any of my drink tickets, giving my seatmates and me as many free drinks as we wanted while talking excitedly all the way from Philly to Frisco.

. . . .

Election night was approaching. I had walked door-to-door, made hundreds of phone calls, given as much money as I could, gotten the word out through social media and wore my Hillary gear everywhere.

When the day finally arrived — November 8, 2016 I was both excited and strangely nervous. John and I had talked so many times about where we wanted to be on what we thought was going to be an historic night. Would we be at a local gathering, at our friends Tricia and Rich's house in the Bay Area, or at a big celebration in San Francisco? In the end we opted to be at home with our favorite munchies, on the couch in our comfortable clothes.

Channel-surfing and monitoring our lap-tops, we watched the results slowly emerge. Our joy, excitement and nervousness turned to dread, shock and immense sadness. I was in total disbelief as it was announced that Donald Trump had won. That night, as I silently slipped into bed, I didn't cry, I didn't rage. I had no mental or physical energy left. I felt completely numb.

In the days and months that followed I went from anger to sadness and through everything in between. I was afraid for our democracy, for women and girls, for immigrants, for people of color, for the LGBTQ community, for our country, and for all the people who are and will be directly hurt by the man Hillary warned was totally unfit to be president. She was right. Every day since that election Trump has proved to be more and more dangerous.

Our country and our world changed on Tuesday November 8, 2016. I wish I had cried that night or in the days after. Maybe I would feel better now if I had. Like a person having lost a loved one or been told they have a terminal diagnosis, I have gone through the stages of grief, including denial. For many months I woke up to the thought that maybe this was all a bad dream — or, rather, a nightmare. For sure my feelings of immense sadness and disappointment will be with me forever.

My plan had been to take a much-needed break after a Hillary victory, and then figure out what I could do to help the first woman president achieve her policy agenda. I would pitch in with renewed energy to fight the policy battles and sexist attitudes that would surely emerge after she took office. Instead, I was feeling lost and deeply depressed.

One day I picked up the phone and was happy to hear a friendly voice.

"Hey Pat, I know we are all depressed but I am calling to see if you wanted to activate your letter writers again?" It was John West.

"Wow, so nice to hear from you! What do you have in mind?"

He proceeded to talk to me about how the Electoral College worked. There are 538 electors, people elected from each state who, after the election, meet to cast their vote for president of the United States. As spelled out in the constitution, the college is supposed to provide the final filter in the presidential election process. Its purpose is to prevent demagogues — like Donald Trump — from assuming the nation's highest office.

It took 270 Electoral College votes to win, and Trump had won 306. Could we persuade thirty-seven Republican electors to flip and not vote for Trump? We had until December 19, the day electors would vote, to make that happen.

"It would be great if you could get people to write letters to these electors. Ask them not to vote for him. What do you think?"

Looking for something to put my energy into, I gave him my usual, well-practiced answer. "Yes, I can do that."

Again I needed a list — this time of the electors and their snail mail addresses. People could email them or post on their Facebook or Twitter pages, but I felt that a physical, hand-written letter would have a bigger impact and not get lost amidst the barrage of electronic correspondence.

I had become a Facebook friend of Rosemary Rocco, a feminist activist from Minnesota whom I still have not met in person. We had talked on the phone a number of times and had quickly become close friends – long lost soul sisters. We had talked about our feelings of powerlessness and that writing to the electors was at least something we could do at this seemingly hopeless moment in history. Throughout my whole life, when in a bind or under pressure, I need to do something — I need to take action.

I was given a spreadsheet of electors, but it was incomplete, which panicked me a bit. How were we going to find the missing contact information? Then Rosemary came to the rescue enlisting the help of LeAnn Brown, a statistician, expert database manager and Democratic activists, who did an amazing job of finding the missing addresses.

Reaching out again to our Hillary people, we provided them each with a list of twenty electors and their mailing addresses, along with brief instructions and a few sample letters.

Meanwhile, thousands of people were calling the White House *requesting that President Obama declassify any and all intelligence related to the emerging news of Russia's interference of the presidential election — and to brief all members of the Electoral College about it before they meet and voted.* Thousands of people were also asking their senators and representatives to sign a letter demanding a U.S. Intelligence briefing for all electors before they voted. There was a massive online petition effort via email, Facebook and Twitter that garnered nearly five million signatures. It urged members of the Electoral College to become "faithless" electors and break from their state to vote for Clinton instead of Trump.

We knew this effort was a true longshot. It had never happened before in the history of the Electoral College that this many electors would choose to vote against their party's candidate. But the stakes were high, so why not try?

The full scope of Russia's hacking of our elections was not known yet. Hillary and President Obama tried unsuccessfully many times during the campaign to let people know about the Russian attacks against the Democratic National Committee and Clinton's campaign, but the media wasn't listening. They were instead obsessed with Hillary's emails and captivated by the "Donald Trump show." It wasn't until mid-March, 2017, four months after the election, that the public first learned that during the election the FBI was already investigating the Trump campaign and Russia's involvement in it.

In addition to the huge odds against our succeeding in convincing thirty-seven Republican electors to change their vote, we faced yet another daunting hurdle. If no candidate got 270 electoral votes, the decision of who would be president would then go to the Republican-controlled House of Representatives. There certainly was no way they were going to vote for Hillary, even if they didn't like Trump.

But as our efforts unfolded I was learning that there were so many people just like me who felt helpless and needed to do something — anything — to ease their pain. I heard from people who said:

Thanks for helping me to feel like I've done something useful.

Thank you so, so much! This is giving me and many others so much hope and no matter what, I can sleep better at night because of your and your colleague's efforts!

Thank you for giving me this opportunity to "do something!" — which I've been looking for since November 9!

And I loved this from one mother:

My 16-year-old daughter decided to write a few respectful letters as well.

This was another example of seeing a need or a problem and figuring out how to address it. Our idea seemed to spread by word of mouth. In just two weeks about 350 thoughtful, committed citizens wrote over eight thousand letters to the key 197 electors in twenty-two states. Each of these electors received about thirty-five personal letters in their mailboxes.

Despite all the efforts of so many, the electors voted to confirm Donald Trump as president, but I did feel a bit better knowing I did what I could.

. . . .

Why did Trump win? This was something everyone was asking. In the months after the election, I immersed myself in reading everything I could get my hands on about it, and concluded that he won because of a multiplicity of factors and events.

It was the way the media covered the candidates. It has been widely reported that the mainstream media was obsessed with covering "everything Trump" and focused an inordinate amount of time on the nonexistent Hillary "email" issue. In addition, during Hillary's run for president in 2016, history had started to repeat itself. Although the mainstream media was not as bad as it had been in 2008, pundits claimed that Hillary's tone during her speech after winning the Iowa caucus was "unpleasant," "angry, bitter, screaming," and suggested that Clinton "may be hard of hearing." Things that would never be said about a male candidate,

But what has not been talked about in the mainstream media is how the strong, active Hillary supporters were being treated. We had to deal with extreme personal harassment from both the right AND the left. In 2016, not only was Hillary being slammed, but her supporters were getting attacked as well. Social media was now the dominant vehicle of mass communication, and female Hillary supporters were being viciously attacked — accused of being "vagina voters", called "cunt", "whore" and worse — on Facebook and Twitter.

It was exhausting. Many supporters told me they didn't put a Hillary bumper sticker on their car for fear of it being keyed or worse. Many were so viciously and personally attacked on social media that they stopped posting about Hillary altogether because they couldn't take it. It was emotionally draining. This election was never just about Hillary; it was about all women. I felt it in every bone in my body.

I agree with my friend Anita Finlay, who wrote:

Those who did battle hard to see Hillary elected, and they were many, were regularly hacked, threatened and harassed (including yours truly). Bullying, shaming and verbal or physical intimidation are effective techniques to stifle women's voices.

As disturbing as all the sexism and misogyny was, I was undaunted, put my head down and powered through — or as the 2016 saying went "She Persisted."

It was also the lies spewed by Trump — way too many to mention — that just enough voters in swing states believed to get him elected.

It was Bernie himself, who kept telling his followers that he could still win the nomination long after he couldn't. And the insinuations from the Sanders campaign that the primary election was rigged by the Democratic National Committee when it wasn't, and that Hillary was in the pocket of Wall Street — a falsehood that fed into the Trump narrative — when she wasn't. This caused her to have to fight both the right and the left at the same time.

It was the destructive effect of FBI Director James Comey saying, on October 28, just ten days before the election, that the FBI had "learned of the existence of emails that appear to be pertinent to the investigation" on the private email server Hillary used as Secretary of State. His statement took over the news cycle, allowing Trump to build on the "crooked Hillary" theme. Then just two days before the election, Comey disclosed the emails hadn't turned up anything new, a clarification that was obviously too little, too late.

It was voter suppression by Republicans and not enough people turning out to vote. It was people voting for a third party — especially in critical swing states. It was the twelve percent of Bernie Sanders supporters who voted for Trump and the eight percent who voted for third party candidate Jill Stein.

As reported in Political Wire, we now know that Sanders supporters who voted for Trump in the General Election were able to push the key swing states of Wisconsin, Michigan, and Pennsylvania over the edge to Trump. If it weren't for those 79,000 votes in these three states, Hillary would be our President.

It was Russian President Vladimir Putin's hatred of Hillary and love of Trump, and the Russian cyber warfare he waged against our free elections that were eventually revealed thanks to Special Counsel Robert Mueller.

And according to an article in the *Washington Post* by Michael Kranish entitled "Inside Russian effort to target Sanders supporters – and help elect Trump" published April 12, 2019, which said

> *...a post-election survey conducted for Ohio State University documented how false stories spread on social media may*

have caused a decline in turnout for Clinton. Only 77 per-
cent of those surveyed who had voted for Barack Obama in
2012 supported Clinton in 2016; 10 percent backed Trump,
4 percent voted for third-party candidates, and 8 percent
did not vote, according to the YouGov survey.

Hillary withstood over twenty-five years of lies and attacks simply because she didn't fit the 1950's image of "the little woman." It
started when she married Bill and kept her last name instead of taking
his. There has been an orchestrated campaign over the years to convince people that she can't be trusted, using the flimsiest of fabrica-
tions, which have never been proven true.

It was that there are more people, both men and women, in our
country who are, consciously or unconsciously more sexist and mi-
sogynistic than any of us realized.

It was all of the above and, I believe, so much more that will be
revealed in the future.

But despite all that, Hillary still won the national popular vote.
With about sixty-six million votes, almost three million more people
voted for Hillary than for Trump! She won more votes than any other
presidential candidate in history except for Obama. To me she will
always be my president.

I have been trying to understand what happened, but my memoir is not the place to explore in depth why Hillary lost. Hillary's
book *What Happened* does that beautifully, and the fact that she
wrote it was a real service to our country and to our democracy. Her
book is an extremely important historical document. I was pleased to
find a companion piece, *The Destruction of Hillary Clinton* by Susan
Bordo, a brilliant book that put all the puzzle pieces together for me
in a clear and concise way. It's a good complement to Hillary's first-
person account.

....

It took me a good six months of many starts and stops to gather the energy and the motivation to become active again. The Women's March in January, 2017, helped me as it did many around the country.

I heard Hillary speak about the book she had written, laying out her personal experience as the candidate, and thought, "It must have been so hard for her to do that. If she can do that, I certainly can get out there again."

This was a perfect example of what Hillary does for so many of us. She models great courage and makes us believe we can do anything and overcome anything. I wondered if that is really what so many "Hillary Haters" fear. Do they fear the upending of the "given order"? Electing a Black MAN president was truly revolutionary. Electing a woman really will be a sign of dismantling the patriarchy. I wonder how many women have felt freed and affirmed by Hillary's candidacy.

Hillary has dared to challenge the given order. She has been a transformational model her whole life, from her commencement speech at Wellesley, the first ever given by a student, to her role as First Lady of Arkansas and to keeping her own name, something that wasn't done in 1975.

As a woman of Hillary's generation, I grew up in the politically progressive San Francisco Bay area, where I watched Hillary with great interest. She was a role model for me as I was rearing three young girls to be strong, fulfilled women. I saw her trying to navigate the gap growing between the traditional stay-at-home moms and the generation of women who were trying to "have it all." Her life was being played out publicly while I was trying to find my way in my secluded private world. From afar I admired her strength and her determination to live the life she wanted, despite the attacks against her.

Hillary has always blazed new trails for what and who women can be, and she bore the brunt of it her whole life. Stepping out of the mold that was familiar and comfortable to many Americans, she wasn't society's idea of a perfect First Lady. We had never seen a First Lady dare to talk about her qualifications and run for office in her own right. Many didn't like her because she committed to stay with her cheating husband, assuming it was because of her own ambition rather than her loyalty to her marriage and her family.

She wasn't the perfect First Lady. She wasn't the perfect Senate candidate. She wasn't the perfect wife and she wasn't the perfect candidate for President.

As a society we have projected our own expectations of womanhood onto her. Why do we want her to be perfect, whatever that is, when we don't demand that of men?

Our need for women to be perfect plays out in so many areas of our lives, starting at a very young age. Books, magazines, TV shows and social media insist we measure up to the so called "ideal woman" in the way we dress, behave and what we aspire to do with our lives. There is a lot of unspoken, and in so many cases unrecognized, pressure every day in women's lives. Our society has a "perfection problem" when it comes to women.

We are conditioned from an early age to seek perfection in ourselves, so why wouldn't we seek it in other women? Especially a woman who aspires to do and be something that we would never consider for ourselves? It is long past time to abandon the "perfection myth" for women running for office, and for that matter, for all of us.

I truly hope that America's women will not demand, either consciously or unconsciously, that a woman candidate be "perfect," but that she be an intelligent, dedicated, courageous and compassionate human being.

. . . .

On January 21, 2017, a cold sunny day in Washington, D.C., a half-million people came from all over the country to join in the Women's March against the Trump administration. They did not march alone — there were "sister" marches in 673 cities around the world, on all seven continents. Almost five million people were involved worldwide in protesting the presidency of Donald Trump. This was the largest march ever, and it was started by one woman, Teresa Shook, who lived in the farthest-flung state of Hawaii. She had an idea, and she posted it on Facebook. Amazingly, I found out that her son was a good friend of my son-in-law and that she had been at my daughter's wedding. It truly is a small world.

I called her up. I wanted to know the history behind her historic action.

"I was so upset after Hillary lost," she said, "that I posted this crazy idea of having a national march against Trump on Facebook. The next morning when I woke up I was in shock to see my post had gone viral! But I was also ecstatic! There was such a buzz of turning the feeling of powerlessness into positive action. It was palpable. We were forever changed by the movement that the Women's March created."

She told me that the next day she picked four women from the hundreds offering to help to be co-hosts. Together they got a state page up on Facebook for each state, with organizers for each, and started building a team for the D.C. march. She continued in the role of liaison between the national and state organizers, a role she could handle from Hawaii.

"I remember one woman, Evvie Harmon, saying she could give me maybe fifteen hours a week," Teresa told me. "We still laugh about that because she ended up working night and day like everyone else did to make the Women's March happen. My goal was to inspire others to get activated – and we have! Women are ushering in a whole new wave of leadership, using their own rules, owning their diversity. It's so awesome to be a part of it all."

I have always believed that one person truly can make a difference. You might not be the one to plant the seed of the largest march in history but millions of individual acts do add up. Why do you think it has become a trend to ask for a three-dollar donation? It's because a million people giving three dollars equals a hell of a lot of money.

The march wasn't meant to be an end but a beginning, a call to action, a call to donate to good causes, contact representatives, get involved with local government, a call to phone, text, write postcards and walk door-to-door for candidates. And a call to run for office. This has all happened! Trump's election has awakened people to the fact that we can't take anything for granted.

The Women's March brought together millions of people all over the country who then became active, involved and who are leading the resistance. Groups like Indivisible, Swing Left, Flippable, Sister Districts, Town Hall Project, Together We Will and Let America Vote have sprung up as a part of the Resistance to Trump and all that he stands for. They are helping people learn how to be citizen activists.

After the Women's March in January, 2017, it was crystal clear that women were incensed that Trump had won — or stolen — the presidency. This helped push a record number of women (mostly Democrats) to run for office. For many, this was the first time they had run for anything.

In a February, 2018, press release, EMILY's List President Stephanie Schriock said:

It's clear that pro-choice Democratic women aren't just interested in winning critical elections in 2018 — they're going to change the political landscape forever. Women are fired up in a way we have never seen before. They can't wait to take action. This historic energy is why EMILY's List has heard from over 34,000 women in just 15 months who want to run for office — not just this year, but in elections to come. They know that making systemic change in this country means that we need to elect waves of Democratic women to office each and every election — and that's exactly what we're going to do here at EMILY's List.

Because of this newfound anger and energy, many of the Republican men who left their seats in 2018 were replaced by Democratic women.

In 1989 there were only twenty-five women in Congress. After the 2018 elections, a record 127 were in office - that is seventy-seven more women in just thirty years. But to give some perspective, that is up from 4.6 percent in 1989 to 23.6 percent in 2018 — meaning we still have a long way to go.

In this new class of women senators and representatives there were many firsts. The first two Muslim women, the youngest woman at age 29, the first two Native American women and the first black woman from Massachusetts elected to congress. And there were the first women House members from Iowa, the first two Latina members from Texas, the first woman senators from Tennessee and Arizona as well as the first woman governors of Maine, Iowa and South Dakota.

According to political scientists, women win elections at the same rates as men. Of course, for that to happen, women have to decide to run for office in the first place. Hillary's loss to an extreme misogynist, and women being galvanized by the Women's March, has caused many more women to make that decision.

"This is all coming out of a moment of realization that elections have consequences and women can't afford to leave politics to someone else," says Debbie Walsh, director of the Center for American Women and Politics at Rutgers University.

It is hard to know the depth of what is happening around the country. There are literally thousands of stories. This is from an August 14, 2017, article in the *Washington Post* by Rhonda Colvin, "Resistance efforts are taking root in pro-Trump country — and women are leading the charge."

> *... Sullivan said a resistance effort has been building in the state* [South Dakota] *since Trump was elected. In January* [2017], *she co-chaired a local march in conjunction with the national women's march, attracting nearly 3,300 demonstrators to downtown Sioux Falls in 30-degree temperatures. Sullivan said the experience — seeing the sea of like-minded people — transformed her from a person who never dreamed of being politically active to someone who uses her spare time to call lawmakers. She is also preparing for her own run for a state legislative seat next year.*

I am happy to say that 32-year-old Kelly Sullivan won her election to the South Dakota House of Representatives.

In writing this chapter I wanted to share what I had done during the election, my feelings about the election and where I was personally in my life. I have chosen to work mostly within the political campaign world, working to elect people who will do their best to help people and make our country and the world a fairer and more just place to live. That is my thing, but it might not be yours. There are so many ways to help. I hope you will find yours.

To help you, I have included a Resource, many organizations that are working on many different issues, in many different ways to improve the lives of people, and save the fragile planet we all live on. My hope is that it will be a useful tool to help you find your way to civic activism.

With Hillary in Oakland, CA after her speech at a rally on May 6, 2016

At the Women's March in San Jose, CA January 2017. From left to right –
John, me, Danielle Suchet, Aida Ebrahimian, Kristin Kohler,
Stephanie Sheldon-Mollinier and her daughter Anaïs Mollinier and
our daughter Sara Bakalian Wildman

EPILOGUE

WHAT COUNTS IS
GETTING BACK UP

Memories are tricky. Time alters perspective and memories get reorganized in our minds. Thankfully, the feelings that were so intense in the moment fade, but it's important to remember them and continue to learn from the events that caused them.

In writing this book I can see how I have always tried to be perfect — as a girl not wanting to be too fat or too smart so that the boys would like me, and later as an adult striving to be the perfect wife, mother and homemaker. It was exhausting and it diverted my attention away from figuring out who I was and what I wanted to do with my life.

What I didn't know when I launched into this project was that it would help me heal some of the emotional wounds I had successfully kept under wraps for so many years. For me, that was the true gift of this labor of love.

I had a lot of anger when I first set out to write this book: anger at my dad, my brothers, my husband, myself. I have none any more.

I have realized that each of us is on our own path, and that the only control I have is over what I do with my life.

I have recognized and dealt with my misplaced anger at my husband. After losing our home and having to move out of the community we had lived in for forty years, ending up in our 60's having to get by each month on a small income, I had a lot of suppressed feelings about the way John and I had lived our lives. I was angry with him for taking me on such a financial rollercoaster ride, and for not being a more stable breadwinner. I was angry with myself for taking so long to recognize my own financial responsibilities to my family. And I was angry with both of us for working so hard to make the world a better place without balancing that with efforts to make a more stable life for our family and a more secure life in our older years.

Now, after recounting the ups and downs of my life with John, I can say I am truly thankful for the man I married forty-nine years ago. We share essential values, including our belief that family is more important than anything else. That I chose someone like John instead of a man like my father when I was so young is a true miracle. Was it the Universe working?

I can see now how my life has been a slow, steady process of coming into my own, of learning who I was — what I was good at and what I was capable of — after a childhood that made those insights difficult to achieve.

My parents grew up affected by the era and culture of the times they lived in as well as many other influences I will never know about. My father's personal burdens kept him from being a helpful, loving parent to me, and my mother's triumphs over her own past influenced me profoundly. When I was young in the 1950's, I intuitively felt her unhappiness, and witnessed her courage in breaking out of a destructive marriage. As a teenager in the 1960's I saw my brave mom start an independent life by taking her three small children to live in Europe.

I watched her go back to school, searching for her own path and her own passion. As an adult I saw her live out a second life as an intellectual, educator, and activist — a life she made for herself and loved. I saw her live with a man twenty years her junior, start a free school, study under leaders in the world of systems science and cybernetics, and become the publisher of their monthly newsletter.

Mom had a saying on her wall: "Life is a journey measured not by one heroic action but by the living of each day to its fullest." She tried to live that way, and, perhaps without knowing it, she instilled that way of life in me. As I listened to my mom's tapes and contemplated her life I was filled with respect and gratitude for who my mother was, for what she went through in her life and for the independent woman she became.

I have come to understand the importance of a loving, caring and attentive father in a girl's life. It would have been nice to have had that. When a girl is a young teenager, at that very formative stage, a father's love and support — or lack of it — can have a huge impact on her life.

My focus on what boys thought of me, and my desire to get their attention, love and approval, looks to me now as if I was trying to replace the love and approval I was not getting from my father.

We don't get to choose our parents. Understanding my father's emotional abuse for what it was doesn't fill the hole that it left in my life. But now, more than twenty years after his death, I have an understanding of the importance of a supportive loving father. I never had that, but it is a relief to be able to say now that I'm done with my dad's garbage. I have peeled away the last layer of the onion.

The family John and I created isn't perfect, but we have a closeness and an open healthy communication that never existed in my childhood.

I can see now that my experience living in Europe at a young age taught me that the world was bigger than my own backyard. I learned to be flexible and resilient, to flow with whatever came my way and to make a cozy space for myself no matter where I was. While my first year there was painful in many ways, my feelings of inadequacy faded during the second year. I learned how to stick it out, like Mom, how to try and make the best of things.

There is no doubt that I am a product of white privilege. I have become more acutely aware of that fact through the process of writing this book. We can't change the color of our skin, where we were born, or the family we were born into. But with self-awareness we can overcome, in our personal lives, some of the cards we were dealt and do what we can to help others who are less fortunate.

The process of writing this book has strengthened my self-confidence. I have come to appreciate my own persistence and resilience, and to believe beyond a doubt that what matters most is not how far you fall or how many times, but that you get back up.

. . . .

In California, medical and recreational marijuana has been legalized and is becoming a booming industry. A few years ago John started working for a cannabis company in Northern California. That enabled us to move from our tiny apartment in Sacramento to Santa Rosa, an hour north of San Francisco, and a thirty-minute drive to the California coast. It's in the heart of Sonoma County, which, along with the County of Napa, is known as California wine country. In every direction, lush green vineyards stretch for miles. I thought then — and still do — that I had died and gone to heaven.

It has become clear to me that you can plan all you want, but you never know what life will bring you. This next adventure has proved that to be true. I would never have guessed this is where I would be at this point in my life. While John is busy developing a cannabis business, I don't know exactly what is around the corner for me. But what I do know is I will continue to work in any way I can to make this a better, more equal, safer, healthier world for everyone.

I had hoped when I started writing my story in 2010 that it would encourage people who have never been active before to become civically involved in whatever issue they care about, at whatever level and in whatever way they choose. My goal was to put a human face on what it was like for me to become an activist. Now more and more people are becoming engaged and I love what I'm seeing.

I wanted to share with you what social and political engagement did for me, from my early days organizing my community to stop an environmentally harmful development; to recognizing the needs of migrant farm workers and organizing a toy drive at my children's school; to organizing a fundraiser to raise thousands of dollars for the pro-choice cause; to helping to establish a county domestic violence commission; to being a part of creating a three county campaign for Hillary Clinton in 2008. I wanted to share how I learned about myself, how I grew as a person, how I had experiences that I could have never imagined and how I met new, lifelong friends whom I will treasure forever.

My lack of self-confidence held me back for way too many years from being the person I truly was. Coming out of my shell has enriched my soul and given me a lifetime of memories.

For me the journey of this book is over. I have learned and grown and am ready for my next adventure. Sharing these stories of my life over the years has been transforming for me. My hope is they benefit you as much as they have benefited me.

My message is: Don't hold yourself back, just do it — whatever your "it" may be, because our country and the world desperately needs you now more than ever.

You don't have to believe everything you think about yourself because so much of what we think about ourselves is from a belief system that was given to us from childhood or from society and it doesn't have to be true. So I would say go for it. Say yes and you will be surprised at what comes out of it. We all have something to offer, we all bring something to the table.

~ Kristin Kolher, Volunteer Administrator for
the nonprofit One Light Global

Everybody can be great...because anybody can serve.
You don't have to have a college degree to serve.
You don't have to make your subject and verb agree to serve.
You only need a heart full of grace. A soul generated by love.

~ Dr. Martin Luther King Jr.

My mom, just before she died. Now, I feel like she is cheering me on from the other side

350

APPENDIX

CIVIC INVOLVEMENT RESOURCES

My story is about making a difference in the world. I couldn't encourage you, my readers, to get involved without offering you some ideas of where to begin. So much good work is being done everywhere but I couldn't include every possible resource so what you will see here are highlights of some of the many organization doing "the good work."

Whatever your experience with social activism or your personal interests, the organizations and resources listed here can give you a place to get started. I have included links that can be accessed more easily by going to the *Civic Involvement* page of my website at http://www.patbakalian.com

My goal is to include groups and organizations that, not only ask for financial donations but, give you a place to volunteer in your local community, or to take action online through social media. There are also links to tools and sites that enable you to be a more informed citizen. I've categorized these resources so you can easily find the area that fits your lifestyle and your passion.

The challenges we face today seem overwhelming. They can make you think that nothing you do will make any difference. I believe that with everyone doing what they can, no matter how small, it will add up to make a huge difference. It's not just what I believe; it's what I have experienced.

Start small - It can be as simple as talking to your neighbors. Finding the right fit for you, and pacing yourself, are keys to being a happy, effective and fulfilled activist. There are many different ways to help: from donating your hard earned money to a cause you believe in, to becoming a mentor to a young person, to registering people to vote, to attending a rally, to making food for volunteers, to calling on your local school board to pass a climate resolution, to gathering gently used toys and giving them to children who are less fortunate as I did.

An informed and engaged population is essential for a strong and viable democracy. It matters that you are involved, because today our country and the world needs you more than ever.

We have seen the good that can happen when people come together to fight hate and divisiveness, help out their neighbors in need and stand up for what is right and just. As Hillary Rodham Clinton said:

Please, never stop believing that fighting for what's right is worth it. It is always worth it.

CATEGORIES OF INTEREST

General Organizations and Tools
To help you to be an engaged citizen

Action Friday: https://actionfriday.tumblr.com/about is an attempt to normalize political engagement and activism. Each Friday they suggest one action to take in the coming week to more deeply involve yourself in local, national, and global activism. These are simple tasks with straightforward instructions. Also, find their *Shy Person's Guide to Calling Representatives* here: http://actionfriday.tumblr.com/post/153358069831/shy-persons-guide-to-calling-representatives

Change.org: https://www.change.org is helping people everywhere connect across geographic and cultural borders to support causes they care about. They are starting campaigns, mobilizing supporters, and working with decision makers to drive solutions. 248,689,426 people taking action and 29,536 victories in 196 countries.

Congress In Your Pocket: http://www.congressinyourpocket.com is an app that provides information on what's happening in Congress from the schedules for votes and committee hearings to information about bills. Plus, they have a variety of resources for political candidates and politically active organizations.

 Countable: https://www.countable.us/about/us makes it quick and easy to understand the laws Congress is considering. They also streamline the process of contacting your lawmaker, so you can tell them how you want them to vote on bills under consideration.
You can use Countable to:

- Read clear and succinct summaries of upcoming and active legislation.
- Directly tell your lawmakers how to vote on those bills by clicking "Yea" or "Nay".
- Follow up on how your elected officials voted on bills, so you can hold them accountable in the next election cycle.

FiveThirtyEight: https://fivethirtyeight.com FiveThirtyEight, sometimes rendered as 538, is a website that focuses on opinion poll analysis, politics, economics, and sports blogging.

FLIPPABLE **Flippable:** https://www.flippable.org/our-plan/ state-strategy Our mission is to turn America blue by building a movement from the ground up focusing on state governments. Because we know you are busy we'll give you data on the most flippable seats and provide meaningful actions to win by spreading awareness, volunteering, and donating. Take action here: https://tinyurl.com/y3z5y6u6

Flip the West: https://www.flipthewest.com is formerly Flip the 14, founded in 2017. They worked closely with like-minded organizations and activists to recruit volunteers and reach voters who might otherwise stay home in the California House districts represented by Republicans. More than 1.5 million voter contacts later, seven House Republicans were replaced by House Democrats in California, helping Democrats take back the House of Representatives. In 2020, they are working to strengthen the work of the Resistance in Arizona, Colorado, Montana, and Texas, while continuing our work in California by organizing meaningful volunteer opportunities to reach voters, recruit volunteers, and provide a number of services to Resistance organizations. Volunteers can do Phone banking, Texting, Postcard-ing, Door-to-door Canvassing, Voter Registration and More. To get involved go here: https://www.flipthewest.com/get-involved

GovTrack: https://www.govtrack.us is an independent website tracking the status of legislation in the United States Congress. Find your representative and senator's legislation that affects you. Learn about and contact your representative and senators and track what Congress is doing. Starting in 2019 they will be tracking Congress's oversight investigations of the executive branch.

Indivisible: https://www.indivisibleguide.com works to elect progressive leaders, realize bold progressive policies, rebuild our democracy, and defeat the Trump agenda. Sign up for the latest updates on how you can take action here: https://indivisible.org/signup. Find your local group here: https://indivisible.org/groups And check out their latest resources to hold your members of Congress and the Trump administration accountable here: https://indivisible.org/resources

Institute for Women's Policy Research (IWPR): https://iwpr.org works with policymakers, scholars, and public interest groups to design, execute, and disseminate research that illuminates economic and social policy issues affecting women and families and to build a network of individuals and organizations that conduct and use women-oriented policy research. The Status of Women in the States provides data on women's progress in 50 states, the District of Columbia, and the United States overall which can be used to raise awareness, improve policies, and promote women's equality. Explore the data here: http://statusofwomendata.org

I Will Vote: https://iwillvote.com is a great tool to check your voter registration status. They take advantage of large gatherings of people to register voters and remind them not take voting for granted, and of the importance of checking their registration status.

 https://www.mobilizeamerica.io/ mobilize-america-home is a partner platform that makes it easy for you to post events you are doing and for volunteers to find opportunities to be civically engaged in their area. Finds events near you here: https://www.mobilize.us

MoveOn.org: is where millions mobilize for a better society—one where everyone can thrive. Whether it's supporting a candidate, passing legislation, or changing our culture, MoveOn members are committed to an inclusive and progressive future. They envision a world marked by equality, sustainability, justice, and love and come from all 50 states and all walks of life. They are at once large and nimble, targeting our resources purposefully, yet pivoting quickly as we identify new opportunities for change and mobilize to seize them. Scroll through this site to find ways to become involved https://front.moveon.org

 https://www.pantsuitnation.org works to build the foundation for a more equitable and engaged democracy. We believe that stories are an essential part of activism. We believe that power is built from ground up, not dictated from the top down. We believe that an equitable democracy of engaged participants is possible and that there are no short term fixes. We take a long path approach to building power and a broad view of civic engagement. We meet people where they are and provide resources to get them where they want to go. Take Action here: https://www.pantsuitnation.org/actions.html

People for the American Way: http://www.pfaw.org and its affiliate, People For the American Way Foundation, are progressive advocacy organizations founded to fight right-wing extremism and defend constitutional values under attack, including free expression, religious liberty, equal justice under the law, and the right to meaningfully participate in our democracy. They are dedicated to Equality, Freedom of speech, Freedom of religion, the right to seek justice in a court of law and the right to cast a vote that counts. Take Action here: http://www.pfaw.org/action-center

Resistbot: https://resist.bot is a service that people in the United States can use to compose and send letters to elected officials from the messaging apps on their mobile phones, with the goal that the task can be completed in "under two minutes".

Rock the Vote: https://www.rockthevote.org is a nonpartisan nonprofit dedicated to building the political power of young people. They have registered and turned out millions of young voters on campuses, in communities, and online. They have successfully fought for — and defended — voting rights and increased access to democracy. They have raised awareness and campaigned for issues that impact the lives of young people. They have pioneered innovative ways to make registration and voting work for the younger generation, and built open-source technology to empower other organizations, as well. Take Action here: https://www.rockthevote.org/action-center

RUN FOR SOMETHING https://runforsomething.net helps recruit and support young diverse progressives to run for down-ballot races in order to build a bench for the future. In 2017 and 2018, we elected candidates in 40 states to offices ranging from state Senate to county Sheriff. Our candidates come from all walks of life– teachers, doctors, activists, artists, parents, and refugees representing communities that have been historically excluded and discouraged from running for political office. We believe in running grassroots-powered campaigns focusing on local issues. Volunteer here: https://runforsomething.net/why/volunteer

 https://sisterdistrict.com focuses on state legislatures because:

1. States are critical to securing fairly drawn districts and fighting back against gerrymandering and voter suppression.
2. States are incubators of strong progressive policies and leaders.
3. State level campaigns are often small and under-nourished — our volunteers' dollars and hard work can have an outsized impact.

Volunteer here: https://sisterdistrict.com/volunteer

Stand On Every Corner: https://standoneverycorner.com is a growing national movement of people coming together to hold regular, peaceful, family-friendly protests in their own neighborhoods. Protect our democracy from corruption and treason. Insist on the rule of law and honesty from elected officials. This movement isn't about left vs. right. Or blue vs. red. It's about right vs. wrong. It's about holding our elected representatives accountable. It's about being there for each other. All it takes is you and a corner. Go here for guidance: https://standoneverycorner.com/frequently-asked-questions

Swing Left: https://swingleft.org about helps you find the most impactful things you can do to help Democrats win the most important elections. The work to take back our government in 2020 and beyond starts NOW—sign up to receive actions you can take. Even if you don't live in a swing district there are ways you can help. Check out this article in the *New Yorker* http://www.newyorker.com/culture/

jia-tolentino/swing-left-and-the-post-election-surge-of-progressive-activism Find a group near you here: https://swingleft.org/groups

 http://twwusa.org is a grassroots civic engagement organization that gets people involved in local governance and drives progressive engagement at all levels. With over 70% of members being new to political engagement, we are cultivating a lifestyle of activism that will not only resist current dangerous policy, but drive sustainable, long-term solutions that encompass our progressive priorities, including both political and social activism. They sponsor local group events and initiatives, fundraise and support candidates, and lobby for progressive initiatives. Tool kit and resources here: http://twwusa.org/resources/activist-toolkit

TOWN HALL PROJECT www.townhallproject.com empowers constituents across the country to have face-to-face conversations with their elected representatives. They are campaign veterans and first time volunteers. They come from a diversity of backgrounds, live across the country, share progressive values and believe strongly in civic engagement. The Town Hall Project researches every district and state for public events with members of Congress. Then they share their findings to promote participation in the democratic process. Get their Town Hall Guide here: https://indivisible.org/resource/town-hall-guide

The Action Network: https://actionnetwork.org is dedicated to building online power for the progressive movement. We don't have clients – we have partners. Use Action Network to: Organize people online and offline, recruit and mobilize new activist, Raise funds to fuel important work and much more. When corporations use their power, influence, and resources to harm workers, consumers of their products, or the environment, The Action Network will activate a network of activists and organizations to hold corporations accountable to their responsibility to create shared prosperity. Find Action Groups near you here: https://actionnetwork.org/groups/search

The Rutgers Eagleton Institute for Politics, Center for American Women and Politics: https://cawp.rutgers.edu/women-elective-office-2019 lists the number of women in elective office, at all levels of government, by state.

Vote Smart: www.votesmart.org provides free, factual, unbiased information on candidates and elected officials to ALL Americans. Vote Smart is an historic undertaking. Citizens come together, not to support one candidate over another, but to defend democracy. It is a gathering of people committed to one purpose: to strengthen the essential component of democracy – access to information. Find ways to volunteer here: https://votesmart.org/volunteer#.XGHrVvlKiyI

5 Calls https://5calls.org helps people call their members of Congress. You enter your city, zip code, or use your smart phone's location service to find your congressional district. The app then provides you with the correct phone numbers to call your representative and two senators. Plus, scripts for a number of timely issues, making it simple to have your voice heard. Every week there will be at least 5 scripts available – so you can make 5 calls!

Children and Families

Alliance for Youth Action: https://www.allianceforyouthaction.org is a nationwide network of organizations building the political power of young people, and the premier youth vote vehicle in the United States. They are local young people's organizations joining together to make each other – and their entire movement – stronger. The Alliance is implementing a targeted campaign to engage and sustain young people electorally. Donate here:
https://www.allianceforyouthaction.org/donate

Boys & Girls Clubs of America: https://www.bgca.org helps millions of kids and teens develop essential skills, make lasting connections and have fun. Club members experience a safe place to learn, play and grow, supportive relationships with caring mentors and enriching programs, experiences and activities. Get involved here: https://www.bgca.org/get-involved/volunteer Donate here: https://www.bgca.org/ways-to-give

Children's Defense Fund (CDF): https://www.childrensdefense.org provides research, advocacy, public education, monitoring of federal agencies, assistance to state and local groups, and community organizing on a wide range of issues that affect children and youth, especially poor and minority children and those with disabilities. Explore the number of ways you can help here: https://www.childrensdefense.org/activism/advocacy/community-organizing To get action alerts go here: https://www.childrensdefense.org/activism/advocacy/speak-up/action-alert-snap And the Fellowship program is open to people of all ages who are ready to put their passion into practice. To become a Child Defender Fellow go here: https://www.childrensdefense.org/activism/advocacy/child-defender-fellowship

First Star: https://www.firststar.org improves the lives of foster youth by partnering with child welfare agencies, universities, and school districts to ensure foster youth have the academic, life skills, and adult supports needed to successfully transition to higher education and adulthood. Learn more here: https://vimeo.com/65436956 For ways to help go here: https://www.firststar.org/how-you-can-help

Girl Scouts of America: https://www.girlscouts.org is a one-of-a-kind leadership development program for girls, with proven results helping girls take the lead in their own lives and in the world. Research shows that girls learn best in an all-girl, girl-led, and girl-friendly environment. Girl Scouts is a place where girls practice different skills, explore their potential, take on leadership positions — and are even feel allowed to fail, dust themselves off, get up, and try again. Get involved here: https://www.girlscouts.org/en/adults/volunteer.html

Girls Inc.: https://girlsinc.org delivers life-changing programs that inspire girls to be strong, smart, and bold. Research-based curricula, delivered by trained professionals, equip girls to achieve academically; lead healthy and physically active lives; manage money; navigate media messages; and discover an interest in science, technology, engineering, and math. The network of local Girls Inc. nonprofit organizations serves 140,000 girls ages 6 - 18 annually. They cannot operate without the hundreds of hours of volunteer service they receive each year from dedicated individuals and community partnerships. Take Action here: https://girlsinc.org/take-action

Families Belong Together: https://www.familiesbelongtogether.org includes nearly 250 organizations from all backgrounds joined together to fight family separation and promote dignity, unity, and compassion for all children and families. This coalition of organizations have raised millions of dollars to help unite immigrant children and families and have mobilized hundreds of thousands people to take action in all 50 states.

Million Women Mentors: https://www.millionwomenmentors.com supports the engagement of millions of Science, Technology, Engineering and Math (STEM) mentors (male and female) to increase the interest and confidence of girls and women to persist and succeed in STEM programs and careers by 2020.

Moms Rising: https://www.momsrising.org is working to achieve economic security for all moms, women, and families in the United States by working for; paid family leave, earned sick days, affordable childcare, an end to the wage and hiring discrimination, better childhood nutrition, health care for all, toxic-free environments, breastfeeding rights, and for a national budget that reflects the contributions of women and moms. Take action here:
https://www.momsrising.org/take-action

National Head Start Association (NHSA): https://www.nhsa.org provides free learning and development services to children ages birth to five and pregnant women from low-income families. Head Start serves over 1 million children and their families in 2,809 programs, employing 225,000 staff and teachers. There are more than 20,000 classrooms throughout the country. Find a Head Start near you to see if there are volunteer opportunities here:
https://www.nhsa.org/why-head-start/head-start-locator

National Partnership for Women and Families:
http://www.nationalpartnership.org promotes fairness in the workplace, reproductive health and rights, access to quality, affordable health care, and policies that help women and men meet the dual demands of work and family. How you can help:
http://www.nationalpartnership.org/support-us/ways-to-give.html

SheHeroes: http://www.sheheroes.org empowers young girls of all backgrounds to dream big, explore their interests and passionately pursue non-traditional careers. Through their online content and video profiles, girls imagine their own potential by engaging with influential stories of exceptional, successful women role models across all fields. Like Sally Ride, they believe: "If you can't see it, you can't be it!" Watch here: https://www.youtube.com/watch?time_continue=104&v=jZ4x6zKmm4o To donate go here: http://www.sheheroes.org/sheheroes-donations

Teen Talking Circles: educates, inspires and empowers young women and men, fosters partnerships between the genders, generations and cultures, and supports youth in positive self-expression and social action for a just, compassionate and sustainable world. Explore how you can get involved here: http://teentalkingcircles.org

Climate Change and the Environment

American Rivers: https://www.americanrivers.org is North America's leading national river-conservation organization. They combine national advocacy with fieldwork in key river basins to deliver the greatest impact. With positions informed by science, they build partnerships and work closely with local river advocates, business and agriculture interests, recreation groups and others to forge win-win solutions. For ways to have an impact go here: https://www.americanrivers.org/make-an-impact

Citizens' Climate Lobby: https://citizensclimatelobby.org is a grass-roots advocacy organization using a respectful, nonpartisan approach to climate education and focused on national policies, particularly advocating for a Carbon Fee and Dividend proposal. With hundreds of chapters, they help ordinary people in exercising their personal and political power by lobby their members of Congress regarding climate. Volunteers include high school students, concerned grandparents, engineers in the Texas natural gas industry, house painters from New England, and farmers from Virginia to California's Central Valley.

Defenders of Wildlife: https://defenders.org works on the ground at the state and local level developing practical, innovative programs that protect and restore imperiled key species and their habitats. Citizen-based advocacy is a linchpin in American democracy. Here are general tips for being an effective voice for wildlife: https://defenders.org/activist

Earth Justice: https://earthjustice.org is the Legal backbone of the environmental movement and represents a wide diversity of clients, from small grassroots groups to large national organizations. Individual donors and foundations enable them to choose cases strategically rather than based on the client's ability to pay. Check out regional offices here: https://tinyurl.com/y5mylpbg And the "Take Action" menu here: https://earthjustice.org/action gives you an easy way to write letters supporting your chosen cause.

Environmental Defense Fund (EDF): https://www.nrdc.org combines the power of more than three million members and online activists with the expertise of some 600 scientists, lawyers, and policy advocates across the globe to ensure the rights of all people to the air, the water, and the wild. Check out Trump Watch, NRDC's official record of the administration's environmental assault here: https://www.nrdc.org/trump-watch For easy ways to take action go here: https://www.nrdc.org/get-involved

Environmental Justice Foundation (EJF): https://ejfoundation.org trains local people and communities who are directly affected to investigate, expose, and combat environmental degradation and abuse. Their work is targeted, direct and effective. They gathered powerful first-hand testimonials from those living on the frontlines of climate change. Get involved here: https://ejfoundation.org/get-involved

Friends of the Earth (FOE): https://foe.org is a global network, representing 74 different countries that defends the environment and champions a healthy and just world. They collaborate with broader movements, because the fight to protect our planet is intrinsically tied to the global struggle for justice. When a political appointee or a threatening piece of legislation looms, they work to stop to it. To take action go here: https://foe.org/take-action

Food & Water Watch: https://www.foodandwaterwatch.org works with concerned individuals across the country to protect our food and water on every level – banning fracking, working to win stated-based GMO labeling, stopping a local water privatization or holding an elected official accountable. Choose your state to find ways to get involved in your area here: https://www.foodandwaterwatch.org/about/get-active-where-you-live They have the tools to help you to get active in your community. Sign up for email updates, and they will tell you when there's a threat in your state and how you can take action to stop it.

Greenpeace USA: https://www.greenpeace.org uses non-violent direct action and creative communication to expose global environmental problems and to promote solutions that are essential to a green and peaceful future. They work with thousands of volunteers who are on the inside track of our campaigns. Whether you've been an activist for decades or you're just starting and want to learn how you can help, they have volunteer opportunities for you here: https://www.greenpeace.org/usa/volunteer-with-greenpeace

League of Conservation Voters (LCV): https://www.lcv.org works to turn environmental values into national, state and local priorities and advocates for sound environmental laws and policies, holds elected officials accountable for their votes and actions, and elects pro-environment candidates who will champion their priority issues. Their scorecard, produced in partnership with leading environmental groups, is the standard bearer to determine the environmental record of all members of Congress. Easy ways to take action here: https://www.lcv.org/take-action

Natural Resources Defense Council (NRDC):
https://www.nrdc.org works to safeguard the earth and the natural systems on which all life depends. They use law, science, and the support of its members to protect the planet's wildlife and wild places and ensure a safe and healthy environment. Watch here: https://www.youtube.com/watch?time_continue=80&v=D7bpH0wB6lc To get involved go here: https://www.nrdc.org/get-involved

NextGen America: https://nextgenamerica.org works to prevent damage to our climate by transitioning to a clean energy economy, based on equality, inclusion, and a shared and sustainable prosperity. They are registering and turning out young voters at an unprecedented rate in eleven states across the country to help elect leaders that work for us. Find out how you can help here: https://nextgenamerica.org/act

Pesticide Action Network (PAN): http://www.panna.org campaigns to replace pesticides with ecologically sound alternatives. They link local and international consumer, labor, health, environment and agriculture groups into an international citizens' action network. Together, they challenge the global proliferation of pesticides, defend basic rights to health and environmental quality, and work to ensure the transition to a just and viable food system. To find ways to help go here: http://www.panna.org/take-action/online-action-center

Population Connection Formerly, Zero Population Growth (ZPG): https://www.populationconnection.org advocates for progressive action to stabilize world population at a level that can be sustained by Earth's resources. Until everyone, everywhere, has access to affordable and appropriate contraceptives, comprehensive reproductive health care, and equal opportunity in education and employment, global environmental crises, food and water shortages, and entrenched poverty will continue unabated. To get involved go here: https://www.populationconnection.org/getinvolved

Power Shift Network: https://powershift.org is a grassroots hub for young climate activists bringing together leaders from the smallest campus groups to the largest national organizations to fight for climate, clean energy, and social justice. They mobilize the collective power of young people. Find out how you can get involved here: https://powershift.org/convergences   To donate go here: https://actionnetwork.org/fundraising/support-a-winning-youth-led-climate-justice-movement

Schools for Climate Action:
https://schoolsforclimateaction.weebly.com is a non-partisan, grass-roots, youth-adult campaign with a mission to empower schools to speak up for climate action. They advocate for elected officials to combat the climate crisis in order to protect current and future generations. They help school boards, student councils, school environmental clubs, PTA's, teachers' unions, and school support organizations to pass resolutions that do 3 things:

1. Drive a paradigm shift so people recognize climate change as a generational justice and equity issue.
2. Clearly articulate the political will for all elected leaders, especially Member of Congress, to support or enact common-sense climate policies (such as carbon pricing, 100% clean energy policies, green infrastructure investments, and just transition plans).
3. Celebrate and expand school district responses to climate change.

For a number of easy things you can do go here:
https://schoolsforclimateaction.weebly.com/take-action.html

Sierra Club: https://www.sierraclub.org works to inspire all Americans to explore, enjoy, and protect the Earth's wild places, to practice and promote responsible use of the Earth's ecosystems and resources, and to work to restore the quality of the natural environment that sustains us. Take action here: https://www.sierraclub.org/take-action

The Climate Reality Project: https://www.climaterealityproject.org launched by former Vice President Al Gore, presents the facts about climate change and its solutions to the general public in an accurate, clear and compelling manner. Watch here: https://www.youtube.com/watch?time_continue=128&v=sujFGXyIbPY Find a chapter near you here: https://www.climaterealityproject.org/chapters

Union of Concerned Scientists: https://www.ucsusa.org develops and implements innovative, practical solutions to some of our planet's most pressing problems, from combating global warming and developing sustainable ways to feed, power, and transport ourselves, to fighting misinformation, advancing racial equity, and reducing the threat of nuclear war. For ways you can help go here: https://www.ucsusa.org/action-center

350.org: https://350.org uses online campaigns, grassroots organizing, and mass public actions to oppose new coal, oil and gas projects, take money out of the companies that are heating up the planet, and build 100% clean energy solutions that work for all. 350's network extends to 188 countries with an emphasis on direct action. Go here to find ways to get involved: https://350.org/get-involved

Disabled Rights

American Association of People with Disabilities (AAPD): https://www.aapd.com is a convener, connector, and catalyst for change, increasing the political and economic power of people with disabilities. They are a cross-disability member organization dedicated to ensuring economic self-sufficiency and political empowerment for the more than 56 million Americans with disabilities.

Disability Rights Advocates (DRA): https://dralegal.org has offices in California and New York and is one of the leading nonprofit disability rights legal centers in the nation. Their mission is to advance equal rights and opportunity for people with all types of disabilities nationwide. To donate go here: https://dralegal.org/donate

Disability Rights Education and Defense Fund (DREDF): https://dredf.org works to advance the civil and human rights of people with disabilities through legal advocacy, training, education, and public policy and legislative development. They are a leading national civil rights law and policy center directed by individuals with disabilities and parents who have children with disabilities. Find resources to help parents and students with disabilities here: https://dredf.org/special-education/special-education-resources

National Disability Right Network (NDRN): https://www.ndrn.org advocates on Capitol Hill for laws that guard against abuse; advocate for basic rights; and ensure accountability in health care, education, employment, housing, transportation, and within the justice system. Easy ways you can help here: https://www.ndrn.org/take-action

Education

American Association of University Women: https://www.aauw.org has been empowering women as individuals and as a community since 1881. For more than 130 years, they have worked together as a national grassroots organization to improve the lives of millions of women and their families. To take action go here: https://www.aauw.org/what-we-do/public-policy/two-minute-activist

Education Is A Right: http://www.right-to-education.org promotes education as a human right, making international and national law accessible to everybody. They conduct research and legal analysis and develop tools and guides to help understand and effectively use human rights mechanisms to claim and enforce the right to education. They build bridges between disciplines (human rights, education and development), actors (CSOs, international organizations, academics), and language communities, linking international, national and local advocacy with practical engagements leading to positive changes on the ground.

National Coalition for Women and Girls in Education: https://www.ncwge.org was formed to educate the public about issues concerning equal rights for women and girls in education; to monitor the enforcement and administration of current legislation related to equal rights for women and girls in education; to perform and publish research and analysis of issues concerning equal rights for women and girls in education, and to take the steps necessary and proper to accomplish these purposes. For a comprehensive list on local, state, and national organizations with opportunities to engage in educational equality for women and girls go to: https://www.ncwge.org/affiliates.html

Progressive Education Network: https://progressiveeducationnetwork.org believes that the purpose of education transcends preparation for college or career. Schools nurture citizens in an increasingly diverse democracy. Within the

complexities of education theory, practice, policy, and politics, we promote a vision of progressive education for the 21st century that: responds to contemporary issues from a progressive educational perspective, welcomes families and communities as partners in children's learning, and promotes diversity, equity, and justice in our schools and society. To donate go here:
https://progressiveeducationnetwork.org/donate

Student Leadership Network:
https://www.studentleadershipnetwork.org empowers a diverse pipeline of young people growing up in low-income communities to access educational opportunities that prepare them to be change agents for themselves, their families, their communities, and our country. Student Leadership Network (formerly known as Young Women's Leadership Network). They impact more than 2,400 students at five all-girls public schools in New York City and nearly 8,000 at 15 national Young Women's Leadership Network affiliates. Moreover, the success of our girls' schools has inspired dozens of single-sex schools to open nationwide. To volunteer go here:
https://www.studentleadershipnetwork.org/volunteer

Elder Advocacy

Alliance for Retired Americans: https://retiredamericans.org is a nationwide grass roots organization, with more than 4.3 million members working together to ensure social and economic justice and full civil rights for all citizens by mobilizing retired union members, seniors and community activists into a nationwide grassroots movement advocating a progressive political and social agenda. Chartered in 36 states, they have members across the country who work to strengthen Medicare, Social Security, and pensions. Learn how to get involved with your state alliance here: https://retiredamericans.org/state-alliances

Create the Good: http://createthegood.org/volunteer-search will take you to a resource for volunteering in your area. By entering "seniors" in the keywords box and your zip code in the next box you'll be directed to a comprehensive list of opportunities to work with seniors in a wide range of settings and services.

Meals on Wheels: https://www.mealsonwheelsamerica.org is often the first line of support for isolated seniors in times of emergency. They provide shelf-stable meals, coordinate evacuation plans or simply checking in to make sure seniors are not forgotten. On their web site a pop-up will appear with a link at the bottom to find Meals on Wheels in your locale so you can get involved.

National Association of Area Agencies on Aging (n4a): https://www.n4a.org provides a range of options that allow older adults to choose the home and community-based services and living arrangements that suit them best. They make it possible for older adults to "age in place" in their homes and communities. Almost every AAA has opportunities for volunteering. You can put in your zip code and link to your local Area Agency on Aging.

SeniorAdvisor.com: https://www.senioradvisor.com/blog/2017/06/15-organizations-working-to-advocate-for-seniors is a list with links to 15 organizations that advocate for seniors. Some of the organizations included in this appendix are included on the Senior Advisor list.

Social Security Works: https://www.socialsecurityworks.org is an organization working to protect and improve the economic security of disadvantaged and at-risk populations. They safeguard the economic security of those dependent, now or in the future, on Social Security and work to maintain Social Security as a vehicle of social justice. Take Action here: https://www.socialsecurityworks.org/category/action

The American Society on Aging (ASA):
https://www.asaging.org/asa-constituent-groups offers education, publications, and training to help people who work with seniors, learn best practices and stay up to date on how to do their work in an effective and compassionate manor. They provide volunteer opportunities for ASA members. The list of ASA Constituent Groups at https://www.asaging.org/asa-constituent-groups will link you to networks, forums and advocacy groups as diverse as the Forum on Religion, Spirituality and Aging https://www.asaging.org/forum-religion-spirituality-and-aging-forsa to the Corp of Accomplished Professionals https://www.asaging.org/corps-accomplished-professionals

Electing Women

Close the Gap California: https://closethegapca.org is a statewide campaign to achieve gender balance in the California Legislature by recruiting progressive women to run. They recruit accomplished women in targeted districts and prepare them to launch competitive campaigns. Their recruits are pro-choice, pro-public school funding and support paths out of poverty and over 75% are women of color. Why Women?

- Women expand a legislature's agenda.

- Women institute transparency and inclusion in proceedings.
- Women add depth and perspective to policy discussions and change the outcome of votes.
- Women get things done.

For volunteer opportunities go here:
https://closethegapca.org/volunteer

Emerge America: https://emergeamerica.org is the nation's premier organization that recruits, trains and provides a powerful network to Democratic women who want to run for office. They inspire women to run and help them hone their skills to win. The mission of Emerge is to increase the number of Democratic women leaders from diverse backgrounds in public office through recruitment, training and providing a powerful network. To get involved go here:
https://emergeamerica.org/get-involved

EMILY's List: https://www.emilyslist.org is a community of more than five million that seeks to elect pro-choice Democratic women. They have systematically defined a strategic approach to winning elections that drives progressive change. They recruit the strongest candidates, support campaigns that can win, study the electorate, and turn out the vote. Go here to support EMILY's List: https://www.emilyslist.org/pages/entry/support-emilys-list And for more information on the Focus 2020 program go to:
https://www.emilyslist.org/focus-2020

She Should Run: https://www.sheshouldrun.org is a non-profit that aims to get more women into elected leadership roles. Thousands of women have raised their hand to run for office or nominated a women leader they know. Our Incubator program supports 14,000 women in finding their unique path to elected office. To help go here: https://www.sheshouldrun.org/250kby2030

Women's Campaign Fund: http://www.wcfonline.org is a national nonpartisan organization that commits to 50/50 representation by women and men in elected offices nationwide by 2028. They are people from all political parties who believe government works best when America is represented by 100% of the available talent, wisdom, and skill – 50/50, men and women, like the population. WCF also operates the 50/50 PAC for women candidates. Not just any women. Women with the proven ability to reach common ground solutions. WCF does not need to speak for all women, for all men, nor for all topics. We champion the ability of more women to speak for themselves, working in equal numbers with men, in every party, in every elected office, at every level of government. To get involved go here: http://www.wcfonline.org/get_involved

Gender, Racial, Economic and Social Justice

Advancement Project: https://advancementproject.org is a next generation, multi-racial civil rights organization that uses innovative tools and strategies to strengthen social movements and achieve high impact policy change. They were founded by a team of veteran civil rights lawyers who believed that structural racism could begin to be dismantled by multi-racial grassroots organizing focused on changing public policies and supported by lawyers and communications strategies. Learn more at: https://advancementproject.org/about-advancement-project

American Civil Liberties Union: https://action.aclu.org works to defend individual rights and liberties guaranteed by the Constitution. Donate here: https://action.aclu.org/donate-aclu?ms=web_horiz_nav_hp

Anti-Defamation League: https://www.adl.org was founded in 1913 to "stop the defamation of the Jewish people and to secure justice and fair treatment to all." Today, it fights against anti-Semitism and bigotry as one of the largest civil rights organizations in the country. For ways you can help go here: https://www.adl.org/takeaction Donate here: https://www.adl.org/ways-to-give

Black Lives Matter: https://blacklivesmatter.com is a chapter-based Global Network, member-led organization whose mission is to build local power and to intervene in violence inflicted on Black communities by the state and vigilantes. They believe that in order to win and bring as many people with us along the way, they must move beyond the narrow nationalism that is all too prevalent in Black communities. They affirm the lives of Black queer and trans folks, disabled folks, undocumented folks, folks with records, women, and all Black lives along the gender spectrum. They are working for a world where Black lives are no longer systematically targeted for demise. Take action here: https://blacklivesmatter.com/take-action

Campaign ZERO: https://www.joincampaignzero.org advocates for policy solutions to end police violence in America. Fill out this survey here: https://staywoke.typeform.com/to/C8sEb7 Use the tools here: https://www.joincampaignzero.org/#action to track legislation impacting your community and hold your representatives accountable for taking meaningful action to end police violence. Campaign ZERO was developed with contributions from activists, protesters and researchers across the nation. This data-informed platform presents comprehensive solutions to end police violence in America. It integrates community demands and policy recommendations from research organizations and President Obama's Task Force on 21st Century Policing. Actions you can take here: https://www.joincampaignzero.org/#action

Color of Change: https://colorofchange.org is the nation's largest online racial justice organization. As a national online force driven by more than 1.4 million members, they move decision-makers in corporations and government to create a more human and less hostile world for Black people in America. By designing strategies powerful enough to fight racism and injustice—in politics and culture, in the workplace and the economy, in criminal justice and community life, and wherever they exist, they are changing both the written and unwritten rules of society. They mobilize our members to end practices and systems that unfairly hold Black people back, and champion solutions that move us all forward. Watch here: https://colorofchange.org/about Become a Color Of Change member here: https://act.colorofchange.org/signup/signup Start a petition here: https://www.organizefor.org

Common Cause: https://www.commoncause.org works for all in every state and each of the 435 congressional districts, with 30 states in their network. In the past year Common Cause activists have helped establish new public financing programs, spread automatic voter registration to five new states, held the Trump administration accountable (including shutting down Trump's election commission) and dozens of other victories. Take action here: https://tinyurl.com/y395tbcw

Courage Campaign: https://www.couragecampaign.org fights for a more progressive California and country. Powered by 1.4 million members, their proven strategy combines digital tools with grass-roots community organizing and powerful messaging. They focus on three priorities:

1. Economic Justice
2. Human Rights
3. Corporate and Political Accountability

They work in California - the largest and most diverse state - to create models for the country. They are not bound by election cycles and are a permanent, independent, multi-issue campaign, winning progressive change today, and building power for the future. Take action here: https://www.couragecampaign.org/take-action

Demand Justice: https://www.demandjustice.org fights for progressive change only made real through the power of citizen activism. Demand Justice empowers citizens to organize around our nation's courts and prevent them from devolving into just another tool of economic and social oppression. They wage fact-based campaigns to defend our right to bodily autonomy and to stop our courts from pursuing an agenda that further enriches the wealthy and corporations at the expense of everyday Americans. They resist those who distort our laws to try to legitimize discrimination against women, communities of color and LGBTQ Americans. And they work to elevate more women and people of color to the federal bench. Donate here: https://secure.actblue.com/donate/demand-justice?refcode=website

Dolores Huerta Foundation (DHF): http://doloreshuerta.org is a 501(c)(3) community benefit organization that organizes at the grassroots level, engaging and developing natural leaders. DHF creates leadership opportunities for community organizing, leadership development, civic engagement, and policy advocacy. DHF is a direct-action organization and hands-on training center for community organizing, leadership development, and policy advocacy. Several of their projects are in agricultural communities of California's Central Valley including Arvin, Lamont, Weedpatch, Lost Hills, Lindsay, Woodlake, and Cutler-Orosi. To learn more watch here: http://doloreshuerta.org/category/dolores-huerta-in-action To donate go here: http://doloreshuerta.org/we-can-do-it-you-can-help

Higher Heights for America:
http://www.higherheightsforamerica.org seeks to elevate Black women's voices to shape and advance progressive policies and politics. By strengthening Black women's civic participation in grassroots advocacy campaigns and the electoral process, Higher Heights for America will create the environment in which more Black women, and other candidates who are committed to advance policies that affect Black women, can be elected to public office. Go here for ways to help: https://www.higherheightsforamerica.org/get_involved

The Southern Poverty Law Center: https://www.splcenter.org is dedicated to fighting hate and bigotry and to seeking justice for the most vulnerable members of our society. Using litigation, education, and other forms of advocacy, the SPLC works toward the day when the ideals of equal justice and equal opportunity will be a reality. SPLC also tracks hate groups. Find information about hate groups in your area here: https://www.splcenter.org/hate-map Their Economic Justice Project is fighting back against deeply engrained policies and practices that exploit or punish the poor simply because of their economic status. Their work has a national reach but is primarily focused on the Deep South. Donate here: https://donate.splcaction.org/sslpage.aspx?pid=1549

NAACP Legal Defense Fund: https://www.naacpldf.org is America's premier legal organization fighting for racial justice. Through litigation, advocacy, and public education, LDF seeks structural changes to expand democracy, eliminate disparities, and achieve racial justice, defends the gains and protections won over the past 75 years of civil rights struggle and works to improve the quality and diversity of judicial and executive appointments. Donate and learn about ways to get involved here: https://www.naacpldf.org/support

National Association for the Advancement of Colored People (NAACP): https://www.naacp.org secures the political, educational, social, and economic equality of rights in order to eliminate race-based discrimination and ensure the health and well-being of all persons. With approximately 2,200 adult branches, youth councils, and college chapters in 50 states, 5 countries and the District of Columbia, the NAACP is actively engaged in increasing the African American responsiveness of citizens to be fully engaged in the democratic process. Sign up to get involved here: https://www.naacp.org/sign-up

Native American Rights Fund: https://www.narf.org has provided legal assistance since 1971 to Indian tribes, organizations, and individuals nationwide who might otherwise have gone without adequate representation and has successfully asserted and defended the most important rights of Indians and tribes in hundreds of major cases, achieving significant results. Donate here: https://www.narf.org/support-us

The Tax March: https://taxmarch.org is a growing national movement that extends far beyond one day of marching. Tired of systems that are rigged in favor of the super-rich? The Tax March movement maintains that any reform to the tax code should be about closing loopholes for the wealthy and big corporations and building an economy that invests in working people. The Republican tax scam passed in December of 2017 does just the opposite. In order to give tax breaks to millionaires, billionaires, and wealthy corporations, the Trump Tax raises taxes for 92 million middle-class families, rips health care away from 13 million people, and threatens life-saving programs millions of Americans rely on. Through on-the-ground organizing nation-wide, representation in town halls, and amplification on social media and in the press, the Tax March will ensure that President Trump and Congress hear us loud and clear. Help spread the word here: https://taxmarch.org/spread-the-word

UnidosUS: https://www.unidosus.org — formerly known as the National Council of La Raza — Since 1968, has remained a trusted, nonpartisan voice for Latinos. They serve the Hispanic community through their research, policy analysis, and state and national advocacy efforts, as well as in our program work in communities nation-wide. They partner with a national network of nearly 300 Affiliates across the country to serve millions of Latinos in the areas of civic engagement, civil rights and immigration, education, workforce and the economy, health, and housing. Open the doors to opportunity for all Americans. Join the UnidosUS *familia* by contributing in a way that's right for you. Give your voice, your time, or a gift. Every contribution makes a difference. https://www.unidosus.org/ways-to-give Watch here: https://www.unidosus.org/about-us/our-history

Gun Safety

Community Justice Action Fund: https://www.cjactionfund.org is building power for and with communities of color to end gun violence.

They are addressing the issue in a holistic, sustainable, and intersectional manner galvanizing the people most affected by the pain to inform solutions that effectively tackle the root causes of gun violence. They work to pass policy on all levels of government that is reflective of communities of color, as well as fight back against any policies that will lead to mass incarceration, or other forms of discrimination. For ways to take action go here: https://www.cjactionfund.org/take-action

Everytown for Gun Safety: https://everytown.org is a movement of Americans working together to end gun violence and build safer communities. Gun violence touches every town in America. For too long, change has been thwarted by the Washington gun lobby and by leaders who refuse to take common-sense steps that will save lives. But something is changing. Nearly six million mayors, moms, cops, teachers, survivors, gun owners, students and everyday Americans have come together to make their own communities safer. Together, we are fighting for the changes that we know will save lives. See actions you can take to prevent gun violence here: https://everytown.org/act

March For Our Lives: Thoughts and prayers aren't going to put a stop to gun violence. It will take all of us advocating for sensible gun violence prevention reforms to make it happen. Go here: https://marchforourlives.com to find ten policies proven to save lives — policies we need to accomplish as soon as possible to ensure the safety of our schools, homes and communities. And, here are five ways you can get involved: https://marchforourlives.com/take-action

Mom's Demand Action for Gun Sense in America: https://momsdemandaction.org is a grassroots movement of Americans fighting for public safety measures that can protect people from gun violence. They work to close the loopholes that jeopardize the safety of our families, and our communities. They work with business leaders to encourage a culture of responsible gun ownership. To take action go here: https://momsdemandaction.org/act

The Brady Campaign to Prevent Gun Violence: https://www.bradyunited.org Complex problems require big thinking. Brady's programs bring people together to address all forms of gun violence. When we work together, we can solve our biggest challenges. Expanding background checks (1 in every 5 gun sales today is conducted without one) and education and dialogue around responsible gun ownership saves American lives. To take action go here: https://www.bradyunited.org/take-action

Healthcare

Environmental Working Group (EWG): https://www.ewg.org empowers people to live healthier lives in a healthier environment. With breakthrough research and education, they drive consumer choice and civic action. They are a non-profit, non-partisan organization dedicated to protecting human health and the environment. Do you know what's in your tap water? What about your shampoo? What's lurking in the cleaners underneath your sink? What pesticides are on your food? EWG's groundbreaking research has changed the debate over environmental health. From households to Capitol Hill, EWG's team of scientists, policy experts, lawyers, communication experts and programmers has worked tirelessly to make sure someone is standing up for public health when government and industry won't. Support their work here:

https://www.ewg.org/support-our-work/ways-to-donate

Families USA: https://familiesusa.org advances its mission by combining policy expertise and partnerships with community, state, and national leaders to forge transformational solutions that improve the health and health care of our nation's families. Their ability to engage a broad network of stakeholders representing consumers, the health care sector, and the business sector is the hallmark of their success, as is their history of working with leaders from both sides of the aisle to tackle the health care problems facing the nation. Congress, federal agencies, and congressional staff rely on our expert advice to understand current policy and to develop new ideas. Share your story here: https://familiesusa.org/share-your-story To donate go here: https://bit.ly/2HlimZl

Health Care Now America: is the national grassroots coalition that ran a five-and-a-half year campaign to pass, protect, and promote the Affordable Care Act (ACA) and fought to protect Medicare and Medicaid, and advocated for fair taxes to support public services. They are organizing grassroots pressure across the country against the GOP's attempt to take away America's health care, and for quality, affordable health care that every family can count on. They believe that the Affordable Care Act must be improved and strengthened, not repealed and are opposed to any measures that would weaken Medicare, Medicaid, and Children's Health Insurance Program (CHIP) and hurt the tens of millions of Americans who depend on these vital programs for their financial and health security. They are organizing grassroots pressure across the country against the GOP's attempt to take away America's health care. The Trump-Republican plan will:

- Take coverage away from tens of millions of Americans
- Replace Medicare with a limited voucher

- Cut $1 trillion from state funds for Medicaid
- Raise the cost of health coverage for almost everyone

To take action go here: http://healthcareforamericanow.org/action

International Medical Corps: https://internationalmedicalcorps.org is a global, nonprofit, humanitarian aid organization dedicated to saving lives and relieving suffering by providing emergency medical services, as well as healthcare training and development programs, to those in great need. Established in 1984 by volunteer doctors and nurses, they are a private group with no political or religious affiliation. To volunteer and/or donate go here:
https://careers.internationalmedicalcorps.org/volunteer.html

Mothers2Mothers (m2m): https://www.m2m.org is bolstering African healthcare systems, while delivering empowerment opportunities for women. They employ, train, and help to empower HIV-positive women as community health workers. These "Mentor Mothers" work in local communities and at understaffed health facilities to ensure that women and their families get the health advice and medication they need, are linked to the right clinical services, and are supported on their treatment journey. This employment enables Mentor Mothers to gain financial security for themselves and their families. By virtue of being professionalised, Mentor Mothers become role models, putting a face to empowered, strong, and healthy HIV-positive women, and thereby helping to reduce HIV-related stigma and discrimination. To donate go here: https://www.m2m.org/donate/from-u-s-and-elsewhere To get involved go here: https://www.m2m.org/get-involved

For more organizations check out this article that will give you information on 15 organizations Changing the World Through Healthcare: https://www.causeartist.com/10-organizations-changing-world-health

The Right Care Alliance (RCA): https://rightcarealliance.org is a grassroots coalition of clinicians, patients, and community members organizing to make health care institutions accountable to communities and put patients, not profits, at the heart of health care. Right Care is a human right. It places the health and wellbeing of patients first. Right Care is affordable and effective. It is compassionate, honest, and safe. Right Care brings healing and comfort to patients, and satisfaction to clinicians. Achieving Right Care will require radically transforming how care is delivered and financed. To get active go here: https://rightcarealliance.org/actions To donate go here: https://secure.everyaction.com/uCm8ND9g80GwjQSmla5WMw2

Immigrant Rights

Border Angels: https://www.borderangels.org is an all-volunteer non-profit that advocates for immigration reform and social justice focusing on the U.S.-Mexico border. It offers educational and awareness programs and migrant outreach programs to San Diego County's immigrant population. For many ways you can support the cause even if you don't live near the U.S.-Mexican border go here: https://www.borderangels.org/volunteers

Define America: https://defineamerican.com is a nonprofit media and culture organization that uses the power of story to transcend politics and shift the conversation about immigrants, identity, and citizenship in a changing America. They have been recognized for using popular culture to influence the immigration debate. Using media consulting, original content development and production, media advocacy, and live events, Define American humanizes the conversation on immigration and fights anti-immigrant hate through storytelling. To date, Define American has consulted on more than 45 films and television projects, such as Grey's Anatomy and Superstore, spanning networks like ABC and NBC and streaming platforms such as Netflix and Hulu. For stories go here: https://defineamerican.com/video To get involved go here: https://defineamerican.com/campaigns To donate go here: https://defineamerican.com/donate

Kids In Need of Defense (KIND): https://supportkind.org works to ensure that no child appears in immigration court without high quality legal representation. They advance laws, policies, and practices that ensure children's protection and uphold their right to due process and fundamental fairness. They promote durable solutions to child migration that are grounded in the best interests of the child, ensuring that no child is forced to involuntarily migrate. Your help could mean the difference between a child who needs protection being sent back to his or her home country where their life may be in danger and the child being able to stay in the United States to live in safety and freedom. To help go here: https://supportkind.org/get-involved

Immigrant Families Together:
https://immigrantfamiliestogether.com is partnering with a number of long-established non-profits, social justice and immigrant advocacy groups, and elected officials around the country to apply their knowledge, experience, connections, and influence to work in collaboration for a single cause: to free mothers and reunite them with their children. They are one of the most comprehen-

sive foundations in providing full assistance to these families. They partner with some the best immigration attorneys in the country. Their entire organization is staffed solely by volunteers. 100% of their funds go directly to provide bonds, living expenses, medical, legal, and supporting urgent needs of like-minded organizations and their operating infrastructure. For many ways to help go here: https://immigrantfamiliestogether.com/how-you-can-help

Miles for Migrants: https://www.miles4migrants.org/mission.php is a non-profit 501(c)(3) charity, dedicated to using donated frequent flyer miles, points and money for the relocation of those displaced by war, persecution, politics and more, to start a new beginning in a new home. Their goal is to help families join their loved ones as quickly as possible, and without undue financial hardship. The refugees and their families that they serve are legally approved by the receiving country's government to travel for migration and/or family reunification purposes but have financial needs that prevent them from purchasing airfare themselves. Their work is on a volunteer-only basis and do not use any funding to cover personal costs for staff, including travel costs to make connections and further our efforts. To donate frequent flier miles go here: https://www.miles4migrants.org/donate.php

RAICES: https://www.raicestexas.org is a 501(c)(3) nonprofit agency that promotes justice by providing free and low-cost legal services to underserved immigrant children, families, and refugees. They combine expertise developed from the daily practice of immigration law with a deep commitment to advocacy. Their diverse staff of 130 attorneys, legal assistants, and support staff provide consultations, direct legal services, representation, assistance and advocacy to communities in Texas and to clients after they leave the state. RAICES staff closed 51,000 cases at no cost to their client. For volunteer opportunities go here: https://www.raicestexas.org/volunteer To donate go here: https://www.raicestexas.org/donate

Team Brownsville: https://www.teambrownsville.org was founded in July 2018, by a small group of like-minded educator volunteers. Since then membership and their mission has expanded with the help of volunteers and donors from around the globe. Team Brownsville volunteers help families and individuals legally seeking asylum in the United States. The team currently manages three programs - Breakfast at the bridge, Dinner at the bridge and Assistance at the bus station. To volunteer go here: https://tinyurl.com/y3qw54yu

The Coalition for Humane Immigrant Rights of Los Angeles (CHIRLA): https://www.chirla.org is an advocacy and organizing group focusing on achieving human, civil, and labor rights for immigrants. Donate here: https://connect.clickandpledge.com Watch here: https://www.youtube.com/watch?v=hWNDlfsN6wk

The Council on American-Islamic Relations (CAIR): https://www.cair.com is the country's largest Muslim civil liberties organization whose vision is to be a leading advocate for justice and mutual understanding and to enhance understanding of Islam, protect civil rights, promote justice, and empower American Muslims. To volunteer go here: https://www.cair.com/volunteer

The National Immigration Forum: https://immigrationforum.org is a leading immigrant advocacy group that offers various programs to integrate immigrants into the workforce and obtain citizenship. Donate here:
https://nationalimmigrationforum.secure.nonprofitsoapbox.com/forum-donate

The National Immigration Law Center: https://www.nilc.org is dedicated to fighting for the rights of low-income immigrants through litigation, policy analysis and advocacy, and various other methods. To get involved and work for the rights of low-income immigrants in our country go here: www.nilc.org/get-involved

The Young Center for Immigrant Children's Rights: www.theyoungcenter.org works to protect the best interests of children who come to the U.S. on their own making sure that wherever they land, whether here in the U.S. or in their home country, they are safe. To make a difference in the life of an unaccompanied immigrant child by volunteering to serve as a Child Advocate in Chicago, Houston, San Antonio, Harlingen, Phoenix, Los Angeles, New York, or Washington, D.C. go to: https://www.theyoungcenter.org/volunteer-at-the-young-center They are especially in need of bilingual speakers of many foreign languages.

United We Dream: https://unitedwedream.org transforms fear into finding your voice and empowers people to develop their leadership, their organizing skills, and to develop our own campaigns to fight for justice and dignity for immigrants and all people. This is achieved through immigrant youth-led campaigns at the local, state, and federal level. To take action go here: https://unitedwedream.org/getinvolved

International/Global Issues

Girl Effect: https://www.girleffect.org is a creative non-profit – experts in media, mobile, brand and international development – working where girls are marginalized and vulnerable. They build youth brands and mobile platforms that millions of girls and boys love and interact with, from apps that build skills, to TV dramas that explore vital issues, to magazines written and distributed by girls. To help go here: https://www.girleffect.org/join-our-community

One Light Global: https://www.onelightglobal.org transforms crisis-impacted communities into cities of inspiration. Through empowered collaboration with marginalized communities that integrates innovative technology with cultural wisdom, they co-create replicable, scalable, sustainable models for how humanity can thrive in our rapidly changing world. To donate go here:
http://www.onelightglobal.org/donate

Rising International: https://risinginternational.org enables women in America who are surviving extreme poverty, gender-based violence, homelessness, and human trafficking to connect with other survivors around the globe. Through the power of entrepreneurship, they help each other to rise. Rising has revolutionized the home party model by using it to alleviate extreme poverty, both locally and globally. Think Avon or Tupperware for a social cause. The world's most forgotten women sell their handmade boutique-quality products online and at Rising Home Parties. Locally, Rising trains women to be Rising Representatives who run their own business selling products made by their global sisters. To donate go here: https://risinginternational.org/rising-donation To host a Rising party go here: https://risinginternational.org/home-parties

The Sisterhood is Global Institute: https://donordirectaction.org was founded in 1984 by Robin Morgan, Simone de Beauvoir, and women from 80 countries. Its Donor Direct Action Fund strengthens women's rights organizations around the world by increasing access to financial resources, political leaders and public visibility, with minimum bureaucracy and maximum impact. To donate go here: https://tinyurl.com/yxktn8un

Women for Women: https://www.womenforwomen.org supports the most marginalized women in countries affected by war and conflict. Their programs enable them to earn and save money, improve health and well-being, influence decisions in their home and community, and connect to networks for support. By utilizing skills, knowledge, and resources, women are able to create sustainable change for themselves, their families, and their community. For ways to help go here: https://www.womenforwomen.org/get-involved

Women in Cities International: https://femmesetvilles.org envisions a world where there is a meaningful participation of a full diversity of women and girls in creating inclusive and equitable cities and communities. They work to generate and exchange knowledge on women's and girls' experiences in urban environments and support the participation of women, girls and other community actors in all processes of urban development and governance. To donate go here: https://femmesetvilles.org/donate

LGBTQ

Gay, Lesbian and Straight Education Network (GLSEN): https://www.glsen.org is focused on k-12 education to improve an education system that too frequently allows its lesbian, gay, bisexual, transgender, queer and questioning (LGBTQ) students to be bullied, discriminated against, or fall through the cracks. Connect to local chapters, information and national resources here: www.glsen.org/chapters

Human Rights Campaign and Human Rights Foundation:
https://www.hrc.org is the largest national lesbian, gay, bisexual, transgender and queer civil rights organization working to achieve LGBTQ equality. By inspiring and engaging individuals and communities, HRC strives to end discrimination against LGBTQ people and realize a world that achieves fundamental fairness and equality for all. For local events and actions and to donate to legal efforts go here: https://www.hrc.org/explore

Parents, Friends & Family of Lesbians & Gays (PFLAG):
https://pflag.org is a national organization with local chapters in almost every state which promotes the health and well-being of gay, lesbian, bisexual and transgendered persons, their families, and friends through support to cope with an adverse society, education to enlighten an ill-informed public, and advocacy to end discrimination and to secure equal civil rights. Connect to local chapters for action, advocacy and support resources here: https://pflag.org/find-a-chapter

The National LGBTQ Task Force: http://www.thetaskforce.org is the oldest LGBTQ organization in the United States. Despite all the progress, millions of LGBTQ people face barriers in every aspect of their lives: in housing, employment, healthcare, retirement, and basic human rights. The Task Force is training and mobilizing millions of activists across our nation to deliver a world where you can be you. Connect to online training resources, take virtual actions and find news of national and regional events.
http://www.thetaskforce.org/about/mission-history.html

Resources for more LGBTQ Information and Actions

Diversity Best Practices:
https://www.diversitybestpractices.com/about-diversity-best-practices
is a division of Working Mother Media, the preeminent organization
for mid to large size organizational diversity thought leaders to share
best practices and develop innovative solutions for culture change.
Through research, resources, benchmarking, publications and events,
Diversity Best Practices offers organizational members information
and strategies on how to implement, grow, measure and create first-
in-class diversity programs.

Media and Freedom of the Press

There are several reputable fact checking sites that specialize in rating
the truthfulness of media content. They are an excellent resource for
verifying or debunking information.

PolitiFact: https://www.politifact.com Fact-checking journalism is
the heart of PolitiFact. Their core principles are independence, transparency, fairness, thorough reporting and clear writing. The reason
they publish is to give citizens the information they need to govern
themselves in a democracy.

Snopes: https://www.snopes.com is the internet's definitive fact-
checking resource. When misinformation obscures the truth and
readers don't know what to trust, Snopes.com's fact checking and
original, investigative reporting lights the way to evidence-based and
contextualized analysis. They always document their sources so read-

ers are empowered to do independent research and make up their own minds. Snopes is an independent publication - the oldest and largest fact-checking site online, widely regarded by journalists, folklorists, and readers as an invaluable research companion. To donate go here: https://www.gofundme.com/savesnopes

FactCheck.org: https://www.factcheck.org is a nonpartisan, nonprofit "consumer advocate" for voters that aims to reduce the level of deception and confusion in U.S. politics. They monitor the factual accuracy of what is said by major U.S. political players in the form of TV ads, debates, speeches, interviews and news releases. Their goal is to apply the best practices of both journalism and scholarship, and to increase public knowledge and understanding.

Media Matters for America: https://www.mediamatters.org is a Web-based, not-for-profit, 501(c)(3) progressive research and information center dedicated to comprehensively monitoring, analyzing, and correcting conservative misinformation in the U.S. media. Using the website as the principal vehicle for disseminating research and information, *Media Matters* posts rapid-response items as well as longer research and analytic reports documenting conservative misinformation throughout the media and works daily to notify activists, journalists, pundits, and the general public about instances of misinformation, providing them with the resources to rebut false claims and to take direct action against offending media institutions. For actions you can take go here: https://www.mediamatters.org/take-action

Reporters Committee for Freedom of the Press: https://www.rcfp.org provides pro bono legal representation, amicus curiae support, and other legal resources to protect First Amendment freedoms and the newsgathering rights of journalists. The Reporters Committee serves the nation's leading news organizations; thousands of reporters, editors, and media lawyers; and many more who use their online and mobile resources. For ways you can help go here: https://www.rcfp.org/ways-to-give-to-the-reporters-committee

Women's eNews: https://womensenews.org is an award-winning nonprofit news service covering issues of particular concern to women and providing women's perspectives on public policy. With writers and readers around the globe Women's eNews' audience stretches from New York City to New Delhi and all points between, reaching an estimated 2.5 million readers each year. Women's eNews editors seek out freelance writers from around the world to write on every topic–politics, religion, economics, health, science, sustainability, education, sports, legislation–and commission them to write articles for distribution each day to subscribers and for posting on their Web site. To donate go here: https://womensenews.org/donate

Men and Masculinity

Coaching Boys Into Men: http://www.coachescorner.org Athletic coaches play an extremely influential and unique role in the lives of men. Because of these relationships, coaches are poised to positively influence how young men think and behave, both on and off the field. Coaching Boys Into Men (CBIM) is the only evidence-based prevention program that trains and motivates high school coaches to teach their young male athletes healthy relationship skills and that violence never equals strength. For ways to help go here: http://www.coachescorner.org/healthy-relationships-advocates

National Organization for Men Against Sexism: http://nomas.org is an activist organization for men and women supporting positive changes for men. NOMAS advocates a perspective that is pro-feminist, gay affirmative, anti-racist, dedicated to enhancing men's lives, and committed to justice on a broad range of social issues including class, age, religion, and physical abilities. To donate and/or become a member go here: http://nomas.org/membership

The Representation Project: http://therepresentationproject.org is a movement that uses film and media content to expose injustices created by gender stereotypes and to shift people's consciousness towards change. Interactive campaigns, strategic partnerships and education initiatives inspire individuals and communities to challenge the status quo and ultimately transform culture so everyone can fulfill their potential. *Miss Representation* is the award-winning documentary that exposes how mainstream media contributes to the underrepresentation of women in positions of power and influence. *The Mask You Live In*, asks: as a society, how are we failing our boys? The film examines how gender stereotypes are interconnected with race, class, and circumstance, and how kids are further influenced by the education system, sports culture, and mass media video games and pornography in particular. Watch here: http://vimeo.com/86728310

Poverty, Housing and Homelessness

Family Promise: https://familypromise.org/find-an-affiliate helps homeless and low-income families achieve sustainable independence through a community-based response. To get involved go here: https://familypromise.org/get-involved

Habitat for Humanity: https://www.habitat.org is a global non-profit housing organization working in local communities across all 50 states in the U.S. and in approximately 70 countries. Habitat's vision is of a world where everyone has a decent place to live. Habitat works toward its vision by building strength, stability and self-reliance in partnership with families in need of decent and affordable housing. To find volunteer, homeownership and ReStore donation and shopping opportunities in your local area go here: https://www.habitat.org/volunteer/near-you/find-your-local-habitat

National Alliance to End Homelessness: https://endhomelessness.org is a nonpartisan, nonprofit organization whose sole purpose is to end homelessness in the United States. They use research and data to find solutions to homelessness; they work with federal and local partners to create a solid base of policy and resources that support those solutions; and then they help communities implement them. Their strength is that they are outcome driven. Take action here: https://endhomelessness.org/help-end-homelessness/take-action

National Low Income Housing Coalition: http://nlihc.org is dedicated solely to achieving socially just public policy that assures people with the lowest incomes in the United States have affordable and decent homes. Their goals are to preserve existing federally assisted homes and housing resources, expand the supply of low-income housing, and establish housing stability as the primary purpose of federal low-income housing policy. To get involved go to the "Take Action" menu here: https://nlihc.org/takeaction

The Southern Poverty Law Center: https://www.splcenter.org is dedicated to fighting hate and bigotry and to seeking justice for the most vulnerable members of our society. Using litigation, education, and other forms of advocacy, the SPLC works toward the day when the ideals of equal justice and equal opportunity will be a reality. To donate go here: https://donate.splcaction.org/sslpage.aspx?pid=1549

The Sylvia Rivera Law Project: https://srlp.org is an organization that addressed the severe poverty and over-incarceration in low-income transgender communities and transgender communities of color, understanding that meaningful political participation for people struggling against gender identity discrimination could only come in partnership with economic justice.

Volunteers for America: https://www.voa.org touches the lives of 1.5 million people in over 400 communities in 46 states as well as the District of Columbia and Puerto Rico each year. They support and empower America's most vulnerable groups, including veterans, at-risk youth, the frail elderly, men and women returning from prison, homeless individuals and families, people with disabilities, and those recovering from addictions. For opportunities to volunteer in several program areas, including taking action to help the homeless and those in need of housing, go here: https://www.voa.org/volunteer

Reproductive Rights

NARAL Pro-Choice America: https://www.prochoiceamerica.org is a political advocacy group focused on fighting for women's reproductive rights and freedom. Their affiliates, working in partnership with NARAL Pro-Choice America, work to protect access to reproductive freedom. From working to pass proactive bills to holding anti-choice legislators accountable, their affiliates are on the frontlines to protecting and expanding reproductive freedom across the country. Click here to volunteer: https://www.prochoiceamerica.org/about/state-affiliates

Planned Parenthood: https://www.plannedparenthood.org is the country's leading sexual and reproductive healthcare provider. For nationwide volunteer opportunities (including as a clinic escort) go here: https://www.plannedparenthood.org/get-involved To donate go here: https://tinyurl.com/y6x6zrzu Local chapters also list more extensive volunteer opportunities, so take a look at your specific chapter for more.

The Center for Reproductive Rights:
https://www.reproductiverights.org uses the power of law to advance reproductive rights as fundamental human rights around the world. They envision a world where every person participates with dignity as an equal member of society, regardless of gender; and where every woman is free to decide whether or when to have children and whether to get married; where access to quality reproductive health care is guaranteed; and where every woman can make these decisions free from coercion or discrimination. Donate here: https://www.reproductiverights.org/about-us/donate Take action here: https://www.reproductiverights.org/take-action

The Guttmacher Institute: https://www.guttmacher.org is a leading research and policy organization committed to advancing sexual and reproductive health and rights in the United States and globally. For research and evidenced-based information visit their website at: https://www.guttmacher.org/about

The National Abortion Federation (NAF):
https://prochoice.org/about-naf is the professional association of abortion providers. Its members include individuals, private and non-

profit clinics, Planned Parenthood affiliates, women's health centers, physicians' offices, and hospitals who together care for approximately half the women who choose abortion in the U.S. and Canada each year. Their members also include public hospitals and both public and private clinics in Mexico City and private clinics in Colombia. To find a provider go here:
https://prochoice.org/think-youre-pregnant/find-a-provider
For education and advocacy information go here:
https://prochoice.org/education-and-advocacy

The National Women's Health Network (NWHN):
https://www.nwhn.org was founded to change the conversation about women's health and to shape policy and support consumer health decisions; monitor the actions of Federal regulatory and funding agencies, the health care industry, and the health professions; identify and expose health care abuses; and mobilize grassroots action for women's health. To safeguard their independence as a trusted voice on women health, the NWHN chooses not to accept financial support from the pharmaceutical industry, medical device manufacturers, or insurance companies. Share your health story here: https://www.nwhn.org/share-your-story Find health fact sheets here: https://www.nwhn.org/fact-sheets

The Reproductive Health Access Project:
https://www.reproductiveaccess.org is a non-profit that trains clinicians to make quality reproductive healthcare more accessible. To donate and get involved go here:
https://www.reproductiveaccess.org/get-involved

Women's Reproductive Rights Assistance Project (WRRAP):
https://wrrap.org provides funds to pre-screened, pre-qualified health

clinics across the nation on behalf of poor and disadvantaged women in need of abortion services or emergency contraceptives, on a case-by-case basis. Their affiliate clinics are members of Planned Parenthood Federation of America (PPFA) and National Abortion Federation (NAF). WRRAP does not demand repayment of funds and they never judge the women they assist. Their mission is to ensure that all women, from all walks of life, are afforded the equal opportunity to gain access to safe, legal abortion services and emergency contraceptives. To volunteer go here: https://wrrap.org/donate-shop-volunteer

Violence and Sexual Assault Against Girls and Women

Futures Without Violence:
https://www.futureswithoutviolence.org/our-mission has been providing groundbreaking programs, policies, and campaigns that empower individuals and organizations working to end violence against women and children around the world. There are many ways to take action and get involved in your community to help prevent violence against women and children. FUTURES was a driving force behind passage of the Violence Against Women Act of 1994 — the nation's first comprehensive federal response to the violence that plagues families and communities. Watch TEDTalk here: https://www.ted.com/talks/leslie_morgan_steiner_why_domestic_violence_victims_don_t_leave Here are a few great ways you can help: https://www.futureswithoutviolence.org/take-action

National Coalition Against Domestic Violence (NCADV):
https://ncadv.org advocates for victims and attempts to change policy

surrounding domestic violence. To donate go here: https://ncadv.org/donate NCADV also provides links to local programs along with research on issues and policies and data research.

National Sexual Violence Resource Center (NSVRC):
https://www.nsvrc.org is the leading nonprofit in providing information and tools to prevent and respond to sexual violence. NSVRC translates research and trends into best practices that help individuals, communities and service providers achieve real and lasting change. Those wanting to volunteer or get active in their community rape crisis center can find links and connections to local resources at: https://www.nsvrc.org/get-involved

Rape, Abuse & Incest National Network (RAINN):
https://www.rainn.org is the country's largest anti-sexual violence organization, which operates the National Sexual Assault Hotline (800-656-HOPE) and programs to help victims of sexual violence. For information about how to volunteer for the hotline or in your community go here: https://www.rainn.org/get-involved To donate go here: https://tinyurl.com/y5zo4akk

The National Alliance to End Sexual Violence (NAESV):
https://www.endsexualviolence.org is the voice in Washington for the 56 state and territorial sexual assault coalitions and 1300 rape crisis centers working to end sexual violence and support survivors. Options for involvement, beyond donating, include signing up for monthly email action alerts, and signing on to a sexual assault policy watch network. https://www.endsexualviolence.org/where-we-stand/how-you-can-effect-change

U.S. Department of Health and Human Services, Office of Women's Health: https://www.womenshealth.gov provides links to state-by-state resources including local program resources. Most local domestic and sexual violence centers and programs offer opportunities for involvement through victim advocacy or policy activism in addition to services for victims and survivors. Find resources and programs in your state that provide support for women who have experienced abuse here: https://www.womenshealth.gov/relationships-and-safety/get-help/state-resources

Voting Rights and Election Reform

America Votes: https://americavotes.org has been the common link between many of the largest and most influential issue and membership organizations in the country. Their work has brought together a wide range of causes and built a unified coalition that has transformed how the progressive community works. Together, they have engaged communities across the country to take action on critical issues – from fighting for working families, to advancing women's healthcare, to protecting the environment and more – and mobilized millions of voters to turn out on Election Day. To find an America Votes operation in your state go to: https://americavotes.org/state-network

Fair Fight 2020: https://fairfight.com/about-fair-fight advocates for election reform, engages in voter education, and encourages turn-out in order to secure the voting rights of all Georgians. The 501(c)(4) arm of the organization, Fair Fight Action, engages in activities such as conducting a vote-by-mail program; educating voters about elections, voting procedures, and voting rights; and facilitating a get-out-the-vote program to mobilize voters to cast their ballots during early voting and on election day. To donate go here: https://secure.actblue.com/donate/fair-fight-1

iVote: https://www.ivoteforamerica.org has one goal: secure voting rights for all Americans. Traditionally, most voting rights groups have focused on challenges in court after rights had been impinged, or defeating efforts to further erode rights. While this is important work, iVote takes a different tack – 'flipping the script' from playing defense on voter suppression efforts to going on offense to secure and expand access to voting. iVote focuses on two vehicles to go on offense for voting rights: Electing Democratic voting rights champions as secretary of state and passing automatic voter registration in states across the country. Donate here: https://secure.actblue.com/contribute/page/ivotefund?recurring=true   Show your support here: https://www.ivoteforamerica.org/sign_up

League of Women Voters: https://www.lwv.org is a nonpartisan organization founded in 1920 by Carrie Chapman Catt during the Nation American Woman Suffrage Association convention. The League encourages informed and active participation in government, works to increase understanding of major public policy issues and influences public policy through education and advocacy. LWV has chapters in over 700 communities in all 50 states and through those chapters, they reached over 10 million voters in 2018. To join the league and find a local chapter go here: www.lwv.org/local-leagues/find-local-league To have your voice heard by elected officials and policy makers and take action on current critical policy issues including voting rights go here: https://www.lwv.org/take-action

The Voter Participation Center: https://www.voterparticipation.org is a central "hub" for voter information and registration, and provides an option for action in your local area by signing up on their email list. The Rising American Electorate — unmarried women, people of color, and millennials — are now the majority of eligible voters. With their groundbreaking research on voter mobilization and issue engagement, the Voter Participation Center has pioneered new ways to get these people to the polls. For information on unregistered voters in your state go to: https://data.voterparticipation.org

Voto Latino: https://votolatino.org is dedicated to empowering communities through civic engagement, issue advocacy and leadership development. Their work has evolved from voter registration to taking on other key issues that impact the Latino community in America such as Voter Education and Registration, Immigration and Citizenship, Social Justice, Health and Professional Development. At Voto Latino they rely on incredible volunteers like you to help them educate, empower and engage Latinos across the country. Sign up to be a volunteer today and they will be in touch with opportunities in your area. To volunteer:
https://secure.everyaction.com/dNSuqhuSbESQiLgFVmy5gQ2
To donate go here: https://secure.actblue.com/donate/vl-website

Women's Equality

American Association of University Women (AAUW):
https://www.aauw.org is the nation's leading voice promoting equity and education for women and girls. Since their founding in 1881, AAUW members have examined and have taken positions on the fundamental issues of the day — educational, social, eco-

nomic, and political. AAUW has local chapters in every state and invites all to participate in actions on a variety of issues. Go to: https://www.aauw.org/what-we-do/public-policy/two-minute-activist

ERA Coalition: http://www.eracoalition.org works with its partner organizations to provide a strong forum for all voices advocating for passage of an equal rights amendment. They represent 76 member and lead organizations, and millions of women and men, and support and help lead the movement for passage of an equal rights amendment through public education and messaging campaigns. Their polling research shows that while 94% of Americans support constitutional equality for women and men, 80% mistakenly think it already exists. To find links to local efforts and for lobbying Congress go here: http://www.eracoalition.org/cosponsors.php To donate go here: https://tinyurl.com/yysosmp5

Feminist Majority: http://www.feminist.org Founded in 1987, The Feminist Majority Foundation (FMF), is a cutting edge organization dedicated to women's equality, reproductive health, and non-violence. In all spheres, FMF utilizes research and action to empower women economically, socially, and politically. They believe that feminists - both women and men, girls and boys - are the majority, but this majority must be empowered. For links to take action locally and nationally go to: http://www.feminist.org/action/index.html

Fund for Women's Equality: http://fundforwomensequality.org promotes legal and lived equality for women in the United States by increasing public understanding of the need for comprehensive, fair and equal treatment of women and girls under the law and the need to end sex inequality in all its forms. The Fund for Women's

Equality is a 501(c)(3) charitable organization. To donate go here: http://fundforwomensequality.org/donate.html

National Organization for Women (NOW): https://now.org is an activist organization, foundation and PAC that advocates for equal rights for women and is the largest organization of feminist grass-roots activists in the United States with hundreds of chapters and hundreds of thousands of members and activists in all 50 states and the District of Columbia. Since their founding in 1966, NOW's purpose is to take action through intersectional grassroots activism to promote feminist ideals, lead societal change, eliminate discrimination, and achieve and protect the equal rights of all women and girls in all aspects of social, political, and economic life. To donate and look for local volunteer programs, like clinic escorting, go to: https://now.org/?state=Select+State&post_type=chapter Take action here: https://now.org/nap For volunteer programs go here: https://now.org/getinvolved For ways to donate go here: https://now.org/more-ways-to-give

National Women's Law Center: https://nwlc.org are advocates, experts, and lawyers who fight for gender justice, taking on issues that are central to the lives of women and girls. They drive change in the courts, in public policy, and in our society, especially for women facing multiple forms of discrimination. Take action here: https://nwlc.org/take-action

The New Agenda: https://thenewagenda.net is dedicated to improving the lives of women and girls by bringing about systemic change in the media, at the workplace, at school and at home. They seek to achieve safety and opportunity for all women by addressing issues which unite us and by advancing women into leadership roles. Find out how to take action here: https://thenewagenda.net/take-action

UltraViolet: https://weareultraviolet.org is a powerful and rapidly growing community of people mobilized to fight sexism and create a more inclusive world that accurately represents all women, from politics and government to media and pop culture. They work on a range of issues — reproductive rights, healthcare, economic security, violence, and racial justice — and center the voices of all women, especially women of color, immigrants, and LGBTQ women. UltraViolet exists to create a cost for sexism and to achieve full equity for all women through culture and policy change.

Women's March: Over 5 Million of us worldwide and over 1 Million in Washington, D.C., came to march, speak and make our voices heard. But it is JUST the BEGINNING! It is time to get our friends, family and community together and leverage that energy. Go to this link https://www.womensmarch.com and sign up for 10 Actions for the first 100 Days. They believe that it is critical to focus on the Congress because - The President proposes, the Congress disposes. Hold Senators and Representatives accountable for their positions and votes.

Workers' Rights

Jobs with Justice: http://www.jwj.org is leading the fight for workers' rights and an economy that benefits everyone. They are the only non-profit of their kind leading strategic campaigns and shaping the public discourse on every front to build power for working people. Jobs With Justice is committed to working nationally and locally, on the ground and online. They win real change for workers by combining innovative communications strategies and solid research and policy advocacy with grassroots action and mobilization. To take action go here: http://www.jwj.org/take-action

National Domestic Workers Alliance (NDWA):
https://www.domesticworkers.org is the nation's leading voice for dignity and fairness for the millions of domestic workers in the United States, most of whom are women. NDWA works for the respect, recognition, and inclusion in labor protections for domestic workers. The national alliance is powered by over 60 affiliate organizations — plus robust local chapters in Atlanta, Durham, and New York — of over 20,000 nannies, housekeepers, and caregivers for the elderly in 36 cities and 17 states. Go here to get involved: https://www.domesticworkers.org/take-action

The Advocates for Human Rights:
http://www.theadvocatesforhumanrights.org/about_us is at the forefront of the world's human rights movement. They are a 501(c)(3) organization that creates and maintains lasting, comprehensive, and holistic change on a local, national, and global scale. Volunteers, partners, supporters, board members, and staff implement international human rights standards to promote civil society and reinforce the rule of law. They have a comprehensive list of and links to vetted organizations focused on workers' rights. To take action go to:
http://www.theadvocatesforhumanrights.org/uploads/workers_rights_take_action.pdf

Solidarity Center:
https://www.solidaritycenter.org/what-we-do/workers-human-rights stands with workers as they defend their right to freedom of associ-

ation, supporting them as they organize, advocate and build worker voice. Their 221 professional staff work in about 60 countries with 400-plus labor unions, pro-worker nongovernmental organizations, legal-aid groups, human rights defenders, women's associations, advocacy coalitions and others to support workers as they exercise their rights, including organizing for safer work sites, demanding living wages and improving laws (and the enforcement of existing laws) that protect working people, and fighting exploitation and abuse. For training, labor union assistance and information on workers' rights go to: https://www.solidaritycenter.org/what-we-do

Sweatfree Communities: https://laborrights.org/our-work/sfc aims to support sweatshop workers globally in their struggles to improve working conditions and achieve respect at work. This campaign does this by encouraging U.S. cities, states and school districts to adopt policies to purchase goods made in humane conditions by workers who are paid decent wages. Sweatfree works to establish purchasing consortiums. You can find links to local efforts at https://laborrights.org/our-work/sfc They also provide helpful information and contacts for advocating with your governmental bodies and local organizations to join a purchasing consortium.

ACKNOWLEDGEMENTS

This book would not exist without the friendship, dedication, and yes, the plain old persistence, of Savanah Forster. My sincere gratitude goes to you for agreeing to take this journey with me, for our endless conversations, edits and rewrites, and for your insightful advice. To know that you were always there for me when I needed it made this book possible.

Sincere thanks go to my dear long-time friends Linda (Cass) Cassineri Desch and her husband Jake Desch, and to Patt and Mike Celayeta, who have been by my side supporting me in too many ways to name. Cass, since fifth grade you have saved me more than once. My teen years would not have been the same without you.

There are also many friends who, recently and over the nine years of writing this book, as I was trying to get my story in book form, helped me in so many ways — large and small — with proof reading, research, editing and advice. They are Tricia Keith-Spiegel, Rosemary Rocco, Ruth Hansten, Shirley Bennett, Diane Wheeler, Beth Aldridge, Michele Larkey, Emily Hansen, Azure Serafini, Mary Beth Angin, Catherine Dodd and the many others whom I interviewed along the way.

I would also like to acknowledge and thank the people in my life who have come along for parts of my journey and who were critical in helping me remember things I had long forgotten. They are Peg Harrington, Rick Leach, Kirk Mitchel, Lucinda Connelly, Gary Hillerson, Marcy Allingham, John Siegel, John West, and my cousin Judy Pierotti. To readers of earlier versions, Libby Rafferty, Chelsea Hardy and Irene Reti, thank you for helping guide my process in figuring out what to keep in and what to leave out and to Liz Beacham who translated my disastrous Swiss report card into English.

When I started this journey I didn't consider myself a writer but felt I had an interesting worthwhile story to share. Two professional editors helped craft my words into a tale that I am proud of and who along the way made me realize that I am a writer. Thanks to Sarah Rabkin and Mary Pattock whose editorial skills helped me create the book that I always wanted it to be. You were both a true pleasure to work with.

And finally, thanks to the thousands of people who volunteer their time all over the country and to my beloved family.

To my daughters Kelly, Sara and Lesha who contributed their thoughts and feeling along the way. You have taught me more than you can imagine about life and how to be a good mother.

To my kick-ass smart, spunky and adorable grandchildren Zoe, Johnny, Mac and Ayla. You have brought such joy to my life at times when your sweet hugs have overwhelmed my heart and soul with love. It is for you that I do this work in hopes that the world you are growing into will be better than it is now.

And to John, my partner in crime. I am incredibly grateful for your patience and support as I spent endless hours, days and months hidden away in my office and away from home doing research. Without your delicious home-cooked meals I would have starved. The crazy journey we have taken together has been a true blessing.

ABOUT THE AUTHOR

Pat Bakalian is a feminist and lifelong activist who started out as a volunteer community organizer in the early 1970s, working to stop harmful development, organizing events in support of women's reproductive rights and helping to create her county's domestic violence commission. Pat was staff on a number of political campaigns, working as a fundraiser, field director and campaign manager. She was a regional outreach consultant for the United States Centers for Disease Control and Prevention under President Bill Clinton. Pat lives in Northern California with John, her husband of forty-nine years. When not writing or engaging in activities to secure women's equal rights or helping to elect Democrats, she spends time with her three daughters, sons-in-law and four grandchildren.